FREEDOM'S RUSH II

More Tales From the Biker and the Beast

To Joanna,
The SC Biker Babe

Foster Kinn

Ride Bold,
Ride Long,
Ride Free

FK

5 Oct 2017

HUGO HOUSE PUBLISHERS, LTD.

Freedom's Rush II—More Tales From the Biker and the Beast by Foster Kinn

ISBN: 978-1-936449-88-0

Library of Congress Control Number: 2017935894

Cover Design & Interior Layout: Ronda Taylor, www.RondaTaylor.com

Photos: Dwight Mikkelsen

Hugo House Publishers
Denver, Colorado
Austin, Texas
www.HugoHousePublishers.com

This book is dedicated to my three children:
Khalin, Lacee and Jasmine.

And always, Rosemary

I would also like to dedicate this book to the memories of

Robert Louis Newman
and
Paige MacKenzie Kelly

CONTENTS

AUTOBIOGRAPHY ix

PREFACE xi

PART I
FOUR CORNERS, FOUR CORNERS, AND MONUMENTS

01 THE FIRST FOUR CORNERS 3

02 THE SECOND FOUR CORNERS #1: SAN YSIDRO, CALIFORNIA 7

03 THE SECOND FOUR CORNERS #2: MADAWASKA, MAINE 13

04 THE SECOND FOUR CORNERS #3: KEY WEST, FLORIDA 19

05 THE SECOND FOUR CORNERS #4: BLAINE, WASHINGTON (OR IS IT?) 25

PART II
EASTERN BEAUTY

06 PLANS 33

07 UP TO THE U.P.! 39

08 HELLUVITS 43

09 TOLERANCE 49

10 TWO CANADAS 57

11 THE WAY LIFE SHOULD BE 59

12 A PRAYER. 65

13 DETOURS 69

14 RESPECT 75

15 PRETTINESS 79

16 FAME 83

17 NOT WHAT I EXPECTED 87

PART III

SOUTHERN CHARM

18 WET. 93

19 FLAT AND STRAIGHT 99

20 LAWS AND CUSTOMS 107

21 STORYTELLING (Or Will Someone *Please* Tell Me Where I Am!) 113

22 LOST AND FOUND 119

23 MAGGIE AND THE DRAGON. 123

24 INSPIRATION. 131

25 LAYERS 137

26 FORTY-EIGHT 141

PART IV

THE ALASKA HIGHWAY—BEFORE, DURING AND BEYOND

27 SERENDIPITY. 149

28 YA GOTTA LOVE IT 155

29 NEW WAYS OF SEEING 159

30 QUIRKS. 163

31 GETTIN' ON. 167

32 ACHIEVEMENTS 173

33 MUD, MUD AND, WELL, MORE MUD 179

34 HEROES. 185

35 FORTY-NINE 193

36 A SINCERE WORD 199

37 PURGATORY 203

38 A WHOLE LOT OF CUTE 209

PART V
ANGELS AND GHOSTS

39 AN ANGEL GETS A RIDE 217

40 REMEMBER 223

41 BLOOD 227

42 WE PULL THROUGH 233

43 WHATEVER HAPPENS, HAPPENS 237

44 THE TANGIBLE AND THE TRANSCENDENT 241

45 A CIVILIZED PEACE 247

PART VI
A BACKWARD GLANCE OVER TRAVELED ROADS

46 INSIGHT 255

47 LEARNING STUFF 263

48 A GOOD MAN 269

49 THE APPALACHIAN KID 273

50 THE BIG FIVE-ZERO 277

51 THE LONG ROAD HOME 285

ABOUT THE AUTHOR 289

INVITATION FOR MORE FREEDOM 291

AUTOBIOGRAPHY

I live in the Temple of Winds.
I stroke clouds,
Scatter dust,
Ripple waters,
Lift the shadows of sorrows.

But I cannot lift the shadows of moons.

I live not in the Winds of Fate.
I utter loudly,
Summon futures,
Sing triumphant,
Cool the fevers of discontent.

But I cannot cool the fevers of lovers.

I live in the Temple of Winds.
Amid the night,
Amid the light,
Amid the half-light.

Alone.

Moving.

Rootless.

PREFACE

The first Freedom's Rush book covered my travels throughout the western half of the United States along with a long side trip to Canada. It wasn't long after it was published that I was asked during a radio interview what I had learned during my travels. I wasn't expecting what came out of my mouth, but I can say it was the truth: The first thing you learn while riding a motorcycle around the United States is that it's a lot bigger than you thought it was.

And what came out of my mouth right after that was something else I wasn't expecting: And I want to see all of it.

So the very next summer, I took off to Canada, an even bigger country than the United States, headed east, then came down into New England and the rest of the Eastern states. The summer after that I visited Florida and the South. And the summer after that?

Well, before I get ahead of myself, I should just let you get onto reading the book itself because it's all about those road trips to the East, the South and beyond. Hope you enjoy it.

$$\infty$$

Publishing a book requires a lot of after-the-writing-is-done hours, too many to count, and the people who put in those hours are invaluable friends and professionals. George Gluchowski, the always-on-top-of-everything publisher; Patricia Ross (The Doctor!), editor extraordinaire and word-nerd-grammar-geek nonpareil; and Ronda Taylor, a genius artist who did a killer job with Dwight Mikkelsen's cover photos.

Three others deserve my gratitude and trust as well and they are Donna Frierson, Diane Austin and Rose Albano.

The Beast would like to especially thank Drew Surina, the Madman Motorcycle Magician of American Speed and Custom in Palmdale, California for always keeping him upright, rumbling strong and invincible.

I want to acknowledge and thank all those who meet and have met the challenge of riding a motorcycle, to those who take the time to read my scribblings, and to my fellow writers and artists who create the beauty that makes our burdens light, our pasts something to smile about, and the future something to look forward to.

Throughout my wanderings, day after day after day, I am continually amazed at how utterly friendly, helpful and cheerful people are. Really. And it doesn't matter where you go. Or how old or young they are. Or the size of their bodies or their beliefs or their gender or their race or their political leanings or their intelligence or their level of education.

You wonder why. Maybe it's the motorcycle, maybe it's the tattoos and the earring; maybe it's the phases of the moon or a roll of the dice or the magic spell of ancient gods. Maybe it's all those things and more.

Or maybe, just maybe, friendly, helpful and cheerful are how people truly are. I think so, and I thank all of them.

Ride Big, Ride Long and Ride Free.

PART I

FOUR CORNERS, FOUR CORNERS, AND MONUMENTS

Afoot and light-hearted I take to the open road,
Healthy, free, the world before me,
The long brown path before me, leading wherever I choose.

Walt Whitman

01

THE FIRST FOUR CORNERS

Desert. That's where we are. The desert. The Great Basin Desert, to be specific, the largest desert in the United States. It's one of my first multi-day rides and the only one in this book where I'm not riding alone. In fact, there are four of us on this trip: My buddy Vic and Scirocco (his bike), and Yours Truly and the Beast (my bike). I'm not leading, Vic is, but that's the natural order of things because before starting out, we tacitly agreed it'd be best if we didn't get lost.

Vic rides like a demon. Not in a fast and reckless way, but in that he's one of those riders who looks at rest areas like they're insults to his manhood and never stops. Probably has one of those titanium butts, I don't know. But I do know my butt's getting sore and I keep hoping he'll pull over for some water and take at least a few minutes to stretch the legs. But he doesn't and never does. He just keeps riding. And I keep following.

So. Here we are. In the desert. It's hot and there's not much of a breeze, but it could be worse because the temperature hasn't quite reached triple digits. Besides, we had a decent lunch and I'm well hydrated so I can almost say that it's somewhat comfy. Almost. And somewhat.

The thing is, there's nothing, really, to take my mind off the monotony because there just isn't that much to see in a desert when you're going fifty to seventy miles-per-hour. Sure, there are low hills, but they're all pretty much the same three shades of brown with an occasional faded green bush.

Miles and miles of nothing but miles and miles is the way my high school geography teacher put it.

Nevertheless, there is a bit of excitement brewing inside of me because our destination is the famous Four Corners, one of the must-go-to places if you're riding throughout the United States. And because crisscrossing this country is exactly my mindset when I'm on the Beast, well, like I said, this is getting exciting.

We arrive just in time to save my butt, though it takes a while to straighten out my limbs and get off the bike. The Four Corners is not a biker place per se, but by the facts that the parking lot is dirt and gravel and half the vehicles are motorcycles, you'd think it was.

There are actually two different Four Corners in the United States. Where we are is the one most often mentioned and is the right-angled meeting point of New Mexico, Arizona, Utah and Colorado. There's a monument here, a small bronze disc that has the names of those four states carved into it.

This bronze disc is embedded in a larger granite disc and around the rim of that disc are carved two words in each state. Starting from Colorado, it reads, HERE MEET, IN FREEDOM, UNDER GOD, FOUR STATES. It's a clever little ditty because you can start reading it at any of the states and it'll make just as much sense. Like if you start from Arizona it reads, "Under God, four states, here meet, in freedom."

Outside that granite disc is an area made out of plain old cement, which is embedded with the four state seals, and the names of those four states are carved into it in big block letters. Outside of that are steps, ramps, benches, fences, flagpoles and a lot of sunlight. Around that area are a bunch of artisan stalls, which offer the only shade for miles around.

Finally, outside those stalls is the Great Basin Desert, which consists of dirt, rocks, even more sunlight and maybe a creosote bush here and there.

The whole place is administered by Navajos and is located at the northeastern edge of the Navajo Reservation where it borders the Ute reservation, which is why you can buy all sorts of Navajo- and Ute-ware while enjoying the shade in those stalls.

Not only that, if you get hungry, there are a number of places to get just about anything made by deep-frying processed flour and sugar. And maybe a cold soda. Sounds more and more like a biker joint all the time.

If you've never visited, it's a good place to put on your to-do list, but take note that it's cash-only, the entrance fee is five bucks, and the nearest ATM is six miles away. Sure, it's out in the middle of nowhere, but it does get a quarter-million visitors a year and is the only place where you can cast your own shadow across four different states.

The area was originally surveyed back in 1868 by a guy named Ehud N. Darling. Three other surveyors were needed to complete the task: Chandler Robbins placed the first marker in 1875; Rollin J. Reeves in 1878; and Howard B. Carpenter in 1901.

Considering the equipment they had to work with, everyone agrees they each did a helluva job, so if you're ever in a tavern with your buddies and in need of a reason to raise your glasses in a toast, those four names will do quite nicely. "To Darling, Robbins, Reeves and Carpenter. Hear, Hear!" However, there's more to the story.

Surveying instruments being what they were over a hundred years ago, those four good men missed the exact location of this unique, four-state meeting point. In 2009, it was determined that the marker was two and a half miles too far to the west. Soon afterward, it was determined that the marker was actually 1,807.14 feet too far to the east. (Boy, those surveying guys and gals really like that accuracy thing, don't they?)

Immediately, there were those who wanted to move the marker to its true location because, you know, accuracy is a good thing, especially to surveying guys and gals. But digging up brass and granite discs, moving artisan stalls, pouring new cement, erecting new flagpoles and fences, tearing down old road signs and posting new ones, and rewriting every map of the Southwestern United States in existence costs money. A lot of money. And who would pay for it? What to do, what to do....

Well, while everyone else was sitting around drumming their fingers on tables, the guys and gals at the National Geodetic Survey (NGS) went to work and found the solution.

A basic tenet of boundary surveying is that once a monument has been established and accepted by the parties involved (in the case of the Four Corners monument, the parties were the four territories and the U.S. Congress), the location of the physical monument is the ultimate authority in delineating a boundary. Issues of legality trump scientific details, and the intended location of the point becomes secondary information. In surveying, monuments rule!

So the lesson is, if you once thought you were right then find out you're wrong, but you still want to be right, build a monument!

THE SECOND FOUR CORNERS #1: SAN YSIDRO, CALIFORNIA

The second Four Corners comprises the four most extremely located cities in the contiguous forty-eight states, which are also must-go-to places. They are

Madawaska, Maine (most northeastern);

Key West, Florida (most southeastern);

San Ysidro, California (most southwestern); and

Blaine, Washington (most northwestern).

Now this is the Four Corners that truly outlines the contiguous forty-eight, and the idea of visiting each one really turned me on when I first found out about them some years ago. (That also explains why the first part of this book is about the Four Corners. Makes sense, right?)

The Southern California Motorcycling Association (SCMA), headed up by the capable and helpful Gonzo Gonzalez, is the official purveyor of this particular Four Corners, and they have come up with a couple of official rides, which you can do on your own or with a group. One of them is the USA Four Corners Tour, for which you have to visit all Four Corners cities in no more than twenty-one days.

The other is called the USA Four Corners Tour True X. This one includes the geographical center of the contiguous forty-eight states, Lebanon, Kansas. What you do is visit Lebanon between visiting each of the four corners cities, which means you end up going to Lebanon three times. For this tour, you're given twenty-six days.

A quick note about Lebanon. According to satellite technology, it's not at the exact center of the contiguous states, but it doesn't matter because, you guessed it, there's a monument there!

I've not done any official SCMA tours, but I have visited all the Four Corners cities. The first one happened some years ago right after I found out about them while sitting in front of my laptop just north of Los Angeles. I chose San Ysidro (san-ee-SEE-drow), California because it was the closest, so one Saturday morning I thought that riding down there would make for a good day ride.

So I jump on the Beast, get on Interstate 405 South, and it's not long before I realize that the 155 miles I have to travel are going to take most of the day. Why? For one reason it's another Hey-it's-Saturday-let's-go-to-the-beach day in Southern California, which means traffic. A lot of traffic. A lot of slow traffic.

I split lanes and it's good (and legal in California), but it's more hazardous than usual because it's the I-405, which means what used to be four lanes each way is now five lanes, which means it's a tight squeeze and there's just no way to slip past some of those rearview mirrors on pickups and trucks that stick out like crash bars on a Goldwing.

The 405 also means questionable road conditions. Cracks and chuckholes filled with bubblegum or taffy or silly putty or whatever the transportation bigwigs in Los Angeles County and Sacramento, our state capital, decide costs the least. All of that to say it's hot, slow and not much fun.

I finally make it past Long Beach, take a right and get onto Highway 1. The traffic is still thick and there are now traffic lights, but the pleasant factor rises a notch because it's right next to the Pacific Ocean, which means it's about ten degrees cooler.

The other advantage is that you get to ride through Newport Beach where, I swear, there's a city ordinance that requires all adult female residents to be forty-nine years old, attend yoga classes four times a week, take a lot of photos of themselves snuggling up to their lovable four-legged furry pets who are their best friends, and whose greatest accomplishment in life is having raised their two sons who are now off to college becoming geophysicists or lawyers or whatever.

And they all enjoy weekend getaways, traveling to exotic locations with five-star hotels, and love to ride horses and snow ski and would love to learn to play golf if only someone would teach them. Last, they have to be blond and have figures in the same proportions as a Barbie Doll. (Yeah, I once joined a dating site.) Anyway....

The traffic remains fairly thick all the way to Laguna Beach, which is a cool place to visit. Lots of incredible art galleries and great restaurants tucked in here and there. If you like to get lost, Laguna Beach is your kind of place and I should know because every time I've been there I've gotten lost. (But then, I sometimes get lost going out to my back yard.) The thing I most like about it, however, is that, despite its quasi-fame and high cost of living, it still has that casual, artists-hanging-out-at-the-beach vibe.

I keep going south and when I get to San Juan Capistrano, the traffic is more biker friendly (fewer cars), and I wonder about the event that used to occur there every March 19th when, as the story goes, the swallows returned home from being in Goya, Argentina all winter. I wonder if that's true. I mean, maybe the swallows consider Goya their real home and San Juan Capistrano as a prime vacation spot, like maybe it's the flying feathers version of Spring Break.

By the bye, only a handful of swallows still return to San Juan Capistrano these days. Evidently, they have discovered better nesting areas elsewhere, like at the Vellano Country Club in Chino Hills, which is a little north. Swallow experts figure that those vacationing birds prefer the newer, higher buildings—hey, penthouse living appeals to everyone—and the food (insects) that that country club offers.

Those same experts are now trying to lure the swallows back to San Juan Capistrano with all sorts of gimmicks, including building fake swallow nests and playing recordings of swallows singing through hidden loudspeakers. To me, that sounds like a lot of busy-ness for something that's quite simple. I'm thinking of writing a letter.

Dear San Juan Capistrano Civic Leaders,

Here is the surest way to get the swallows to come back to your fair city. Build a really tall monument!

Sincerely Yours,

Foster

It's right after San Juan Capistrano that I stop in Dana Point, which, from the looks of the two women I see while filling up my tank, might be another Newport Beach type place. The traffic lightens up and I soon pass by the San Onofre (san-uh-NO-fray) nuclear power plant and wonder how many air conditioning units it's powering and how nice it'd be to sit in front of one of them for a while.

I pass by Oceanside, Carlsbad and Encinitas and when I get to Del Mar, I wonder what's the most amount of money anyone has ever won in one day at that famous horse racing track. As I'm wrangling my way through the whirling traffic in San Diego, National City and Chula Vista, all I can think about is staying alive. Finally, TA-DA!, I see the city limit sign for San Ysidro! Yes!

I pull into a Taco Bell and immediately a guy holding a can of whatever in a paper bag walks over. He's old. Really old. So old I'm thinking he's been here ever since Sir Francis Drake first touched down on the California coast in 1579, so he must know everything about San Ysidro.

Me: Say! Do you know if there's a monument in San Ysidro?

San Ysidro Elder Historian: A monument for what?

Me: For being one of the four corners.

San Ysidro Elder Historian: The four corners of what?

Me: The contiguous forty-eight states.

San Ysidro Elder Historian: What's that?

Me: The forty-eight states that border at least one other state.

San Ysidro Elder Historian: *(Furrows eyebrows and thinks hard)* San Ysidro's not a state.

Me: Right. But it *is* the southwestern-most city in the contiguous forty-eight states.

San Ysidro Elder Historian: What's that mean again?

After it goes on a while longer I gladly give him five bucks as a consultation fee when I realize I've learned another valuable lesson about traveling around the country. If you want to find out about monuments, don't ask a really old person who's drinking out of a can inside a paper bag.

Regrettably, there is no Four Corners monument in San Ysidro, which leads me to think that this is an exceptional money-making opportunity. Why not buy a plot of land at the southwestern end of the city, build a monument, and charge people five bucks to park there? If the Four Corners Monument in the Great Basin Desert can get over a million dollars in parking fees a year, why not here?

What I later find out is that when bikers go there while on a Four Corners Tour, they get a photo of themselves and their bikes in front of one of the three post offices with the zip code showing. Some day I'll have to go back and get that photo because, you know, you have to be able to prove these things.

03

THE SECOND FOUR CORNERS #2: MADAWASKA, MAINE

The second Four Corners city I visited was Madawaska (mad-uh-WASS-kuh), Maine in the summer of 2013. In an effort to be accurate, I'll point out that Madawaska's population is under 5,000 so it's actually a town and not a city, but that doesn't disqualify it because, hey, they have a monument! And a damn nice one it is.

My route to get here went through Canada and getting back into the good ol' USofA turns out to be a bit of a chore because I keep getting lost over and over again in Edmundston, which is right on the border. It's my fault, though. I made the mistake of expecting a sign, a big sign with "United States" and an arrow on it.

Maybe it's just me, but I'm thinking, you know, the United States is a big country (the third or fourth largest in the world depending on how you do your calculations) so maybe a big sign would be appropriate, but there isn't one. Not even a small one that I can see.

I'm trying my hardest to follow the directions on my smart phone, but I guess I'm not smart enough because I don't see some of the streets the map says are there. But then maybe I can't see them because it's a couple of hours after sunset and there's no moon out. I don't know.

Nevertheless, it's not entirely frustrating because this part of Edmundston is quaint. Happy people walking around, unique shops, cute lampposts, well-trimmed shrubbery, and flowers in flower pots on every corner. One thing is that moderately and even cheaply priced eateries are often called Chez Something-or-Other. It's interesting because in Southern California, where I live, when an eatery is called Chez Something-or-Other, you can bet a buck you'll spend half your paycheck on lunch.

I end up wandering through some neighborhoods and it's more and more quaint with many wood paneled, two-story houses painted white, blue and red. I see a young man lying on his back, working on an old Plymouth RoadRunner, and hope he'll soon be driving it around, wooing the young ladies and being the envy of all the other young men.

I begin to look for very small streets with very small street signs hidden by trees and finally, after riding down a few very small streets, I see a small sign that says "U.S.A." Yes! Victory! I cross over the St. John River on an arched bridge called, coincidentally enough, the Edmundston-Madawaska Bridge, which is one of those bridges with steel mesh instead of asphalt.

I'm not a fan of these types of bridges and can't imagine any biker would be. The steel surfaces are vertically ribbed and will cause a motorcycle to wiggle, but it doesn't have to be a problem—you just relax and go with it. However, when it's wet, the metal gets slippery so it's a good idea to really slow down, sometimes do the old duck walk. Or, if there's a sidewalk, ride on that.

Tonight, thankfully, it's not raining or slippery so I safely wobble to the U.S. customs office and have a jovial chat with the four customs officials, a young man and three women.

One of the things you're sometimes asked when going from one country to another is how much money you have. I'm guessing it's because the customs guys and gals don't want anyone coming into their country who can't pay their own way. The customs official who asks me this is the young man and because he's a bit fidgety, I figure he's new on the job and a good candidate for a little schtick.

> **Young Newbie Customs Official:** (*In a proper and official tone*) May I ask if you have enough money for your stay in the United States?
>
> **Me:** Well dang, I hope so. If I don't my mortgage company's gonna be pissed.

Young Newbie Customs Official: *(The three women customs officials look over, smiling)* Oh no, I just need to make sure you have enough for food, gas and a room.

Me: *(Reaching into my pocket and pull out all the bills and coins, about twenty-five Canadian dollars.)* This is all I have.

Young Newbie Customs Official: Oh, that's Canadian money. You'll need American dollars.

Me: Oh. Uh, is this like a payola thing? I mean, you know, how much are we talking about?

Young Newbie Customs Official: *(The young man is red-faced and the ladies are laughing)* Oh no no no, I don't want any money from you!

Me: So you don't need to know how much money I have?

Young Newbie Customs Official: No, I mean yes, but no. I just need to know if you have enough for a room.

Me: Uhhh okay, now it's starting to sound like a proposition.

Young Newbie Customs Official: *(Now the ladies are laughing out loud)* No no no! It's not a proposition. We just need to know if you can afford a place to stay.

Me: We?

Young Newbie Customs Official: Yeah, the customs office, the customs officers here.

Me: *(Look around and count the customs officials plus myself)* So I need to get a room for five people? Sounds like one helluva party, I'm all in!

Young Newbie Customs Official: No no no, just for yourself.

Me: So I'm not invited to the party?

I finally let him off the hook and a few minutes later, I'm finally back in the good ol' USofA.

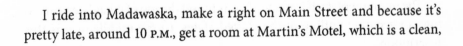

I ride into Madawaska, make a right on Main Street and because it's pretty late, around 10 P.M., get a room at Martin's Motel, which is a clean, friendly and privately owned place that really feels like home. Small but cozy room, comfy bed, cute wallpaper, and everything works like it should; the coffee maker, the faucets, the lights, hot water, vending machines, everything. Except I can't close the curtains over the only window, which means when I step out of the bathroom after a shower, my pure white butt is right there for anyone outside to ogle at, though I can't imagine why anyone would want to.

The first thing I do the following morning is take a short tour of the countryside to the west. The sparse traffic never slows me down and the road itself, US Highway 1, is nice and easy, but I'm not bored because it's all so pastorally picturesque and perfectly partitioned with two-story, wood-paneled houses, grassy fields, healthy trees and lazily rolling hills in the distance. Even the weeds look like they've been fertilized and trimmed. But what impresses me the most is that it's so clean. Not a piece of litter or a stroke of graffiti anywhere. Mother Nature and Mankind in harmony.

After an hour or so, I ride back into town heading down Main Street looking for the Four Corners Monument but can't find it. I'm not worried, though, because I often can't find things and it's got to be around here someplace. Around 11 A.M., I go to the McDonald's (there's only one) and ask a local resident. He gives me directions, I ride for a minute, and whaddya know!, there it is, right up a small incline.

If you ever go to Madawaska, something I urge you to, and have the same problem just do this. Go to McDonald's and if you stand facing Main Street, it's on the opposite side about a hundred yards to your left, cater-corner from a gas station called Larry's One Stop.

∽

The Madawaska Four Corners Monument is done the way a monument should be done, meaning it's tailor-made for motorcycles. Ride up that small incline, make a left then a left U-turn and, bam, there you are, right in front of the monument ready to pose for photos. (If you're in a car, you make a right to the parking lot and have to walk to the monument.)

The monument itself is made of granite and the top of it has been carved into an accurate outline of the United States. In the middle of it is this inscription.

MADAWASKA MAINE
ESTABLISHED IN 1869
FOUNDED BY ACADIANS
FONDÉE PAR LES ACADIENS

Below that is a rectangular inscription that reads

THE MOST NORTHEASTERN
TOWN OF THE UNITED STATES
ONE OF THE FOUR CORNERS

Below that is a flower pot sitting on the base, on the front of which is a black marble slab inscribed with Plourde's Harley-Davidson and the Harley-Davidson bar and shield.

I park the Beast in front of the monument then stroll around the clean and cleverly designed park. There's an information wall, two gazebos covering stone tables and benches, potted flowers, flags, trees, a fountain and a double swing set. Around the fountain and through the thick grass are broad walkways covered with granite walking stones that are inscribed with names, dates and messages from those who've visited.

After some minutes, a biker couple from New Jersey show up. They offer to take pictures of me and the Beast in front of the monument (afterward, I return the favor) and while standing there, I realize I'm probably as far away from home as I could be and still be in the contiguous forty-eight states.

After our informal photo shoot, I go to the Plourde's Harley-Davidson store, which is not quite two miles past McDonald's and on the right. The actual dealership is about fifty miles south in Caribou, but the store here in Madawaska is one of what I call boutique H-D places, which means there's no service department and no bikes for sale.

They do, however, sell t-shirts, leather, t-shirts, jewelry, t-shirts, shot glasses, t-shirts, H-D bric-a-brac, and more t-shirts. I do buy a t-shirt, but the real reason for my visit is to get an official Yes-I-Visited-the-Madawaska-Four-Corners-Park certificate, which is actually signed by the governor of Maine. How cool is that?

At the park's website (madawaskafourcorners.org), you can buy your own granite walking stone and get it inscribed with whatever you want (well, within reason) and that's what I did. Mine says:

FOSTER KINN
AND THE BEAST
28 AUGUST, 2013
RIDE BIG
RIDE LONG
RIDE FREE

[A quick note. A year after I was there, the proprietor, Joe LaChance, who sports one of those delightful Maine accents, along with the rest of the good Madawaska Monument folks, put up an arched sign over the entrance so it's now easy to find.]

THE SECOND FOUR CORNERS #3: KEY WEST, FLORIDA

The third Four Corners city I visited was Key West, Florida. After spending the night in Homestead in Southern Florida, I head south on Highway 1 and because there are only 108 miles to go, I'm figuring to get down there before lunchtime.

Once I get past the thick pedestrian and automobile traffic of Key Largo, Highway 1 starts heading mostly west and it's here that your senses expand way out. It is a truly grand feeling, having the Gulf of Mexico cuddled up to your right and the Atlantic Ocean to your left. However that feeling lasts but ten minutes because when I get to Tavernier there's more traffic (pedestrians and slow cars) along with road maintenance.

It continues to be a slow go for a while with no one getting close to the moderate speed limit of forty-five miles-per-hour. The heat and humidity are weighing on me and it's not long before I'm in serious need of hydration, so I pull over at a gas station in Islamorada (EES-la-moh-RAH-da) and park next to another biker who's standing next to his bike in the shade.

When I pull up, he's looking intently at a map, an actual paper map, and I mention to him that's it's nice to see someone else finding his way around using the old fashioned method. He smiles and says he prefers it, that GPS and Google maps lower the sense of discovery, something with which I agree. He also tells me that he's a sixth grade school teacher in Michigan and uses the photos from his long distance rides when he teaches geography. What a cool thing to do!

In the spirit of trivia, I check on the name Islamorada and it has nothing to do with Islam. Rather, it was named by early Spanish explorers and means Island Home (Isla Morada) and some time ago was nicknamed Purple Island. Why, I don't know, but I do know it was the home of baseball great Ted Williams for forty-five years starting in 1943. The things you learn on the road!

After cooling down and hydrating up, I continue my slow, westerly trek to the end of the Keys. It's not long before all the heat, humidity and slowness again get to me and, to be honest, I'm feeling pretty miserable. I've often said that I prefer cold weather to hot, not because I'd rather be cold, but because it's easier to warm up than it is to cool down.

You can do any number of things to get warm. Put on an extra layer of clothing, flap your arms, sing at the top of your lungs, pull over and do some pushups and so on. No, you never get totally comfortable, but the simple fact that you're *doing* something calms down your thoughts and makes you feel more in control.

But in hot and heavy weather like this, most of what you do to cool down involves doing nothing; any physical activity, including singing, will only make you more hot and there's a limit to how many clothes you can take off. So it's mostly a sit-and-hope type of thing, which is contrary to the heart-pumping activity of riding a motorcycle.

When I pull over in Big Coppitt Key to drink some water, a commonly heard comment occurs to me: It's a nice place to visit, but you wouldn't want to live there. I look around at clusters of healthy trees providing shade for nice beach homes with air conditioning and realize that for me it's the opposite here: It's a nice place to live, but I don't much like visiting.

Enough bellyaching.

I finally make it to Key West with a sense of accomplishment. I park in the partying part of town, walk around a while but don't do any partying because it's still daylight and if I drink just one beer, I'd have trouble finding my bike. So, regrettably, I have no wild-times-with-scantily-clad-babes stories to relate, but I will say that if you're into partying with scantily-clad babes (or if you're partial to scantily-clad, muscle-bound hunks), you might want to put this area of Key West on your prime spot list.

The next place I visit is the Hemingway House. Ernest Hemingway is one of my heroes, not only for his writing, but also for how he never backed off from living an adventurous life, so I spend a lot of time looking around. Wonderful place. Shade from trees, comfortable grounds, breezes flowing in and out of all the rooms, an elevated walkway to his studio, and it's within a block of his favorite watering hole, Sloppy Joe's.

The residents are mostly six-toed cats, many of whom are descendants of Hemingway's first cat, Snow White. They live the ideal cat life, eating the best food, grooming themselves, chasing mice or lazing about without a care in the world.

∽

Next, I finally head on down to the most famous Four Corners monument, which resembles a large ocean buoy that proudly states

Southernmost
Point
Continental
U.S.A.
Key West, FL
Home of the Sunset

Above that it says, "90 Miles to Cuba" and above that is an emblem made up of a conch shell inside a yellow triangle on which is written "The Conch Republic."

To the left is a line of people waiting to stand next to it and get their pictures taken. It's a civilized affair because without any kind of verbal or written instructions, the person in back of you will take your photo and the person in back of them will take theirs. What happens with the last person in line at the end of the day, I don't know, but I'm sure he or she works out something.

I do get some photos of me standing in front of the monument, but what I really want is a photo of me sitting on the Beast in front of the monument.

The problem is that there's no place to park on the sidewalk (too many kids running around) and the curb in front is painted red. Normally that wouldn't worry me much, but I'd heard that the Key West police are eager to hand out traffic tickets.

Finally, I decide on a plan, walk up to a guy who's just hanging around and ask him if he'd like to make five bucks. He looks at me suspiciously so I quickly add that I just want a photo of me and my bike. He agrees, I hand him my camera and five bucks and have him stand across the street. I ride around the block to make sure no cops are around then stop next to the red curb for about a half-minute while he shutters away.

Nine of his ten photos are either way off angle or out of focus or both, and the tenth one has his finger in front of the lens. (I guess I'm not good at hiring the right people.) So I find another guy and offer the same proposition. He refuses the money and ends up taking some excellent photos, one of which is my all-time favorite of me and the Beast.

It's late afternoon and time for some food, so I head on over to the Stoned Crab. Cool place. I sit outside watching the paddle boarders and hoping to see a manatee but, alas, never do. On the menu, they brag that stone crabs are one of the few sustainable food-producing animals because you can chop off one leg and it'll grow back in a year.

Now, I know that "sustainable" is a popular and positive buzzword these days, but I wonder how the crabs feel about it. I mean, sure, they don't have nerves like we do and can't feel pain like we do, but geez, getting a leg cut off once a year has to be at least annoying, if not downright abusive.

I end up ordering three large crab legs and make a prodigious mess with the crab pliers but don't care because there's no one around to impress. The thing is, my meal comes with nothing else. No bun, no soup, no salad, no veggies (fine by me!), no anything except water. All for the price of eighty-nine bucks.

Eighty-nine dollars for three crab legs and water gets me thinking that motels rooms in Key West probably begin at twice that, so I decide to back-track on Highway 1 for a while to find cheaper accommodations.

It's raining as I head back toward the mainland, but after being hot and miserable all day, it's refreshing. I end up in Looe Key (not a misspelling and pronounced LOO-ee KEE) where, despite it being a Sunday night, there's a well attended bar, a live band, and the Dodger game is on the TV. Love it here!

About that "Conch Republic" triangle on top of the Key West monument. What exactly that was (or is) bugged me for a while so I finally looked it up and its backstory is one of the most hilariously wacky stories in U.S. history.

In April 1982, the Unites States Border Patrol set up a roadblock at the southern tip of the mainland. The reason was because of all the cocaine coming into the U.S., but it ended up being a nuisance for the Florida Keys residents. In fact, it may be the only time in history that American citizens had to show their passports to travel *inside* the United States.

Key West mayor, Dennis Wardlow, along with some other local political and legal types, requested an injunction to lift the blockade, but it was denied. When he left the federal courthouse, Mayor Wardlow proclaimed to the gathered crowd and TV reporters that on noon of the following day, April 23rd, The Florida Keys would secede from the United States and forever be known as the Conch Republic.

The next day Mayor Wardlow did just that, thereby becoming Prime Minister Wardlow, and he christened the new nation by breaking a loaf of stale bread over the head of a man dressed in a U.S. Navy uniform. Thus the rebellion began, a rebellion unlike any other in history.

After a minute (just one minute), the din of celebration died down, at which time Prime Minister Wardlow officially surrendered to a Navy admiral who happened to be there. He then demanded one billion dollars in reparations so the Keys could rebuild after the devastations caused by their one-minute war of secession from the United States.

The Keys never got the money but as fantastic as it sounds, because the U.S. government never formally rejected the secession, the Conch Republic is still today a bonafide country with internationally recognized passports and its citizens can hold dual citizenship with the United States. My, oh my.

05

THE SECOND FOUR CORNERS #4: BLAINE, WASHINGTON (OR IS IT?)

It wasn't until 2015 that I visited Blaine, Washington, the last of my Four Corners visits. I'm heading north out of Seattle and the first order of business is to get past the slow-go big city traffic and the questionable road conditions. Plus it's raining. And lane-splitting is illegal in Washington. But as I look at the faces of the commuters, I realize again, as we all have, that despite all that, my mode of transportation is the superior one.

It's not until I'm north of Everett and Marysville that the traffic and the road surface settle down and smooth out. It's still raining, but it seems appropriate because, in my mind at least, Washington and rain go together like clutch and throttle control.

Despite the quarreling clouds, I get a good look at the surroundings. Trees all over, grass covered hillsides, smart-looking farms, wooden structures, very few billboards, and a local place selling homemade apple cider.

When riding in the rain, I sometimes get a cozy feeling similar to being inside and warm when it's cold and wet outside, and that's how it is now. It's one of those times when the rumble from your bike calms your nerves and evens out your heart and you get the feeling that you and the rest of the world are rolling along just fine.

I finally get to Blaine and pull off the freeway onto Harrison Avenue. There's no monument here so, as with San Ysidro, I need to find the post office. I'm looking for a place to park so I can get out my map when, whoops!, right there is an American flag waving above zip code 98230. So I ride around the block, park, and get some photos of the Beast in front of the front doors that have the zip code above them.

I feel accomplished. It may sound silly to say that about something that wasn't difficult and offers no fame or money. The thing is, visiting all the four corners cities was something I'd wanted to do for no other reason than to do it. And that's what I did.

It wouldn't be right to end this chapter without addressing the dispute about Blaine being the northwestern-most city, a dispute that would go away if the civic leaders in Blaine would just hurry up and build a monument. Just like San Ysidro, it'd be a great investment with all the money flowing into their coffers from the hundreds of thousands of monument visitors a year. Anyway, here's the gist.

We all learned back in grammar school that the western two-thirds of the boundary between the United States and Canada is the 49th parallel. (It goes from Buffalo Point, Manitoba to a point in the Salish Sea.) Back in the mid-1800s, when this was agreed upon, all the government types figured a straight boundary line was a good idea, and I'm sure it was, but you have to wonder if any of them ever looked at a map because no more than twenty miles west of Blaine, across the Strait of Georgia, is a little, southern-pointing peninsula called Point Roberts.

Point Roberts is below the 49th parallel. This means that its fewer-than-five square miles are part of the United States, specifically the state of Washington. But because it's separated by water from Washington, there are only four possible ways to get there: swim, sail, fly or ride (or drive) through Canada.

Let's face it, swimming twenty miles is out of the question for almost everyone. Sailing there might put you in the hands of customs officials (I don't know) and as far as I can tell there's no ferry service. It's the same with flying there and landing on the grass runway of the Point Roberts Airpark.

Besides, those who swim, sail and fly are a small minority and even if you did one of those, you wouldn't have a motorcycle to ride so why bother?

All of this means that nearly everyone who wants to visit must cross an international border into Canada then another one into Point Roberts. And coming back, they'd have to reverse that.

To do four international border crossings in one day seems like a hassle, and it is, but I want to make sure that my last Four Corners visit is a valid one no matter what city becomes the official, monument-hosting Four Corners representative in the northwest.

Besides, there's another reason. I did a Google search on the place and discovered a persistent rumor that Point Roberts is the prime location for people in witness protection. Makes sense because if you're a hit man with a criminal record looking to rub out an informant, it's doubtful that the Canadian Border Guards would let you enter their country. Intrigue! So I venture forth.

I arrive in Point Roberts, get a map and ride around. Servicing the 1300 residents are a grocery store, five gas stations, one medium sized restaurant, a few very small ones, a well-populated Marina and an 18-hole golf course. No McDonald's, no Costco, no WalMart, no Starbucks, no strip malls. Excellent!

The roads are narrow and tree-lined, and the homes close to the beach look like beach homes while the inland homes look more like mountain homes. The beach, if you can call it that, at the southern side of the peninsula is mostly rock and driftwood, but Maple Beach on the eastern side is mostly sand lapped by small waves. I never got a good look at the western side.

One time I see something unusual and end up asking a local resident about it.

> **Me:** Say, I just saw something unusual and wondered if I could ask you about it.
>
> **Point Roberts Guy:** Sure! What was it?
>
> **Me:** A pure black squirrel. Never seen one before.
>
> **Point Roberts Guy:** Oh, they're all over.
>
> **Me:** Really?
>
> **Point Roberts Guy:** Yeah. They taste a lot better than the brown ones, too.

Me: They do?

Point Roberts Guy: Yeah! You know how the brown ones are sour and tough, right?

Me: Okay.

Point Roberts Guy: Well, the black ones are sweet and tender. They barbecue real nice, too.

Me: Well, there ya go!

After that, I take another look at my map and see that the main attractions in Point Roberts form their own miniature Four Corners. Clockwise from the northeast they are Maple Beach, Lily Point, Lighthouse Park and Monument Park.

Wait! *Monument* Park? There's a monument here? Point Roberts actually trumped Blaine and built a monument? Woah!

I immediately climb on the Beast, head west, and on the way send good luck wishes to all the black squirrels I see. I get there quickly, walk down a path and, sure enough, the monument exists! A nice, solid obelisk reaching up to the heavens saying, "Yep, I'm here!"

The problem is that everything written on it and on the plaque nearby is about it being Marker One of the U.S./Canadian border. In other words, there's nothing around here saying Point Roberts is the most northwestern city, which makes me wonder if it's a valid Four Corners Monument.

Then another question occurs to me. Sure, Washington is part of the contiguous forty-eight states, but Point Roberts isn't connected to it. Does all that interposing water disqualify Point Roberts?

I'm confused so I ask my biker/writer friend Gary, a Washington resident, but he says nothing to clarify the situation. He points out that if you disregard Point Roberts because of the water, you'd have to do the same for Key West. (When going to law school, he majored Finding Loopholes.)

Then to make matters as clear as used motorcycle oil, he tells me about Cape Flattery, which sits at the northwestern point of the Olympic peninsula. Blaine and Point Roberts are farther north, but Cape Flattery is much farther west. Then he asks an unanswerable question, "Who's to say that north is a more valid direction than west?"

Not only that, he tells me that on the way to Cape Flattery there's a road sign that says it's the most northwestern point, but that just brings up another question without a definitive answer: Does a sign qualify as a monument?

Now I'm really confused. There are three possible locations for the most northwestern point in the United States, but none of them have an unquestionably valid monument, which means there's no carved-in-stone location for the most northwestern city.

Regrettably, I can't visit Cape Flattery on this trip because I'm in a time crunch to get home. Someday, though, I'll make the trek because I want to have all my Four Corners bases covered. Besides, from the photos I've seen, it's a beautiful place.

Later, I realize there's a growing anxiety deep inside of me, a swirling of unanswerable questions and confusions. My fervent wish is that someday someone, *please anyone*, in the Pacific Northwest will hurry up and build a valid Four Corners monument so I can sleep well at night.

∝

At my first gas stop on the way home, I'm still gleaming with pride. When you're in that kind of mood, a conversation with a stranger is easy and that's exactly what I find myself having with a lady who's drinking coffee and smoking a cigarette. It's not long before I mention what I'd just done. Her shocked and disapproving reaction is not unusual. "You did all that *on a motorcycle?*"

I smile. It's common to hear non-bikers remark that they cannot see any value in riding a motorcycle. The sentiment is understandable because until you ride, it's difficult, perhaps impossible, to understand the connection between motorcycling and Freedom.

Further, both motorcycling and Freedom are sometimes, perhaps oftentimes, hard and dangerous. None of us likes being painfully cold or getting a sunburnt face, or being wind-battered hour after hour, day after day and how it hardens our skin; or our eyes getting sore from the glaring sun while every muscle is on the verge of cramping. And let's face it, asphalt is unforgiving, and winds blow and rains fall without regard for you or me.

Despite the hazards of Freedom, we yearn for it and relish how it makes us grow. In a similar way, we ride motorcycles not *because* of the hazards, rather we ride because of what facing them does for us. We endure, push through and rise above, and come upon realities about ourselves that no one else can give us, realities as personal as our own DNA.

There is great joy in conquering a challenging road and in mastering those twisted canyons, blind curves, rough road surfaces, and yes, visiting all Four Corners cities. We often gravitate to such paths because it is within those challenges that we find that we are capable of more, that we possess the wisdom to successfully apply our skills to previously unknown tasks.

Ultimately, what we long for is to test ourselves and the chance to succeed. And every time we climb on our bikes, we are tested, even when conditions are perfect.

Too, riding a motorcycle is a tribute, a tip of the helmet, as it were, to our rugged ancestors who challenge us through the dust of centuries, proof that we have not succumbed to the safety nets of civilization.

PART II

EASTERN BEAUTY

*You know a moment is important
when it is making your mind go numb with Beauty.*

Friedrich Nietzsche

———

Let Beauty be your end.

Jack London

06

PLANS

Despite what my family and friends may think, I'm good at making and
following plans. Not only that, I like plans. Really. That is, as long as
they're not too detailed. Actually, to be honest, plans without details are my
favorites. But then maybe a detail-less plan isn't a plan at all, I don't know, but
if that's the case, I wouldn't know what to call it so I'll just go with "Plans."

My current Plan (and it's a good one) is to find an enjoyable route up
to Canada, then ride in that country for a while (always a good idea), then
meander around a part of the United States the Beast and I have never
ridden in: New England and the rest of the eastern states.

It all begins on the last day of the Black Hills Motorcycle Rally in South
Dakota. (Yeah, that'd be Sturgis.) It's around noon when I wake up, step
out of my tent and see that all my neighbors have already left, but I take a
few moments to say a warm and silent farewell to them anyway.

An hour or so later, the souvenirs have been wrapped up and sent home,
the Beast is loaded up and strapped down and I make my way through the
mud of the Buffalo Chip Campground. It's raining as I get onto Interstate
90 East so I'm wet and dirty and even though I woke up at noon, I'm un-
derslept. Yeah, one of those late nights that ends after sunrise.

But dang it, I'm feeling fine because the first part of "The Plan" is to catch
a mind-blowing sunset over the Missouri River, thereby adding another
sweet memory to the many I have of the Big Muddy.

On the way, I breathe the peace from a land that soothes you with its serenity, a land that demands to remain unbroken, a land as tough as we all yearn to be.

∝

I do get some photos of a mind-blowing sunset after taking a dirt road to a cliffside on the western edge of Chamberlain, South Dakota, and the following morning, I'm rolling along Interstate 90 without a worry. The temperature's a tad warm but comfortable enough, the road's in excellent shape, there's very little traffic, and I'm right where I belong, atop the Beast, smiling big and feeling fine.

And I run out of gas.

It's embarrassing. After all, I'm supposed to be an adult and one of the things real adults are not supposed to do is run out of gas. I'm so embarrassed that I can't bring myself to ask for help from the people in the passing cars. In fact, I can't even look at them because I know what they're saying. "Oh look, George, a stupid adult on a motorcycle ran out of gas."

It doesn't make sense because I should get at least 170 miles per tank, but my trip odometer is at 135. And that doesn't include the reserve tank, which to my chagrin, is already open and used up. Why? I don't know! I never keep that lever open!

I'm a hundred yards from the next exit, another two hundred from a lone gas station, and absolutely do not want to push my bike that far. So I start rocking the Beast left and right hoping that a drop of gas hiding in a crevice will somehow fall into the carburetor. I crank the engine but nothing. More rocking and cranking but nothing. Two more times I rock and crank but still nothing. Finally, on the fifth try, the engine fires up.

I make it off the freeway but get only half way to the gas station. More rocking and cranking and on the fourth try, another success. The engine stops again, but I have just enough momentum to reach a gas pump.

I fill up the tank and the pump shows the maximum for the Beast: 5.1 gallons. That comes out to twenty-seven miles per gallon, which is crazy because I average thirty-six miles to the gallon and with freeway riding, commonly get over forty. I can't imagine what the problem is. The engine sounds fine (great!) so instead of calling a tow truck, I decide I can make it to the Harley dealership in Mankato, Minnesota without causing any damage.

I check the mileage at the next three gas stops and it ranges from normal down to twenty-three miles per gallon. Now it's ridiculously crazy. I mean, Cadillacs get better gas mileage than that. Maybe even the space shuttle.

After crossing into Minnesota, I pull over at the first rest stop and get into a conversation with Paul and Marty, two bikers going home to Ohio after a week in Sturgis. Their bikes are piled ridiculously high with everything from tents and fishing rods to umbrellas and lawn chairs. (Somewhere in there I think I see a kitchen sink.) What's even more impressive is that they each used only four bungee straps and some duct tape.

I walk around to check out their handiwork and am in awe. I swear, if you gave them a dozen bungee straps and two rolls of duct tape, they could strap the entirety of Manhattan on the back of a Vespa scooter.

A Helluvit is the taking of a route for no reason other than you want to. The thinking is usually along the lines of, "Well dang, there's a road, why not?" or "Gosh, that seems like a good direction." Oftentimes, they lead to something uninspiring and when that happens, your most exciting thought is, "Uh, oh-kay, I'm here." Occasionally, however, you'll come to a pretty creek or pond or a unique cluster of trees and this is the payoff, something you'll remember forever. But wherever you end up, it's all good because doing something just for the helluvit is a rush of freedom.

Despite the low gas mileage, I take a few Helluvit side trips, the last being a short one to Minneopa Falls, which is not far from Mankato. Wonderful place! Wonderful not only because the park ranger on duty is a biker and lets me in for free, but because of the beautiful lawns, the picnic tables under gazebos, and the rustic walkways, steps and bridges that lead you all around the place. True, the falls of Minneopa may be on the small side, but they're falls nonetheless and I like waterfalls.

I get a room in Mankato and go to the dealership the following morning. The mechanic, a friendly fellow, comes out, we shake paws, then he rolls the Beast into the service bay. Ten minutes later he comes out with a big grin and invites me in to have a look.

The air filter is dirty. Really dirty. A gum wrapper, a paper receipt, parts of a plastic bag, cellophane, weeds, hardened dirt, the works. In fact, it's so dirty that after he finishes cleaning it, the resulting puddle of crud looks like the bottom of a twenty-year-old dumpster in downtown Detroit. (Thank you Sturgis!) He also cleans out the gas line and the carburetor and I'm handed a bill so low that I question it, but the service manager assures me it's correct. I like Mankato.

With my gas mileage back to normal, I head east, then south, then cross over the Mississippi River at La Crosse and roll into Wisconsin where the Great River Road (Highway 35) parallels the river through the Mississippi River Blufflands, also known as Wisconsin's West Coast.

It's a two-lane, not-too-wide road with low mountains and inviting hollows on the left. Sprinkled throughout are small towns and quaint hamlets, the buildings of which are a cross between seaside bungalows and mountain retreats. Today, the weather varies from the mid 60s to the high 70s and there's a cool, lazy breeze all along the way.

I pull over in a brick-lined turnout to take some photos and, as I always do, read the information signs. It's here that I learn the amazing facts that bald eagles mate for life and build nests six feet across and ten feet high in only four days. With due respect to Paul and Marty, the two bikers I met earlier, bald eagles do all this without bungee straps or duct tape.

To my right is a railroad line and just beyond that is the Mighty Mississippi, my constant companion for these sixty miles. Despite the never-ending human traffic on either side, the daily trains, the busy boat docks, the countless fishermen, the thousands of tugboats and pleasure boats, the enormous commerce, the histories good and bad, the Mississippi remains resolute and calmly travels his chosen route as if he's the Lord of North America. And I believe he is.

At Prairie du Chien (officially pronounced as prair-doo-SHEEN, but I heard it as prair-duh-SHOON), I head east on Highway 18, another unencumbered two-lane road, and end up in Madison, a place which exemplifies the word terrific.

It *is* a cool city, but for me, the primary reason for all this terrific-ness is the company and conversation of my terrifically talented friend, Mars. In fact, Mars is so terrific, that, even though she conscientiously maintains a healthy-but-not-quite-vegan diet, she takes me to a place where I have a terrific man-burger and man-fries.

The next day is a short one because I make it only to Green Bay. My primary reason for being here is to have a look at the most famous football stadium in the world, Lambeau Field. Despite several wrong turns, I finally find the dark green and brown landmark and twice ride around it taking photos. All the while I can hear Vince Lombardi's voice: Thuh Green. Bay. Packahs.

Last, let me say that the countrysides of Minnesota and Wisconsin in the summertime are so scenic and ideally American that they make you feel like you're in a Norman Rockwell painting. The towns, townships and unincorporated areas are rustic and clean, healthy trees are never more than a short walk away, and the hale and hearty farms stretch out all over the loping landscape.

And fitting right in with all this, the family homes are all surrounded by enormous, robust lawns. You know that old line: "Whatcha been doin'?" "Oh, just watchin' the grass grow." Well, it's so fertile here I'm thinking you could actually do that. I'm also thinking that whoever sells tractor mowers in this area must have a booming business.

UP TO THE U.P.!

The state of Michigan is divided into two land masses connected by the glorious, five-mile long Mackinac Bridge. The northwestern one sits atop Wisconsin and is called the Upper Peninsula, or the U.P. I've heard and read many times that it's a beautiful place and, well, doncha love it when everything you've been told about an area is true? Rivers and streams, lakes and ponds, blue skies and white clouds, great roads and perfect weather. My, oh my.

I'm on Highway 141, which doesn't go over the Mackinac Bridge, but it does pass through one picturesque area after another that are scattered about with more Norman Rockwell-like towns and townships. Riding on the low hills and through the shallow valleys, the broad turns are pure pleasure and the closest worry is hundreds of miles away.

I stop at a roadside fruit and vegetable stand in L'Anse (pronounced Lawns) and buy a tub of perfectly ripe, just picked cherries called Michigan Sweet Blacks which, I admit, do have a perfectly sweet taste, yesirree. I continue around the southwestern end of L'Anse Bay then take a short Helluvit ride around the village of Baraga, which was named after a Catholic Bishop who wrote the very first book using the Native American Ottawa language. (You *never* stop learning when you ride a motorcycle.)

I end my ride for the day in Houghton, pronounced "HOE-tn" by the local folks. While there, I learn that a dentist named Jack 'Doc' Gibson formed the world's first professional hockey team in Houghton in 1904. Five minutes later there was a brawl that resulted in three ejections and two double majors.

The folks here are conversationally playful and call themselves Yoopers (U.P.-ers). You know they're proud of the moniker because you can get Yooper t-shirts, Yooper bumper stickers, and bottled water called Yooper Water (ONCE A YOOPER, ALWAYS A YOOPER!), which is so good it'll smooth your wrinkles, straighten your teeth and cure baldness. Or so I was told.

The following morning I head north on Highway 41 to Copper Harbor, forty-seven miles away. Of course, it's not the same Highway 41 that leads from Fresno up to Yosemite in California, but if you're looking for beauty as a common factor, it may as well be. The road is in excellent shape and is never truly straight, but all the curves are on the gentle side so braking is optional. Too, it's never totally flat so your route is either up-down-up-lean-left or down-up-down-lean-right. Nestled on both sides are trees so full of growth that you feel like you're cuddled up in an enormous down comforter.

And then. And then you lean around another curve and ride the last twelve miles.

This is outright spectacular. You simply could not find a more perfect route for cruising. The road's shoulders disappear so the trees are even closer than before; so close that each one leans over to kiss its sweetheart on the other side, creating a canopy of loveliness, while the soft sunlight polka-dots its way through the leaves and the scent of pine cleans out any coarseness you may harbor.

And just when you think it can't get any better, you round another curve and right there, on your left, the sparkling, emerald-colored Lake Medora bursts into view. It's a sucker punch of aesthetics that nearly knocks me out.

I arrive in Copper Harbor, which sits as pretty as you please on the shore of Lake Superior and, whaddya know!, there's an arts and crafts fair going on in the park. I'm thinking, "Can this day be any more perfect?" The live music is excellent and so is the food, though the cuisine is way different from what you find at a motorcycle rally. I gotta say that after spending a week in Sturgis, it's weird to be at a public event where you can buy a vegetable.

Another excellent thing is the conversational skill of the local residents, all of whom seem to have at least one dog. (Dogs, I find out, can also be Yoopers.) I ask one of them (a person, not a dog) about the winters here, if it snows much. He says, "Oh, it's not too bad. Last year we got only 136 inches."

I ride around the area and end up on the narrow and cozy Lake Manganese Road which, as I correctly predicted, leads to Lake Manganese. (How do-oo I do it?) The only others visiting the lake are a husband and wife who are throwing sticks and tennis balls into the water for their five Yooper dogs to fetch. Tell ya what, there is no better picture of "ecstatic" than dogs fetching sticks and tennis balls in the water.

I head back to the party in the park, ignore the vegetables, get a sausage dog (my second for the day), chat with a few two- and four-legged Yoopers, then backtrack on Highway 41 a bit. It's not long before I come to Gay Lac la Belle Road, hang a left and find myself surrounded by more prettiness than you think is possible.

I soon come to a small but proud waterfall, Haven Falls, in a small but proud park right next to the road and think, "Is there no end to the 'perfect' around here?" After a while, Gay Lac la Belle begins following the forested shoreline of Lake Superior and, sure enough, all the "perfect" of a perfect day keeps on coming on.

After several miles I see two women walking alongside the road poking around in the grass and weeds. Later on, there are two more people doing the same thing. Then two more and then a family with a bunch of kids. I can't figure out what they're doing and finally pull over and ask two ladies, a mother and daughter, what the heck they're all up to. Smiling, they show me their four buckets full of wild blueberries, which will soon find their way into homemade blueberry pies.

Really? Wild blueberries? Yooper neighbors picking wild blueberries on a Sunday afternoon so they can bake blueberry pies? Well, I'd say a perfect day just got even more perfect.

08

HELLUVITS

Ideal riding weather. That's what I'm thinking as soon as I wake up and open the front door of my motel. The sun makes it a tad on the warm side, but the clean, cool breezes lower the temperature right into that narrow band of, like I said, ideal. The only item needed to make it an all around ideal day is a ride through some gorgeous scenery and that's exactly what I intend to do in the second largest country in the world.

Crossing the border into Canada at Sault Ste. Marie (soo-saynt-muh-REE) is the opposite of what it looked like it was going to be. There're only me and a family of four so you'd think the border guards would take the opportunity to fully scrutinize everyone, but instead, they just want our passports and aren't interested in asking any questions.

Then you'd think that with so few people and no interest in them, it'd go quickly, but that's not the case, either. Instead, the border guard keeps our passports in a pile on his desk without ever peeking inside.

So it's a wait-and-watch-the-clock affair. It's quiet and I soon start hearing the ticking of that clock and, well, you know how that goes. Once you notice the ticking of a clock there's simply no way to un-notice it.

The plastic chair isn't that uncomfortable, but after only a few minutes of ticking, I'm antsy, so I get up to go outside for a walk. Before I'm half way to the glass door, the border guard snaps back my attention by calling me "Sir!" with a voice that cuts like a rusted chainsaw. I stop and turn around.

He tells me I have to stay inside because on the other side of those glass doors is Canada and I've not yet been allowed to go there. And I'm not allowed to go back to the American side, either. And he keeps calling me "sir," which has always made me feel awkward. Or old. Or both. Anyway, I don't argue because, well, he's a border guard and I'm not, and his job is to guard the border and my job is to convince him that I'm not the kind of person he needs to guard against. Besides, he has a gun.

Forty-five tedious, clock-ticking minutes later, I legally walk through those glass doors, make a quick getaway through the city, hop onto Highway 17B and into the Ontario countryside. And a lovely countryside it is. There are a lot of farms, and though it may not be as wild with growth as what I've seen in some other parts of the province, it's nevertheless filled with flourishing plant life, deftly evolving clouds, and a matrix of unspoiled rivers and lakes.

As I said, the weather is ideal and despite the bumpy road surface that's urging me to keep a moderate pace, I feel unrestricted, like I'm running with scissors next to a pool and no parents are around to stop me.

At times like this, it'd be great to go helmet-less, but that's illegal in Canada and if I get caught, I might get deported to the United States and then I wouldn't get to enjoy this bountiful country. And if I get only a ticket, it'd make a deep cut into my already meager budget. Nevertheless, helmet-clad or open-air, it's a supremely pleasant ride through a countryside that amplifies the freedoms of riding.

At first, I mostly stay on the Trans-Canada Highway (Highway 17 in Ontario), where for every road sign in English, there's one in French, and I wonder if that's the reason for the high taxes here. I mean, they have to somehow pay for all those extra road signs, right?

The only annoying thing is road repair every ten or so miles. Really, if there's anything that'll lower your enthusiasm along with your daily mileage (or kilometerage) it's waiting for a pilot car to pilot you through sand, mud and gravel.

That's not to say I'm against pilot cars, I'm not. In fact, I like them because their rear tires create the safest possible path through those unpaved surfaces. Besides, I'm glad they're repairing the roads because there's hardly a decent stretch of pavement longer than a half mile. (For you Canadians, that's .8 kilometers.) Normally, numerous delays like this tend to arouse an annoyed mindset, but that's not happening today because this is Canada, home of placid lands under tranquil skies.

One stop I make is in Bruce Mines, which has a population of under 600. It's a cute place so I hang out for a while, chat with a few locals and find out that the fine for not cleaning up after your dog is $150. I'm thinking that a fine that high can mean only one thing: the dogs of Bruce Mines are the size of elephants.

The folks I talk with are quintessential Canadians, meaning they're quick to smile, know how to start a friendly conversation ("You're from America, eh?") and how to properly end one ("Have a blessed stay in Canada, eh!"). One of them, a lady working at the Nugget Food Store, tells me I should continue down Highway 17 and spend the night in Blind River because, "It's big. They even have a hospital."

I begin taking some Helluvits, nothing extensive or noteworthy, and some hours later find out that Blind River has a population of 3600 so the lady back at the Nugget Food Store was right. (Hey, if you live in a town with 600 people, a town with 3600 *is* big.) And not only do those 3600 citizens have a hospital, they managed to pony up the funds to build a pretty fountain right in the middle of the river Blind, which flows into the North Channel of Lake Huron.

Though it happens almost every day, it's always gratifying to meet up with other bikers and have a spirited conversation and Canadian bikers are some of the best, especially when you're drinking brews on a motel veranda at the end of the day.

Claude is one of those animated guys who never sits down, who can eat ten thousand calories a day and never gain a pound, and who'll get all pumped up about the slightest thing, like an extra tomato slice on his burger. He tells us about how he had lowered the plexiglass face guard on his helmet just seconds before a four inch piece of metal fell off a truck and smacked into it. Without that face guard, he'd have been a goner. In a few seconds of solemnity, he says he doesn't normally thank God, but in this instance he did. Then he runs into his room, gets his helmet, and with a big smile shows us that cracked face guard like it's a sculpture worthy of Michelangelo.

Martin, who's on his way back home after riding the Alaska Highway, is a bohemian philosopher type of biker, relaxedly leaning back in his chair like he's stretched out on a water bed. He tells us that during his trip, he rode into Montana and Wyoming where a hornet got stuck under his sunglasses and stung his eye three times, but thankfully, the swelling went down after only a day.

I'm too embarrassed to tell them that my biggest escapade so far on this trip was running out of gas so I tell them about an "exciting" accident I had a couple of years ago.

After a while, Toby, a fine painter of flowers and a lover of Classical music, joins us. Her husband is a well-known Cherokee painter and she's filled her van with his paintings to deliver them to an exhibit in Ottawa. After an hour or so, Claude and Martin go to their rooms, but Toby and I continue talking for a long time, mostly about Chopin (she's a serious fan) and the advantages and disadvantages of painting with oils verses acrylics. Wonderful.

The next day, after taking a few more Helluvits and again coming across nothing worth writing about, I end up at a motel in North Bay right on the beach of Lake Nipissing, but don't get too impressed. The place is pretty much a dump and a safe haven for mosquitos.

The beach, however, is nice and clean as is the lake, so I don my swim trunks and wade into the water, which is that ideal temperature between too warm and too cool. I keep wading farther and farther away from shore hoping to get somewhere deep enough for a swim. (I'm forever in need of exercise.) Eventually, I'm a hundred meters out, but the waterline is still only at my knees, so I wade back to the beach figuring the bones got enough of a workout.

It's been a good day (except for the mosquitos) and I'm enjoying that satisfying combination of tiredness and exhilaration. I read a bit, write a bit, brush my teeth, shower, pack away my dirty clothes, and take out the clean ones for tomorrow.

Then, just before going to bed, I discover I've already used the last of the toilet paper in my room. Then I discover that the motel office is deserted and then discover that the folks running the place are long gone. I start knocking on my neighbors' doors and finally find a guy in white underwear and a wife-beater tank top who has an extra roll and thereby comes to the rescue. Ah, the life!

$$\infty$$

The next day is my last day in Ontario and I want to find one last side road, take one last Helluvit, that leads to a sparkling view of a lake or river, a last bit of magic, as it were. I'm back on Highway 17, but none of the roads crossing it hold any kind of draw. Finally, I see one that promises to be magical.

It bends and bends some more until Highway 17 is way out of sight. After a few more turns, the bumpy pavement turns to dirt and rock and about a hundred meters later it deadends next to a corral in which are seven healthy, attentive horses. Well, when you're outside taking photos, you get what you're given, so I figure my last Ontario photo is going to be the iron horse (the Beast) having a chat with those seven horses.

I no sooner get out my camera when, on the other side of the corral, two dogs start running toward me. Big, muscular, loudly barking dogs who are hellbent on eating a human leg for lunch. I shove the case beneath my jacket, put the camera between my teeth and climb back on the Beast. I'm pointed in the wrong direction so I commence making a three-point turn on a gravel and dirt road that's only ten feet wide, an unsteady and slow maneuver at best.

The dogs are closing in, saliva dripping off their razor sharp teeth and the horses look like they're watching the winning goal in the seventh game of the Stanley Cup. When I'm finally pointed in the right direction and take off, the dogs are right there, nipping at my boots. Thankfully, I make it out alive, both legs intact.

Getting back on the 17, I start thinking about this and come upon some deep wisdom that ranks in importance with checking for toilet paper *before* you sit down in a public restroom. For your own safety, my friends, whenever you come to a deadend, turn your bike around *before* you get off.

TOLERANCE

Not long afterward is when I run into the only bad weather in Canada, a rockin' thunderstorm in the southwestern outskirts of Ottawa. The wind is howling, the traffic is fast and thick, and the road is in terrible shape including two miles where the pavement is missing. I'm thinking I had a better chance of survival with the dogs.

When riding in conditions like this, it's understandable to think, "What the heck am I doing on a motorcycle?" Well, if you ride, the answers are obvious and many of them have to do with Freedom.

This may sound crazy, and it may very well be, but it's during crazy conditions like this that I often think about the connection between riding a motorcycle and Freedom, and how motorcycles have become a symbol of Freedom, even to those who don't ride. In fact, riding a motorcycle may be the purest and most accessible incarnation of Freedom—it begins the moment you kick up your kickstand. Truly, the Freedom Avatar is a biker.

The fundamental reason for this is that Freedom *does not* offer security, comfort or wealth, and neither do motorcycles. That's not to say that Freedom and motorcycles prohibit those things, they don't, but that security, comfort and wealth are not integral parts of Freedom or motorcycles.

For instance, the Beast is the most comfortable bike I've ever ridden, but honestly, it's not nearly as comfortable as the leather chair I'm sitting on as I write this. Comfort is a relative thing. And security? Sure, we do a lot of things to make ourselves more secure, but we'll never be as safe as sitting behind an air bag in a car or a truck. Security is relative as well.

It's that thought about security that gets me thinking I ought to put my attention back on the road, so that's what I do. It soon smoothens out, thank goodness, and I make it through Ottawa and to the other side of the storm, eventually riding into the province of Quebec and stopping for the evening in Gatineau.

In many aspects, Quebec is a different country. The moment, and I mean the very instant, you cross into that province, everyone is speaking French. All the road signs are only in French, too, replete with all sorts of diacritical marks and a white king's (or queen's) crown, so I'm thinking the taxes must be lower here than in Ontario because they don't have to pay for all those extra signs in English.

At my last stop for the day, a big (and I mean really big), gnarly-looking, scowling, muscle-bound, tattoo-covered biker saunters over and with a pleasantly lilting voice says, "Bon jour!" The look on my face is probably similar to the look on his when I say "How do!"

My first book, Freedom's Rush, is almost ready to go to the printers so it's in Gatineau where, even though the editing and proofreading are done, I spend three days scouring the whole thing, trying to make sure I didn't screw up too much. Plus there are some other publishing type chores I need to do, like get a photo of myself and write a short bio for the back cover.

The motel I choose is on the outskirts of the city and connected to a small, dingy casino. After slowly looking me up and down with an oh-gawd-this-is-hard-to-tolerate look on her face, the French-speaking desk lady gives me the room farthest away from the front office in a wing of the building where I'm the only resident. It's fine by me, though, because there's hot water, the electricity works, and I don't have to put up with the frequent ding-a-lings of the slot machines.

I get everything done for the book, including a selfie portrait taken behind a McDonald's parking lot, but the hardest task is writing that short bio. For some inexplicable reason, my publisher rejects the first version.

> *Foster Kinn is the second most interesting man in the world. He recently developed a five-dollar, one-time-only pill that cures cancer, AIDS, and the common cold, then bequeathed it to humanity as a gift, but was then targeted for assassination by wealthy, nefarious humans and alien slave traders. He is currently fighting hordes of heavily armed mercenaries in various jungles of the world with only a toothpick and a cigarette lighter. The last report was that he is winning. He also likes long walks on the beach, dinner with wine by candlelight, and puppy breath. He is a Taurus with Capricorn rising.*

What, pray tell, is wrong with that? Anyway, I eventually write an acceptable bio and I'm finally ready to get back outside and enjoy the province of Quebec.

I get a late start, zigzag my way to Papineauville, stop at a roadside food place for a bowl of poutine, which is french fries with gravy and cheese curds—the Canadian equivalent of chili cheese fries but healthier—and have a chat with a friendly group of English-speaking riders.

We talk for a while about, what else, the joys and hazards of riding motorcycles and a little bit about the ridiculously high taxes in Quebec, which I find out are higher than the ones in Ontario. This gets me to thinking that maybe there *are* some road signs in English somewhere around here. Either that or sign makers get overtime pay for making all those diacritical marks that the French language requires.

It also gets me thinking about my meager budget and the fact that in addition to security and comfort, wealth is not guaranteed by riding a motorcycle either.

(If you're trying to convince your sweetheart that you'll save money by buying a motorcycle, don't have him or her read this.) I'll just say it right now. Not only is riding a motorcycle *not* going to make you rich, it's not even going to save you money. True, we get better gas mileage than most cars, but what the about other things you have to buy, like the gear you need and the biggest cost item, tires?

Speaking of tires, mine last anywhere from 8-12,000 miles while most automobile tires last 60-80,000 miles. I've paid up to $450 for a back tire alone while you can get an excellent car tire for less than half that.

Further, the average life of a motorcycle is 80-100,000 miles, but many cars will last a quarter of a million miles. Factor in all those things against what you'll save on gas and you'll come to the same conclusion as every other biker has: owning a motorcycle is *not* cheaper than owning a car.

Add that to all the high taxes in Canada and I'm thinking that to be a biker living up here, you have to be one dedicated, hardtail son of a gun. And when I look at my new Canadian biker buddies, that's exactly how they strike me.

After lunch, they offer to let me ride with them, I say I'd love to, and off we go. Not long afterward, we make a short stop for something cool to drink and it's here that I tell them that I want to get way on the other side of Montreal before the sun sets. They look at each other for some moments, then one of them looks directly at me.

Canadian Biker Dude: You'll never make it.

Me: Uh, okay.

Canadian Biker Dude: I'm serious. It's impossible for a foreigner.

Me: Impossible?

Canadian Biker Dude: Yeah. You'll get lost.

Me: Makes sense, that's something I'm good at.

Good guys and one gal that they are, they offer to lead me through the maze of downtown Montreal freeways. When we descend into that Gordian Knot of cement and crazy traffic, I realize they were right. I would have gotten lost. Several times. In fact, left on my own I may still be there.

One by one, they bid adieu as they take the offramps leading to their homes and eventually I'm back to depending on my own sense of direction.

Or rather lack of it. I had intended to stay close to the St. Lawrence River, but not surprisingly, my non-sense of direction takes me to the farmlands well south of it. It's a pretty and fertile area, but I've a hankering to get back to water, so I check the map then head north on Highway 55.

Just before the river is a Harley dealership in Bécancour, so I go in and buy a t-shirt. (I swear, t-shirts at Harley dealerships are like industrial-strength magnets.) When I get to the cash register, I stop and stare, mouth open, mesmerized by the girl behind it because she's the spitting image of Daenerys Targaryen from the TV show Game of Thrones. You know, Khaleesi, the blond chick with the dragons.

I fantasize about chopping off the heads of her three rivals and presenting them to her as a gift—you'd have to be a fan of the show to get that—but I don't. Instead, I try to be witty, which doesn't work, and charming, but that doesn't work either. So I just pay for the shirt, thank her for being pretty, then ride over the first-rate Laviolette Bridge and head west on Highway 138.

I run into some rain outside of Quebec City, but it's not cold or hard so I don't mind it much. As I get closer to the city, however, the commuter traffic gets more and more aggressive so when I see a sign for Prémont Harley, I figure it's as good a place as any to get away from all that. Besides, I can get another t-shirt or two. Maybe meet another Khaleesi and have another go at being witty and charming. Who knows?

Prémont Harley is huge and housed in a two-story, metal structure designed in a modern way with a tower at one end. I walk all around, but alas, see no one who resembles Khaleesi. Nevertheless, I do get a t-shirt (only one, they're more expensive than usual) and spend a long time checking out the large collection of old and vintage motorcycles on the second floor.

It's dusk and still raining when they close up shop so I decide to get a room for the night, but it's not as easy as it usually is. The problem is that this is a newish, sort of upscale area. Nothing wrong with that, of course, but it does mean there are no cheap motels and when you have a budget like mine, cheap motels are pretty much a necessity.

But then, this is Canada and with all the high taxes, especially in the province of Quebec, there is no such thing as cheap, so when it comes to getting a room, the cheapest you can get is a lower priced expensive one.

I ride around a bit and soon discover that not only are there no cheap motels, there are no motels at all, only hotels. With an H. Meaning multiple floors. And elevators with mirrors. And bell hops. And chocolates on the pillows, soap cakes embossed with fleur-de-lis, hospitality service managers who'll bring dinner to you room, and dimly lit lounges where you and your friends can drink wine and talk about what a wonderful hotel you're staying in.

Having no choice, I go ahead and walk into one and am immediately greeted by another check-in gal who, when she first sees me, also gets an oh-gawd-this-is-hard-to-tolerate look on her face. Boy, the amenities you get for an additional hundred bucks a night are remarkable.

The following morning, I continue east on Highway 138 and once I get out of the metropolitan area, it becomes a classic route. Forested mountains on my left, picturesque villages and towns to my right, and beyond them the majestic St. Lawrence River proudly holds the boundary between Canada and the United States. The road goes up-down-left-right through the mountains while the weather couldn't be better. It's like riding through a picture-perfect postcard so I stop often to take photos (anyone would) and to just enjoy being here.

I'd decided last night that it would be a good idea to take the ferry from Saint-Simeon (sahn-see-mee-OWN) to Rivière-du-Loup (wish I knew how to pronounce that), then ride south and cross the border into Maine. It's around lunchtime when I arrive, pull up to the dock and watch the ferry sailing away. Yep, I missed the departure time by five minutes. Someday, I should start planning things.

I buy a ticket for the next ferry, which leaves in three hours. I don't want to lose my first place in line so I park the Beast then walk back up the hill to a walk-up counter and get an ice cream. I eat it. Sit some. Get another one, eat it and sit some more. I'm bored. I decide I don't need to be first in line so I retrieve the Beast and take a short tour of southeastern Quebec.

Now *this* is a Helluvit! Though there's not much population, it's clear that the people here aren't disconnected in the least from the rest of the world. I ride by wood paneled houses with steep roofs, satellite dishes, elevated porches, split rail fences, and kids' toys on lawns. And there's a cute and clean steepled church painted yellow. And all around, like a gathering of old friends, are the birch and fir trees of the exquisite Acadian Forest.

Riding here is transcendental—you really do enter another dimension. The air is different, lighter, and there are places where the trees are so close and thick that even at its brightest, the sun can only freckle the road with light. And you keep looking at the horizon, the elusive "over there," yearning for it, as if at the top of the next hill, you'll begin to fly.

I get back to Saint-Simeon just in time for the ferry and ride down the ramp into the hull with three other riders, two of whom are father and son. The son tells me that in 1969 his dad did an Iron Butt ride before there were such things. He had just gotten a brand new Honda CB250 and with no windshield rode it 1,100 miles down the Atlantic coast in only twenty hours. I look at Dad and say, "Dayum, you are one helluva tough rider." With a red face and a modest smile, he shakes his head and says, "Oh, I don't know."

This part of the St. Lawrence River is actually called the St. Lawrence Seaway, the wide estuary that connects the river with the Atlantic Ocean, which means it's now filled with salty ocean water. The waters are calm and the trip takes over an hour so I lie down for a snooze on a bench on the second deck.

I'm awakened when a fellow with a booming voice yells, "Oh my Gawd!" I get up in a bit of a panic thinking someone fell overboard and run to the back of the ship along with most everyone else. What we see is amazing: a half dozen whales popping through the surface wishing us "Bon Voyage!"

10

TWO CANADAS

I truly dislike being the bearer of bad news—I almost didn't include this chapter in the book—but someone has to do this. It should be daily headline news, but of course, it's being ignored by all media everywhere.

This gritty, seemingly irresolvable issue is the one of the "Two Canadas" title of this chapter. As I wrote above, crossing from Ontario into Quebec is like going to a different country. Over the years, the differences between these two, Western Canada and Eastern Canada, have spawned a bit of distrust and even some hostility on both sides, and nothing, it seems, is being done to alleviate the situation.

Now believe it or not, I've discovered the root of the problem and you can trust me on this. The entire issue swirls around three common food places in Canada: Subway, McDonald's and Tim Hortons. Yeah, you noticed it, didn't you. Tim Hortons has no possessive apostrophe.

The nerve! It's so brazenly wrong, so contrary to decency, that it's difficult to just look at the name. How can they get away with this? Where are our civic leaders when we need them most? Subway doesn't need a possessive apostrophe, of course, and McDonald's does it right and has one. So we have no choice but to blame Tim Horton(')s with the moral decay of our world.

Now, it's true that Tim Horton(')s does have great coffee and good food, healthy too, and the founder is an ex-hockey player, but I just can't bring myself to support them. I mean, I do have some integrity. But when I think about aligning with McDonald's, well, I'm not too keen on doing that, either.

And if I end up supporting Subway, the neutral Switzerland in all this, I'll feel wishy-washy. I honestly do not know what to do.

To make matters worse, I find out that Tim Horton(')s's parent company is Burger King. What?! Burger King in the United States is aiding and abetting Tim Horton(')s? Treason!

What a sad, sad state of affairs. The battle lines have already been drawn and every day, the animosities between the Possessive-Apostrophe and No-Possessive-Apostrophe camps grow and no one, it seems, wants to do anything about it. And who's going to end up suffering the most? That's right, the people. You and me. The good and hardworking folks who just want to live a peaceful life with properly used possessive apostrophes. And let's not forget about the children. What will happen to our children?

Just today I discover that Tim Horton(')s has invaded the United States without a peep of protest. Where this will lead is anyone's guess, but I do have some advice. World War Possessive Apostrophe is coming, my friends, so take heed: protect your grammar books and hide your children, this is going to get ugly.

THE WAY LIFE SHOULD BE

When you consider all the factors involved (weather, traffic, surface conditions, personal health and so on) a road, like a river, is never the same, moment-by-moment becoming something other than what it was, so that every momentary turn of our wheels takes us over the threshold into the unknown.

It's no wonder, then—if I may respond to Conrad's Lord Jim—that riding a motorcycle takes vengeance on half-shut eyes, deadened ears and dormant thoughts. And as you become more aware you become more alive and become more connected with everything around you. It makes sense because motorcycling mirrors the actions of the universe.

Something others have noted is that, in a technical sense, riding a motorcycle could be defined as balancing the force of forward motion with the outward force of a turn with the downward force of gravity. And right now, the universe is doing a similar balancing act, albeit on a larger scale, as it holds colossal forces in equilibrium.

When nature's equilibrium gets upset, we have anything from a few raindrops to an all-out cataclysm. And what happens afterward? Nature settles down and finds a new equilibrium. In a smaller sense, it's the same with riding a motorcycle. When we don't balance the forces involved, we experience anything from taking a turn a few inches too wide to an all-out crash. And afterward, just like nature, we settle into another equilibrium in the sense that we go back to balancing those forces and no longer take that turn too wide. Or crash.

Ultimately, the center-point of riding and of life itself *is* Freedom. Freedom is the very core of our heart of hearts and when you get on your bike and roll on the throttle, there's a charge that runs up through you that connects you to all things, solid and abstract, grand and trifling, sacred and profane.

This ... is to be Good
Great and Joyous, Beautiful and Free;
This is alone Life, Joy, Empire, and Victory.

Shelley

───⤬───

I'm in Maine wandering left and right of US Highway 1. The temperature is perfect (mid-60s to mid-70s) and though it's mostly overcast, I run into only a teeny bit of moisture. The roads are in decent shape and the drivers are watchful for motorcycles. Not even once was I tailgated.

I think of the long distance to home and wish my family and friends were riding with me so we could marvel together at this countryside where your lungs quickly become addicted to the vigorous air.

All around is a keen, silent rush to grow and mature before Winter brings her short days and silent sheath of white. The land is ribboned with rivers and streams and freckled with lakes and ponds; the mountains are low and in the distance they are like great folds of deep green velvet, the ever-present trees bowing with the weight of growth. I half expect the verdant views to disappear around the next bend, but thankfully, they never do.

Truly, Maine is one of those states where it's clearly evident that nothing weaves the exquisite quite like Mother Nature.

Too, the citizens reflect the crisp and clean countryside, though you could argue that it's the other way around. The ones I met and saw were industrious and courteous. There is no hubris here so what you see is, indeed, what you get. The state motto is apropos: Maine, The Way Life Should Be. I'm inclined to agree.

By the bye, if you're ever in Caribou looking for excitement, the Lion's Club has bingo on Monday nights.

I cross the southern border of Maine and allow me to say this right now: In New England, it's simply not possible to put in the amount of miles per day you will in, say, Arizona, Texas or Utah. Slow moving delivery trucks on narrow, two-lane roads and small towns every ten or so miles, each with two or three stop signs and maybe a stoplight. But you don't mind because, tell ya what, New England is jam packed with an amazing amount of Pretty.

At Gorham in New Hampshire, I take a left on Highway 16 and that fine route takes me into the White Mountains. It's raining most of the time, but it's one of those rains that makes you feel comfy and cozy, and with all the trees crowding the road it's like when you were a kid after a long day of jumping in every mud puddle within a half mile radius and you're finally home, planning future triumphs inside a blanket tent. And your mom is baking cookies.

I pass by the Mount Washington Hotel where the famous (or infamous) Bretton Woods Agreement was signed in 1944. It's an enormous luxury hotel and I think about spending the night there. But then, on my budget I might be able to afford a broom closet, so I keep riding.

About the Bretton Woods Agreement. I don't like making political statements, but I will say that everyone should know about this international monetary agreement because it's something that deeply affects all of us, more so today than back then.

Enough with the politics.

Highway 16 gently goes up and down as it weaves through the mountains and it's not physically draining in the least. I end my day in the lively and personable community of Conway at the Schoolhouse Motel, which is aptly named because right when I check in, the owner gives me a delightful forty-five minute history lesson of the area. A perfect way to end an outstanding day of riding.

The next day, I head south and when I get to Meredith, I check the map and find out I'm only ten miles from Laconia. (By the bye, if you're into family-type water fun, Meredith is a place you might want to check out.)

Laconia is the site of the oldest bike rally in the world (the first one was in 1923) and hundreds of thousands of bikers attend every year. This year's rally was a couple of months ago, but I figure I'll go on over there and see the place anyway.

I get to Laconia but see absolutely nothing about a bike rally. After riding around for a while, you guessed it, I'm lost. No worries, though. I'll just pull into a gas station and get directions from someone working there.

Now, if you've ever been to New England, or know someone from there, you know that their style of speech is unique and that if the letter r is in the body of a word, they'll pronounce it as if it's an h. You know the old line: Pahk yuh cah in Hahvahd Yahd.

> **Me:** Say, do you know how I can get to the place where the Laconia Bike Rally is held?
>
> **Laconia Gas Station Guy:** Right. Yuh wanna get tuh Wizz Beach. Go down datta way *(he points)* and tuhn left at the sixth light. Yuh can't miss it.
>
> **Me:** Thanks!
>
> **Laconia Gas Station Guy:** Sixth light, tuhn left.

So I go down dattaway, but at the third light the road forks and I don't know which fork to take, so I walk into a convenience store.

> **Me:** Say, do you know how I can get to the place where the Laconia Bike Rally is held?
>
> **Laconia Convenience Store Lady:** Right. Yuh wanna get tuh Wizz Beach. Go down datta way *(she points)* and tuhn left at the thuhd light. Yuh can't miss it.
>
> **Me:** Thanks!
>
> **Laconia Convenience Store Lady:** Thuhd light, tuhn left.

So I go down dattaway, turn left at the third light and Wizz Beach is … uh, yeah, there it is, *Weirs* Beach!

Lakeside Avenue is the main drag and it's easy to see why bikers like coming here. Mostly mom-and-pop type eateries, gift shops, an arcade, and American flags hanging from lampposts and telephone poles. I walk down one side and back up the other at a comfortable pace with a smile on my face, and the only thing I wish is that there was more of it.

My walk ends at the corner of Lakeside and Highway 3 and right next to a water park is a place, don't know the name, that sells fried dough, ice cream and pizza. It all sounds scrumptious and makes me think about sitting here for a couple of hours and eating some of everything. However, I come by a dash of discipline, decide it's time for a healthy diet and get only a vanilla ice cream cone. Double scoop. Big scoops, too.

It's the kind of ice cream cone where you have to keep spinning it around, real quick-like, so you can lick the melted parts before they drip onto you fingers, but you never quite get all of them in time, but it doesn't matter because what you're really looking forward to is the half-soaked, bottom part of the cone where those little square chambers are filled with melted heaven, and when you finally get to it, you pop it into your mouth and you hear that dull crunch when you bite down and it all swirls around inside your mouth and squishes against your cheeks and you want it to last forever.

12

A PRAYER

My good friend, Debba, has a great line. New England has four distinct seasons: Rain, Snow, Mud and Construction. As far as I can tell, she's right. Evidently, I'm here at the end of Construction and the beginning of Rain and, just as you'd expect, the weather goes from unblemished-and-dry to wet-and-wet and back again.

One thing you come to appreciate when riding around the country is small town marketing campaigns. Really, they're the best. I'm tooling along Highway 104 in New Hampshire and ride past a local diner with a sign out front that reads, DON'T GO BACON MY HEART, which gets me singing that old Elton John/Bernie Taupin tune *Don't Go Breakin' My Heart*. What little I remember of the lyrics has nothing to do with riding a motorcycle or with where I am, but it's an enjoyable activity in an enjoyable countryside nonetheless.

All along, nested amid the forests, are quaint and clean small towns. There are roadside fruit and vegetable stands, more American flags on telephone poles and lampposts, garage sales, cafes featuring sweet corn and homemade maple syrup, historical sights, a plethora of mom-and-pop shops, and a rest area with a bathroom that looks like a log cabin. (When you're on the road, you get excited over things like that.)

When I get on the gently sloping and meandering Highway 4, it gets misty, which for a motorcycle is worse than rain. (Rain picks up the slick petrochemical residue out of the asphalt and washes it away; mist picks it up and just leaves it there.) Then, not long afterward, a robust rain begins to fall.

Now, I'll admit to a mercurial relationship with rain. Sometimes, riding in it is cozy, mellow even, like it was yesterday. Other times, it feels like the clouds are hurling little ball bearings at my helmet in Morse Code: DON'T TRUST YOUR TIRES, DON'T TRUST YOUR TIRES! It's seriously unnerving and that's what it feels like now.

One time I catch sight of a narrow stream that's down a short, rocky cliff and for some reason, that image gets stuck in my head as an ominous prophecy.

Because of all that, I'm riding pretty darn slow and cars are lining up behind me. I want to do the polite thing and pull over, but it's hard to find a shoulder that's more than a foot wide. Nevertheless, whenever possible, which isn't often, I do pull over so the merry and dry car drivers can continue at a faster pace.

A thunderstorm hits hard, really hard, and about a mile later I see a gas station, pull in and park under the roof next to the gas pump. The lone employee manning the place, a young woman in her late teens, is standing under the eave smoking a cigarette. I ask her if it's okay if I leave my bike under the roof until the thunderstorm passes, that if a car comes in they can go to the other side of the pump. She says it's okay as long as I don't tell her boss that she's smoking. (The boss turns out to be her dad.)

Twenty or so minutes later the rainfall slows down a little and I take off. As before, I'm going slower than the speed limit, cars are lining up behind me and there's really no safe place to pull over. And in my mind that image of the creek with hard flowing water has become a wide and deep river with Class V rapids.

Then, in a flash, it begins raining so hard I can barely see my own windshield. It's like I'm riding through an out-of-control carwash and twelve pound shot-puts are falling on my helmet without any Morse Code messages. I've no idea where the next curve is or even if I'm still going straight, and I'm guessing cars are still closing in behind me and if the visibility is only a couple of feet, there's no way they can see me. Now I have no choice but to pull over and wait for the storm to pass.

As I'm inching toward the side of the road, essentially blind, it occurs to me that this section of the road *may not have* a side to it, that maybe it goes straight down a three hundred foot rocky cliffside and into a violent, death-laden river. Moments later, as my front tire goes over the side of the pavement, I'm terrified out of my wits so I scream the plea for help and safety to the motorcycle gods, a solemn prayer that is known to motorcyclists everywhere. "OH! SHIT!"

Some minutes later, the rain lets up a bit and I see I'm on a somewhat level section of grass midway between a couple of mailboxes and a fire hydrant. I also notice that, thankfully, I'm still alive.

Safety tip: When you're in trouble, scream that plea to the motorcycle gods as loudly as you can.

Later, I find myself in the middle of the third thundershower of the day and it's here that I come upon a new realization about life: There are vastly different levels of wet.

Science tells us that the average amount of water in a human body is 60-65% and that that percentage can vary. It makes sense. Wash your hands, you're up to 67%; brush your teeth, you're up to 69%; go for an hour swim, you're up to 78%. Ride through three New England thunderstorms in one day and you've morphed into nothing more than a traveling collection of water molecules.

When Highway 4 comes to Interstate 89, I'm thinking, "It's an Interstate, there's gotta be a motel around here someplace," and decide to stop at the first one no matter if it's dumpy and cheap or upscale and expensive. I pull off at the first exit and still can't see much of anything other than rapidly moving, vertical ribbons of wetness. Finally, and just in time, I notice a sign for a Courtyard by Marriott, so I pull in.

When I step into the upscale lobby, I don't know how to act because I can't remember the last time I was in a lobby this nice. I'm feeling a little awkward and what makes it more so, is that everyone else stares like I just stepped, fully clothed, out of a swimming pool. I mean, the squishing of my boots is louder than the flat screen TV on the wall. But even though I don't fit in with the fancy surroundings, the check-in gal is genuinely pleasant.

Pleasant, Upscale Check-in Gal: Wow! Looks like you ran into some rain!

Me: I'll say!

Pleasant, Upscale Check-in Gal: What do you do when it rains like this?

Me: Oh, you know, you get wet.

Pleasant, Upscale Check-in Gal: You must be one tough rider, that's all I can say!

Me: Oh, it's not that hard. *(Translation: I think I need to change my underwear.)*

She gives me a room at the very back of the hotel as far away as possible from everyone else and with the way I look, I can't blame her. When I get there, however, I discover the real reason is that these rooms have back doors that open right onto the back parking lot, so you're never more than a dozen steps away from your bike. Not only was the check-in gal pleasant, she was thoughtful.

Everything, and I mean ev-ver-ee-thing, in my bags is soaked through and through. I can use the bathroom towels to dry all the metal and plastic, but for the clothes, I'm going to need a clothes dryer. So I call the check-in gal and ask where the laundromat is, but she says they don't have one. I'm guessing it's because people who stay in nice hotels don't like to bother themselves with dirty clothes. Either that or they're smart enough to not ride motorcycles in torrential rains.

I check to see if the housekeeping people are still around, thinking they might let me use their industrial-sized dryer, but they've all gone home for the day and their washroom is locked. So there I am, a giant water molecule sitting on the bed wondering what to do.

The only solution I come up with is to stretch bungee straps across the room, hang up the clothes and turn on the heater full blast. So I do that, and boy, does the air get hot. Seriously hot. I'm thinking that the hotel owners must have taken all the money they saved by not building a laundromat and spent it on nuclear powered room heaters.

The thing is, it's going to take hours and hours for everything to dry, which means leaving the heater on all night. Well, that makes it too hot to sleep so I open the back door to let in some cool night air, but finding the exact right width to leave the door open is tricky. Too wide makes it too cold for the clothes to dry, too narrow makes it too hot for me to sleep. It's an old school thermostat thing.

13

DETOURS

The next day is the kind you dream about. Crystalline sky, clouds like cathedrals of ivory, benevolent temperature, and cool breezes that are like kisses from an angel. Mostly, however, I'm glad it's dry, even though there are shallow puddles here and there and my boots are still a little moist.

I don't get started until noon for a ride across Massachusetts and into central Connecticut where I'm going to visit my friends, Debba and Greg, for a couple of days. I'm especially looking forward to it because, in addition to being two of the best folks around, they promised me two Greg Burgers, which are supposed to be among the best in the world. Thankfully, it's not far.

Along the way, something doesn't seem right, but I'm feeling fine and scooting right along, fully enjoying the ride. Every now and again, however, the thought pops into my head that I should stop and find out what it is that's making me feel that something's amiss. But I don't want to stop, so I don't.

Yep, it's one of those times when I should have listened to my gut because it's not until I pull over for gas in Hooksett and pull out a map that I discover I'm on Interstate 89 headed to Boston instead of Interstate 91 headed to central Connecticut. (Tell ya what, if getting lost was a marketable skill, I'd be rich.) Getting back on track means seventy-five extra miles, but what better place to undo your getting-lost-ness than in New Hampshire on a glorious day?

So I backtrack a bit then just before Hopkinton, cut southwest on Highways 202 and 9 and what a pretty and pleasant route I've stumbled upon. Except for a quarter mile patch that's like riding on ball bearings, I'm cruising in a perfectly cruising way, meaning easy sweepers, unobtrusive traffic and invigorating air.

One interesting thing about riding through untroubled areas like this is that you find all sorts of things to keep you happily occupied. Like when I cross over the Contookook River, I start thinking of all the other words that have ten letters and five of them are the same. I don't come up with any, but you know, it was fun anyway. I keep going, enjoying everything, including how some dark clouds are beginning to mingle with white ones to the south.

Right after the Connecticut River I fall in with the speedy traffic on Interstate 91, finally going in the right direction, and right after that, I'm in Massachusetts, the only state I can never spell right on the first attempt.

Tennessee used to be like that until I spent a whole afternoon working on it. Mississippi was tough until I learned that silly saying in grammar school: "M-i-crooked letter-crooked letter-i-crooked letter-crooked letter-i-hump-back-humpback-i." Connecticut was easy once my brother pointed out that it's made up with the three words Connect, I and Cut. But Massachusetts? No way. I mean, it takes me at least three attempts every time.

Spelling issues notwithstanding, on this day Massachusetts is healthy and pretty. The white and gray clouds continually morph their shapes against a stark blue sky and the meadows of the not-so-distant hills are a shimmering green backdrop for the darker green trees that lie on them in patterns we humans have yet to fathom.

It's not long before I'm under mostly gray clouds and it starts raining, but in contrast to what I ran into in New Hampshire, it's a mild, almost happy rain. Also, the road is in good shape and so are my tires, so I'm not bothered in the least. The truth is, despite the circuitous route and that rain, I'm having a darn good riding day and easily make it in time for those world-class Greg Burgers.

Debba, Greg and their two dogs, Sioux and Cheyenne, all live in a fantastic place in a fantastic neighborhood that is so, so New England, primarily because it seems like they're in a wilderness. But then, to my west coast eyes,

New England is mostly wilderness. I mean, when you see similar places in California, you *are* in an uninhabited wilderness, but in New England, a wilderness is the common setting for a neighborhood. You know, with chimneys, mailboxes, elementary schools and neighbors mowing their lawns. The thing is, there are so many trees that you never see many of the homes, so it always *feels* like you're riding through a wilderness. But then, I guess you *are* in a wilderness, but it's a neighborhood, too.

About those Greg Burgers. Oh my! Watching Greg prepare his burgers is like watching a master magician. Each thick patty is inspired with the exact right amount of spices and he does it all with a nonchalant flair, like he's done it a million times. While they're grilling, he flips them at the exact right moment so that not one iota of flavor is lost. And the taste? For two reasons, they *are* among the best I've ever eaten. In addition to having the perfect taste and texture, they have the perfect volume. (In other words, they're big.) Second, I've eaten so many McDonald's burgers lately that I'd forgotten what meat tastes like.

The next morning, I find out that Debba is in charge of breakfast. There are only three of us, but the table is big enough for six and it's covered with Debba's vast breakfast spread, which includes this homemade cherry cake thing for dessert. (Yeah, dessert after breakfast.) I keep eating and eating and eat so much I can feel my clothes shrinking by the moment.

I love sitting with them on their large and covered wooden porch, a perfect setting for unstressed conversations. In the evening, raccoons, skunks, foxes and deer walk up to the back fence to check us out and eat the table scraps Greg has left for them. And all the time, birds fly up to munch on Greg's bird food and, just like that, Greg, who has photographed almost fifty different species, will say what kind of bird it is and even if it's male or female. Exactly *how* he learned to tell the difference is something I'm afraid to ask.

On my last day, I'm alone on the porch with Sioux and Cheyenne and begin to think about baseball, which, for me, isn't unusual, especially during summertime. Of all the things written about baseball, my favorite piece is by the late Bartlett Giamatti. Giamatti was a professor of English Renaissance Literature at Yale, a life-long baseball fan, and was unanimously elected as major league's baseball commissioner just 154 days before he passed away.

Baseball will break your heart. It is designed to break your heart. The game begins in the Spring when everything else begins, and it blossoms in the Summer, filling the afternoons and evenings, and then as soon as the chill rains come, it stops and leaves you to face the Fall alone. You count on it, you rely on it to buffer the passage of time, to keep the memory of sunshine and skies alive, and then, when the days are all twilight, when you need it the most, it stops.

Y'know, there *is* something about baseball that makes everything—you and me and everyone else—okay. When you go to the ballpark and catch your first glimpse of that diamond, a certain love steals into your thoughts and all the dissonances of life disappear, and for the next few hours, you can be someone else or more of yourself, you can yell or be silent, be an expert or a novice, gregarious or a loner. It's a game that's bigger than the players, bigger than the ballparks, bigger than champions or second-placers, a paradigm of togetherness and triumphs, disagreements and disappointments. Life itself.

I check a map and find out that I'm only a little over a hundred miles from Fenway Park, the legendary home of the Boston Red Sox. Well, if you know baseball, you know that Fenway is akin to a religious shrine, so I get on the phone and reserve a ticket for their game against the Detroit Tigers the following night.

One reason I'm pleased with the plan is that the distance is short enough that I can take some Helluvits throughout the verdant Connecticut countryside, which is the motorcycle cruising equivalent of eating a Dodger Dog at Dodger Stadium, meaning it's the equivalent of taking the sacrament.

The following morning, filled with good memories, burgers and cherry cake, I say farewell to Debba, Greg, Sioux and Cheyenne then head east and a tad north. As I'm filling the gas tank in Brooklyn (the one in Connecticut, not New York), I figure I have enough time to visit Rhode Island, so I keep going east.

Rhode Island may be the smallest state in the union, but it more than makes up for its lack of square mileage with some of the loveliest routes you'll find anywhere. (For one thing, 59% of the land is covered with trees.)

Throughout most of the state, I'm on winding, two-lane roads that pass by lakes full of life, among trees full of wisdom, and over streams and rivers full of character. The drivers are courteous (always appreciate that) and the air is so clean it'll raise your IQ ten points.

Maybe it's because all my permanent places of residence have been in always-in-need-of-more-water California that I'm again amazed at how lush landscapes like this are settings for neighborhoods. I can only imagine what it's like to be home and at any moment you can play on your XBox, take a short walk in the woods to a great fishing spot, or take a nap while your IQ goes up.

14

RESPECT

A side note about Boston. I visited years ago and fell in love with it. So much history, so much personality, and so many things that make it unique. I walked around for one whole day and remember seeing a good amount of statues, including a dragon and a pear. I don't know the story behind them, but I'm sure they're as colorful as the city itself. However, the statue I remember best is the one of Samuel Adams.

What got to me most about it was the inscription on the side of the pedestal.

A STATESMAN,
INCORRUPTIBLE AND FEARLESS.

Wouldn't we all want future generations to say that about us? I wonder how many politicians today would deserve such praise.

As I get to the outskirts of Boston, I start feeling lost because, you know, I am. Riding through manufacturing and industrial areas, along a river flowing against my direction of travel, hassling one-way streets, can't get over to make a right turn I want to make, drivers looking at me as if my indecisions are a personal insult. Sigh. Typical big city traffic. I keep stopping to consult a map and only by luck and bull-headedness do I keep getting closer and closer to Fenway Park.

The commuter traffic is as thick and slow as clam chowder, it seems like there's a red light every sixty feet six inches, and it takes two or three light changes to get through an intersection. I'm thinking that if I make a wrong turn, it could take a half hour to get back on track, so I start looking for some knowledgeable help.

It's a tough task because with it being a hot afternoon, all the car drivers have their air conditioners on and their windows rolled up. Except for this one guy in an open-air, blue Jeep Cherokee a block in front of me. I break the law, split lanes and pull up alongside of him.

I ask him if he knows how to get to Fenway Park and if he knows of any motels close by. Turns out he's going to the game himself. At the next several lights, we talk a lot about baseball, and find out that he'll be sitting in left field and I'll be in right.

Baseball and motorcycle fan that he is, he says he doesn't want me to get lost again and he's happy to go out of his way and lead me through a half dozen lights to a Howard Johnson's Hotel that's within a block of the right field entrance. And that's exactly what he does. I never got your name, Mr. Blue Jeep Cherokee, but you're a good man!

At $170 a night, this particular Howard Johnson's on Boylston Street is more than three times what I'm used to paying for a room. On top of that, they charge another twenty bucks a day for parking, even though I park in a no-parking spot. But I'm fairly beat and the thought of again wrangling with downtown Boston traffic to find a cheaper place has no appeal whatsoever, so I pony up the coinage.

Now, I've been sweating all day so, you know, the "bouquet" of air following me around is, well, challenging (okay, I stink), and along with everyone else within a twenty foot radius, the check-in guy can't help but notice this. To his credit, he's actually friendly and it's clear that he's been working on the art of being tactful when he says, "So, uh, I hope you have time to, ahem, freshen up before the game." I reply, "Oh no worries, I'll be sure to change my socks."

The room is small, stuffy and non-sparkly with age, so I go outside to stretch out the bones and watch the pedestrian and automobile traffic and all the other goings-on. I'm sitting on a low brick wall, haggard and aroma handicapped, when an upscale, middle-aged couple walk by and into the trying-to-be upscale Howard Johnson's Chinese restaurant. I notice the wife whisper something to the husband and twenty minutes later, he hands me a thirty dollar Chinese dinner and wishes me better times ahead. Charity, ya gotta love it.

Fenway Park is a must-visit place even if you're not a fan of the game. Just like the city, there's so much history, so much culture, so much personality. The whole park has been totally refurbished, but they did it in such a way that it still looks like it was back in 1912 when it was first built. Even the new, high-tech scoreboards are made to look like painted wood. And between innings, a guy with a ladder walks through a door in the left field fence and changes the scores on the scoreboard of all the other major league games by hand, just the way it was done way back when.

The Big Concourse under the center and right field bleachers is like a wide boulevard in baseball paradise with vendors hawking kielbasa (love the crunch of every bite), burgers, lobster rolls, Fenway Franks and kettle corn. The walls are lined with displays of old and new Red Sox posters, paraphernalia, souvenirs, jerseys, and photos of Williams, Yaz, Fisk, Foxx, Rice, Smoky Joe, and every other great player from the past one hundred plus years.

The Big Concourse leads right onto Yawkey Way (the official address of Fenway), which is like a grand baseball bazaar in a dream. Smiling fans and smiling families of fans bubble with excitement as they weave in and out of each other heading to their seats. When I walk up the tunnel and see the Green Monster for the first time, I get goosebumps.

My seat is just beyond Pesky Pole (if I catch a ball, it's a home run) and seated around me are a group of engineers (civil-type, not train-type), and though I tell them I'm a Dodger fan, they welcome me like an old friend, share their peanuts and buy me a beer. Of course, telling them I taught my kids to hate the Yankees probably has a lot to do with it, I'm sure. (The Red Sox and Yankees are history-long rivals.)

The supervisor, Bob, was the one who put together their company-paid night out and he tells me all sorts of Red Sox history and trivia, including the fact that in all of Major League Baseball, we're sitting in the only seats that don't face home plate. (It *is* odd, having to look ninety degrees to my left to watch a pitch.)

With two first place teams going at it, the game is amazing. There are a total of nine home runs (eight by Boston) including two by David Ortiz, better known as Big Papi. That's right, Big Papi hit two home runs, one of them a grand slam, which is something to tell your grandkids about. Boston ended up winning 20-4 and it's the most runs scored I've ever seen in person. (Well, since my kids were in Little League.)

Big Papi also gets the 2000th hit of his career, a double in the sixth inning. As he stands on second base, the packed house and the players in both dugouts give him a standing ovation. And what does that big, strong man do? He cries.

15

PRETTINESS

The day after the Red Sox/Tigers game, I head northeast to Vermont, my last New England state. When I get there, I find that, true to the form of her five sister states, she is relaxed and neighborly and again proves, as I wrote above, that nothing weaves the exquisite quite like Mother Nature.

As is the case with the rest of this part of the country, the small Vermont roads connecting the every-now-and-again small towns mean a lot of stopping and slow-going, but honestly, it's so lovely here than you don't care. The mountains are a beguiling allegory, the greenery a gentle chaos, the air an aphrodisiac.

After the name of Highway 9 changes to Molly Stark Trail (cute name!), I get off the Beast and spend a good while enjoying the areas around Big Pond and Bugbee Pond. In places like this, you can't help but take photos—you want these views to last forever—but I hang around mostly because one of the fine things in life is to freshen up your sensibilities surrounded by personable trees, trails and ponds.

There's about an hour of daylight left when I get back on the Beast heading west for some lodging. When the road goes back to being Highway 9, I check the odometer and see I've covered 140 miles, which is fifteen miles more than my daily average for New England. Again, I smile when I compare that to the 2-400 mile days bikers in the southwest and midwest commonly do. The thing is that here, with all the two-lane roads, slow moving trucks and small towns with stop signs, 100-140 miles *is* a full day of riding.

Now, my low daily mileage is not something I'm concerned about in the least. The only reason I know what it is, is because I like mentally playing games with numbers. And that little odometer guy with his constantly changing face is sitting right there challenging me with all sorts number puzzles. No, mileage truly has nothing to do with these rides I take. In fact, the only time mileage should ever be of a concern is when you have to be somewhere at a certain time and date, but that's seldom the case.

Soon, I come to the cute and quaint town of Bennington. There are old stone walls, buildings of red brick and wood panels, several blocks of nothing but locally owned shops, sidewalk trees, houses (many two-storied) with raised porches and enclosed verandas, the Walloomsac River and streets named Maple, Pleasant, Spring, School and Silver.

I check into the Kirkside Motel and the owner, just like that motel owner in New Hampshire, gives me a colorful history lesson of the town. Afterward, I unload then take off to take some photos of the coming sunset. I find the perfect spot in Pownal off of Barber Pond Road that, coincidentally enough, passes by a small lake called Barber Pond. (Love it when things work out like that.)

The sunset turns out to be mostly a dud, except for one small sliver of pink that's reflected in the glassy dark blue waters. It's not disappointing, though, because the air is so dang healthy that it's like the one place in the world where you could never get sick. In fact, I'm so comfortable here that I decide to spend another day riding in and around this fine town. Alas, I never get a good sunset photo.

Despite the ultimately pleasurable riding of the last week and a half, those 100-140 mile days have gotten me in the mood to feel some top gear speed, so the first thing I do when I leave Bennington is beeline it to Interstate 90 West and crank it across upstate New York. It's interesting because even though I'm on an interstate and no longer in New England, the beauty of the land hasn't diminished, proving once again that Mother Nature doesn't give a whit about mankind's borders.

I pull into the fast lane going eighty miles-per-hour and because the traffic is sensible and zipping along, I fit right in. Soon, it begins to rain so I slow down to sixty, but now I'm alone in the fast lane so that's where I stay. A while later, I notice some staggered headlights in my rearview mirror closing in pretty fast so I pull over. Flying by me at ninety to one hundred is a group of six Hells Angels. I look at them and think, man, going that fast in the rain and never being more than an arm's length from two or three other riders requires some real trust.

I pull over at the Junius Ponds Travel Plaza for gas and food. The only reason I mention this is because I want to compliment the Roy Rogers Restaurant for their double cheeseburgers. Unlike McDonald's, the patties actually taste like meat, which makes for a right fine treat. Not as good as a Greg Burger, but hey, I'm happy to chow it down.

The end of the day finds me in the big city of Buffalo. I stay on the bigger streets because that's where the motels usually are and finally find one that looks cheap enough. The problem is that the road in front of it is so chewed up that the surface is like an array of metal spikes. And there's a one-foot drop into it. So I do what any self-respecting, law abiding biker would do, and ride on the sidewalk until I get to the parking lot.

16

FAME

Niagara Falls! Today's the day for my long-awaited first visit. I'm excited. I love waterfalls and, as we've all heard our entire lives, Niagara Falls is one of the grandest. Thankfully, the day is rain free as I twice cross over the Niagara River on Interstate 190. Between those two bridges is Grand Island and it is here that I begin to replay that old Three Stooges skit in my head.

> Niagara Falls!
> Slowly I turned,
> And step by step,
> Inch by inch…

Okay, so it's not the most sophisticated noggin-banger, but it does make the time go by a little faster.

I get to Niagara Falls Park, which has a bit of a theme park atmosphere to it, find my way out of the parking lot, walk around a little, and finally find the actual falls, of which there are three: American Falls, Bridal Veil Falls and Canadian (or Horseshoe) Falls. I stand for a long while just looking. It truly is spectacular and there is no way anyone could be disappointed with this.

I browse the few museums and learn a lot of facts.

- 150,000 gallons of water fall every second. (It's a good thing there are a lot of restrooms around.)
- The flow of water totally stopped in 1848 due to an ice jam in the river.

- The flow of water was totally stopped for several months by engineers in 1969. They wanted to see if they could remove the rocks from the bottom so the falls would fall farther and be more spectacular and create more electricity. They decided against it.

- Nicola Tesla (there's a statue of him) designed the power plants in Niagara Falls.

- In 1876, Maria Spelterini walked on a tightrope across Niagara Gorge while wearing peach baskets on her feet. (How does someone even think of doing something like this?)

- Niagara Falls Park is the oldest state park in the US. It was designed by Frederick Law Olmstead, the same guy who designed Central Park in New York City and Fenway Park in Boston. What a cool set of gigs!

- If the sun is out, there are rainbows.

However, the most interesting fact I come across has to do with Annie Edson Taylor, a sixty-three-year-old schoolteacher from Michigan, who somehow got the idea of going over the falls in a barrel. I know, it's something else that just doesn't seem like a good idea. I mean, which is more crazy, walking on a tightrope with peach baskets on your feet or tumbling down 167 feet in a barrel?

Anyway, there was some logic behind Annie's decision. By doing this, she figured to become famous and make a lot of money for her retirement; if she didn't make it, she wouldn't need any retirement money.

So on October 24, 1901, she climbs into her barrel, someone pushes her into the river and a few minutes later she's tumbling over Niagara Falls. And she makes it! She actually makes it and becomes the first person ever to survive a fall down the falls. Good for you, Annie! Now, good idea or not (she never did make any money from it) you have to admit that that's one tough schoolteacher. I mean, it's scary to think about what she did when her students got your, you're and yore mixed up.

All in all, I'm there for about four hours and during that time a curious thing happens three different times and I'm certain it's because of two policies I adopted while up in Canada, which are working out really well.

First, I stopped shaving because, let's be honest, it's a hassle. Second, because I was sometimes riding through rain, I figured I could wear my clothes a couple or three days longer than usual because the rain washes out all the dirt and grime so they keep getting clean. You know, that biker's laundry thing I mentioned in my first book. (Please tell me that makes sense.) Besides, doing laundry is more of a hassle than shaving. And if you think I'm going to stop and get a haircut … Hah!

Anyway, I'm there for about an hour when a couple walks up.

> **Niagara Falls Lady:** Excuse me. We don't mean to bother you, but are you, like, famous or something?
>
> **Me:** Uh, I don't think so.
>
> **Niagara Falls Lady:** Are you sure?
>
> **Me:** Uh, well, yeah. But I haven't been following the news lately so you never know.
>
> **Niagara Falls Guy:** So what you're saying is that you are famous.
>
> **Me:** Oh no, I was just trying to be, you know, humorous.
>
> **Niagara Falls Lady:** What is your name?
>
> **Me:** Foster Kinn.
>
> **Niagara Falls Guy:** Is that your real name?
>
> **Me:** *(Now this gives me pause because, after all, Foster Kinn is a pseudonym and for some inexplicable reason I feel like I need to tell the truth)* Well okay, Foster Kinn is a pseudonym, but that doesn't mean I'm not Foster Kinn. I mean, I *am* him and he's me and we're, you know, the same person.
>
> **Niagara Falls Lady:** So you are famous!

It gets even more odd when it happens two more times. I'm not joking. On two separate occasions, once by another couple and once by a mom herding four kids around, I'm asked if I'm some sort of television or movie star or something like that. It's sort of cool, I guess, but it also makes me feel bad because they get disappointed when I tell them the truth. But they keep looking at me like maybe I *am* famous and just trying to be incognito.

Anyway, from those three encounters I learn another important fact about life: Nothing shouts out "Celebrity!" as loudly as being a biker in desperate need of a shave, a haircut and clean clothes.

17

NOT WHAT I EXPECTED

After Niagara Falls, I make my way south through a Pennsylvania countryside untouched by greed or vanity. The views are similar to New England's but on a grander scale. It's interesting because no matter how much greenery there is, I never tire of it. It's in times and places such as this that we again become aware that Beauty is the fuel of the human motor, the antidote to weariness, and the lifting of spirits.

It's warm bordering on hot so a lazy pace seems appropriate and that's exactly the way I'm rolling. All along, there's a settled and relaxed feeling, not a ruffle coming from anywhere except at this one stop where it felt like I just walked into a horror film.

I'm standing next to the Beast eating my lunch when I see a four-inch long, dark brown something or other on the wall of the convenience store. Curious, I walk over and when I get close enough to see what it is, about jump out of my skin. I ask the first six people walking by if they know what it is. None do, but they all walk a wide arc around it.

The seventh guy, however, teaches high school entomology so he knows everything about insects and he tells me it's a flying hellgrammite. I tell him the hell part of the name is fitting and it looks like the love child of a mosquito from Jupiter and an F-16 fighter jet.

Then he tells me it's a male hellgrammite and they're not dangerous to humans because their long pincers can't penetrate human skin. The females are another story. Their pincers are short so they *can* puncture human skin and they like to hang out down by the river and attack campers at night. Even though it's daytime and I'm not camping, I start nervously looking over my shoulder. I'm being hunted, I know it.

The weather is still ideal when I make my way over to Highway 6 where the traffic is flowing as easily as a hot knife through pumpkin pie. I take a good, long look all around and, man, is it pretty. And this gets me to thinking about how the last two weeks have been not at all what I expected.

When I was a young boy I got the impression, along with probably every other west coast kid, that the Eastern United States was nothing but tall buildings, rude taxi drivers, cement, and too many people. It's understandable, being that most every photo and film we'd see of the East was of downtown Manhattan. It's probably similar to how young east coast kids come to think of California as nothing but movie stars, surfers, and curvaceous blonds in convertible sports cars.

As I grew up, I'd see photos and films of the non-stereotyped parts of the East. The stately Adirondacks, the wooded countrysides, the fall colors, the sunrise over the Atlantic Ocean. It was a good thing to see all of that, educational to be sure, but now that I've been riding here for over a week, I realize that films and photos are meager substitutes for the real thing. For that reason, my tour of the Eastern United States has opened my eyes more than once every day. Whatever aesthetic sense I may possess continues to be dazzled over and over and over.

In Coudersport, I pull over for a snack, check the map and find out there's a town on the Susquehanna Beltway called Jersey Shore. Jersey Shore? In Pennsylvania? Ya know, sometimes you see a town name and just have to go, right? It's not far, about seventy-five miles, and Cherry Springs Road seems like an excellent choice for how to get there.

Cherry Springs Road, a narrow two-lane affair that goes through the Susquehannock State Forest, is pretty much void of traffic, the curves are on the broad side, the patches in the pavement are done well (thank you!), and the prettiness of the aged and settled hills keeps coming at me and finding its way into my rearview mirrors.

Just after I arrive, I get a nice photo of the West Branch of the Susquehanna River then roll into town. It seems like a nice place, the clouds above giving it a homelike feel. I'm at a gas station having another snack when a fellow pulls in and parks next to me. His wife goes inside to get whatever and there's a baby in a car seat in the back. He rolls down his window and, just like that, starts a conversation.

> **Jersey Shore Pennsylvanian Fellow:** People in Pennsylvanuh sure are stupid, ain't they?
>
> **Me:** *(Pondering the unintended irony)* Well, uh, I don't know. Haven't been here that long.
>
> **Jersey Shore Pennsylvanian Fellow:** Where you from?
>
> **Me:** Southern California.
>
> **Jersey Shore Pennsylvanian Fellow:** Sheeit. Californuh ain't as stupid as Pennsylvanuh, I c'n tell ya that. I really gotta get me outta here. Maybe Al'bama or Miss'ippi. Didja know you c'n kill a man down there and not go to jail fer it?
>
> **Me:** Ya know, I did not know that.
>
> **Jersey Shore Pennsylvanian Fellow:** It's true. Is it like that in Florida?
>
> **Me:** Uh, I don't know. I'm from Southern California.
>
> **Jersey Shore Pennsylvanian Fellow:** Right. Y'see that guy on the sidewalk over there? He's stupid. Y'know how I c'n tell? He lives in Pennsylvanuh.
>
> **Me:** Okay.
>
> **Jersey Shore Pennsylvanian Fellow:** Damn, I gotta get me outta here. C'n you kill a man in Texas and get away with it?
>
> **Me:** Uh, I don't think so.
>
> **Jersey Shore Pennsylvanian Fellow:** I thought you was from there.
>
> **Me:** No, I'm from California.
>
> **Jersey Shore Pennsylvanian Fellow:** Californuh? Sheeit, I gotta get me outta here. Too many stupid people around.

Me: Right.

Jersey Shore Pennsylvanian Fellow: Al'bama, Miss'ippi, that's where I'm goin'. Ain't no stupid people down there.

On and on it goes until his wife comes back and gives me a rolling-eye look like, "He's harmless, just talks like that." The baby in the back seat has the same look.

PART III

SOUTHERN CHARM

*A good traveler has no fixed plans
and is not intent on arriving.*

Lao Tzu

———

*If you know where you're going,
you'll get there.
If you don't know where you're going,
you can get everywhere.*

db Mikkelsen

18

WET

It's summertime, which means it's riding time and I'm beelining it east on Interstate 10. The idea is to get from Southern California to Key West as quickly as possible so I can complete that phase of my Four Corners tour I wrote about earlier, then take my time riding the rest of Florida and meandering throughout the South.

There are, however, two stops in Texas I need to make. The first is to visit Jette, Gammon and Kirsten (my sister, her Texan and my niece) in the Texas Hill Country. Wouldn't miss the good times with those good folks for anything. Then there's all that great Texas food. Wouldn't miss that, either.

The second stop is to hook up with some friends in Houston for a music gig. Work-wise, it lasts for only a few hours; fun-wise it lasts for four days.

After Houston, I get back to my beelining ways, hell-bent on getting to Key West. At least that was the idea.

Interstate 10 cuts across the bottom parts of Louisiana, Mississippi and Alabama and riding here is like entering another dimension. When I cross over the elevated freeway between Lafayette and Baton Rouge, the endless swamps left and right are arousing an urge for a Helluvit because I'm feeling a type of curiosity I've never felt before, as if that water-laden mystery is calling my name. But I'm dedicated to getting to Key West before taking any kind of Helluvit, so I keep going.

I'd already decided to skip New Orleans so right after Baton Rouge, I keep going east on Interstate 12 and not long after that I hear the swamps calling my name again. Well, I can't ignore it any longer. Helluvits are, after all, a part of my philosophy so I decide to delay my superslab, beelining ways for a while and head south into the Livingston Parish in Louisiana.

The whole area seems to exist solely for the brown and slow moving Tickfaw River (love the name) and farther south for the Amite River. The countryside is amazingly alive and when I stop on the first bridge to take photos, I see my first alligator.

Like I said, it's a Helluvit ride so I'm following every whim, exploring this road and that, and when possible, talking with the residents. I have a chat about the local geography with a tall, hard-muscled fellow named T-Boy and another one with Marie, a dedicated photographer, down at the Boopalus Bar next to the Tickfaw.

Eventually, I'm back on the I-10, but it's not long before I shun the superslab again and head south through the Mississippi countryside. For a minute, I roll off the throttle so as to concentrate my thoughts into a personal homage to all the superior Mississippi writers who have changed our lives: Twain, Faulkner, Hughes, Chopin, Welty, Williams and the most recent, Larry Brown. Their words seem to have sprung from the river itself, ever-growing and wrought with irony, humor and understanding.

I cross the terrific Bay St. Louis Bridge and at the end of it is Henderson Point, which is at the western end of Pass Christian. I like it here so I ride down the narrow roads in an area that's a cross between a beach neighborhood and a rural neighborhood. I nod to the guys remodeling homes and working on cars and boats, and come across the remains of a house fire.

I ride up the circular, brick driveway, make my way across the cement foundation of what used to be a living room and dining room, through the kitchen and down a brick walkway to a dilapidated old wharf. It's here that the Beast and I get our first close-up look at the soft and warm waters of the Gulf of Mexico.

Afterward, I follow the coastline for a while next to miles and miles of blindingly white sand in Long Beach, then at Gulfport head back to the I-10. Cutting across southern Alabama seems to last the proverbial blink of an eye (it's only seventy or so miles), so there're definitely some Alabama Helluvits in my future.

I cross the border into Florida's Panhandle and it's not long before I realize that there are seven different types of weather in Florida.

- Hot humidity
- Hot misting rain
- Hot sprinkling rain
- Hot regular rain
- Hot heavy rain
- Hot cloudburst
- Hot monsoon waterfall

Now, believe it or not, riding in wet heat like this is fairly pleasant because the moisture cools your skin, but within two minutes of getting off your bike, you're splashing around in your own sweat. In other words, it doesn't matter what time of day or night it is, you're going to be covered with water and half of it will have come out of your own hide.

I spend the night in Pensacola and wake up to a morning temperature in the low 90s so I'm wearing nothing but a t-shirt and my patch vest. (Oh stop your hearts from pitter-pattering, I'm wearing jeans and boots, too.) It begins to rain so I do what I always do and slow down a bit for safety. The other reason is that around sixty miles-per-hour, raindrops become painful. At eighty miles-per-hour it feels like you're being attacked by an army of acupuncture ninjas.

So there I am riding just under sixty in a hard rain with my hazard lights blinking because, as we all know, truck drivers never slow down in the rain and I *so much* want them to see me. It's about five minutes later when I'm greeted with my first Floridian monsoon waterfall. Within seconds my visibility is down to five feet and the only way I can stay on the freeway is to follow the white guideline on the right.

This is nerve-wracking. I mean, geez, if all I can see is that thin white line, how are those ninety miles-per-hour truck drivers behind me going to see my itty-bitty flashing lights? A couple of miles later, I come upon a sanctuary in the form of an overpass, pull to the shoulder and back up the Beast to the thin sliver of space that's not being pounded by rain. I'm soaked to the bone and have no way to dry off anything, but hey, at least I no longer have to worry about those 18-wheelers.

Parking on the shoulder of an Interstate is illegal and I'm hoping no Florida State Troopers drive by, but wouldn't you know it, one does. But he's cool. When he slows down, I give him a thumbs-up and he nods as if to say, "Yeah, I know why you're there. Good move," and he speeds away.

I stay on the I-10 through the panhandle and at Tallahassee head south on Highways 27 and 98. It's here that I began to not feel well, mostly a beaten down feeling with a thick head, so I expand my salt and water routine in Perry and again in Cross City. I feel better, though nowhere close to one hundred percent, and come to realize that part of the heat I'm enduring is a fever.

I've not gone far when I pull over again, this time at a Chevron Station in Fanning Springs. I'm outside, sitting on the curb next to the Beast when Chet, clutching a can inside a paper bag, comes over, sits next to me and begins telling me stories of the good ol' days when he used to ride a Moto Guzzi Eldorado. Everything about it was great except for the fact that his wife hated it and kept bugging him to get rid of it because he was "going to get into an accident someday."

One Friday night he comes back into town from working the oil rigs in the Gulf, but before going home, he starts playing poker while drinking shots and beer. Yeah, bad combination. He ends up losing his entire paycheck but is too terrified to tell his wife, so he comes up with a watertight plan.

He calls a buddy and convinces him to buy his "Goose" for the price of his paycheck plus four hundred dollars (it was a good deal) on the condition that he can't ride it for two weeks. Then he calls his wife and tells her he was drinking a little and got into an accident but not to worry because he's okay, but the bike is totaled. The good news is that his friend will give him four hundred dollars for it and haul it away. Also, because he'd been drinking, he decided to spend the night at his friend's place.

He then tells her the most important thing, which was that she was right all along, that he should never have gotten the bike in the first place. The next morning he and his friend go to the bank, get the money, and he deposits his "paycheck" plus the four hundred into his account.

Two weeks later, they see his friend riding the "Goose" and his wife asks if that was his bike. He says it is and that his friend did a heck of a job of fixing it up in only two weeks. She never suspected anything other than what he told her.

Chet looks at me and asks, "Ever do anything that stupid?" I tell him, "Oh yeah. We all have."

Chet's stories brighten my spirits, but I'm still not feeling well. Nevertheless, I keep going at a good pace because I'd promised to meet my friend, Jay-Jay, in Dunedin the next day and figure a good night's sleep will make it all better. The route is nothing but flat and straight, but at least the Florida transportation bigwigs had the good sense to line the roads with trees and a thick carpet of grass so it could be worse.

FLAT AND STRAIGHT

The long night's sleep was what I needed (along with some garlic and oregano water) so the next day I'm feeling pretty damn chipper. I've three hours before I meet up with Jay-Jay so I figure I'll ride along Florida's west coast for a while and see what's there.

It's nice to ride along the ocean, anyone would agree, but the traffic here is about as slow-go-no-go as you can get. It's also hot and though I appreciate the ocean breezes, they're not doing much in the way of cooling me down.

I stop for an ice cream, pull out my map and see a place called Kensington Park. Sipping a cold lemonade while sitting under a tree in a park sounds like a fine idea, but when I get there I find out Kensington Park is not a park but the name of a city. A city with a lot of traffic, a lot of heat billowing up from the pavement, and no ocean breezes. (Sometimes my stupidity amazes me.)

So I turn around, head back to Dunedin and find my way to the small Edgewater Park, which is next to where I'm to meet up with Jay-Jay. I take advantage of the fact that I'm a half hour early by cooling off in the shade of a tree and finally enjoying some lemonade.

Jay-Jay has lived an interesting life. She's from England via South Africa and when you first meet her it's apparent that she enjoys the finer things. Unique clothes, smart home furnishings, designer nails, and the kind of skillfully coiffed hair that looks totally natural and not coiffed. She even has two pure white cats and with the names of Summer and Breeze, they're about as cool as cool cats can get.

Jay-Jay is cool, too, and despite the finery and sophistication she's used to, she has no problem hanging with a sweat-covered biker and talking about whatever comes up. And she won't even bat an eye if you say "fuck" now and again.

We're at the fairly upscale Bon Appetit Restaurant and Bar, sitting outside, enjoying the weather, our drinks (some sort of elaborate something for Jay-Jay and beer for me), the view of the small harbor, and the frequent visits of a witty waiter when a guy carrying a sketch pad and pencils walks on over.

Paul tells us that he likes to go to places just like this and sketch some of the people he sees, which are mostly pretty women, and when he's done he gives them the drawings and refuses to accept any money. (If there are no pretty women around, he'll sketch a building or a boat or a chandelier or whatever.)

He shows us some of his work and he's actually a fine artist and all his drawings have a life-like precision that's top-notch. Jay-Jay is also impressed by the fact that he gives strangers unexpected gifts along with a delightful memory that they'll carry around forever. Of course, being burdened with a guy's mind, I think that the real reason he does this to get to know all those pretty women.

Paul's a retired marine with a devil-may-care attitude so he fits right in with our conversation. We talk about motorcycles (he used to ride) and many of the crazy things life hands you and you hand back. Jay-Jay and he talk about a few goings-on in the area and though I miss their inside jokes, I'm able to contribute an occasional remark that makes Paul chuckle and Jay-Jay say, "Oh gawd!"

As Jay-Jay strolls to the bar to get another drink, Paul and I immediately engage in some highly complimentary comments (i.e. highly suggestive guy-type stuff) about her prodigious and appealing contour. Alas, I can't tell you what we said because Jay-Jay will read this some day and for some inexplicable reason she thinks I have a fairly decent mind and I'd like it to stay that way.

I meet up with several other friends on the west coast of Florida, but there's one in particular I want to mention because she does something that flat out makes my day.

Tullia is one of those few people who makes you wonder where they came from because she is simply too good for this world, not an unkind blemish in her soul. A terrific conversationalist, a damn good painter and writer herself, and a tireless supporter of artists of all kinds.

And what does she do that puts a permanent smile on my face? As soon as I get to her place, she offers me all the cold lemonade I want. I'll just say it right here: If you ever want to make this biker happy, get me a tall glass of cold lemonade. Or a lot of 'em.

The following morning, I head south on US Highway 41 with the idea of seeing the Everglades. There's still a lot of traffic all the way to the other side of Sarasota, but it's moving along well and I'm making good time. The thing is, the continuously flat and straight streets and highways are annoying and the more they bother me, the more my fever comes back.

I arrive at the Everglades around noon and find out that Highway 41 is also called the Tamiami Trail. When I first see the word, I figure it's pronounced TAH-mee-AH-mee and has a Native American derivation, but alas, it doesn't. The original idea for the name was the Tampa to Miami Highway and the highway designer guys made a combined form (<u>TAM</u>pa-m<u>IAMI</u>) so I guess the pronunciation is actually TAM-eye-AM-ee. But then, maybe some people do pronounce it TAH-mee-AH-mee, I don't know.

Despite its unique moniker, the Tamiami Trail/Highway 41 is just like every other road in Florida: flat, straight and close to sea level. I wish I could get used to this type of route, but I can't.

Boring roads notwithstanding, this a fascinating place. The Everglades have a sinister, beguiling beauty, shadows dark and mysterious; a holocaust of secrets upon secrets upon secrets, and you can't help but wonder how many layers there are, how many are yet to come.

To really see the Everglades, you have to get away from the roads, something I did several times. Fortunately, you don't have to wade through mud, water, sawgrass, alligators or panthers (panthers?) because every now and again there are park/rest areas, a few with elevated walkways.

I pull into one place that's a dirt and gravel loop that stretches a hundred yards or so. Next to it is a pond, but believe me, it's not the kind of pond you would want to sit beside and have a picnic. As I walk around taking photos, I'm constantly attacked by swarms of these little black flies that love to feast on human skin.

Later, I ask a lady working at the Miccosukee Indian Village about them and she tells me that the locals call them Bitch Flies. It's an appropriate name because they're as aggressive as a wealthy and jilted, past-her-prime trophy wife with an over-priced divorce attorney.

The best views I get of the Everglades are courtesy of the Kirby Storter Roadside Park. It has an elevated, half-mile long boardwalk with several small outlets, one with a thatched roof to give you some shade. As you walk along its curving path, you come to places where the growth is so thick and tangled with cypress trees that it's impossible to tell where the waterline is.

I walk all the way to the end and as I'm walking back, running toward me is a beautiful, bosomy young woman in a tight t-shirt. It's a delightful sight and especially enjoyable when she smiles and says "Hi!" I feel like Dudley Moore watching Bo Derek run along the beach in that movie *10*. Regrettably, my encounter comes to a different ending from Dudley's because I never see her again.

But what about alligators? Glad you asked. Trust me, go there, keep your eyes open and you'll see some. And panthers? Yeah, there are supposed to be panthers in the Everglades but don't count on seeing any. No resident I talk with has ever seen a panther and the closest I come to seeing one is a road sign that reads, PANTHER CROSSING 5 MILES.

After my tour of the Everglades, I spend the night in Florida City, which is at the bottom of the mainland part of the state. The next day is when I head to Key West, a trip that is covered in the Four Corners chapter. However, I'm thinking that now would be a good time to say something about my encounters with Florida cops.

Three times I could have gotten, and maybe should have gotten, a traffic ticket but didn't, and I thank Florida's finest for that. The first was that time I escaped the blinding rain by hiding under an overpass on the shoulder of Interstate 10. The second was in the rain just after I rolled into Homestead.

> **Me:** What's up?
>
> **Florida City Traffic Cop:** Do you know what the speed limit is?
>
> **Me:** Forty-five!
>
> **Florida City Traffic Cop:** It's thirty.
>
> **Me:** It is?
>
> **Florida City Traffic Cop:** Yes.
>
> **Me:** Really?
>
> **Florida City Traffic Cop:** Yes.
>
> **Me:** Are you sure?
>
> **Florida City Traffic Cop:** (*Looks at me like he's thinking "You're actually asking me that?"*) You didn't see that thirty mile-per-hour sign?
>
> **Me:** Uh, no.
>
> **Florida City Traffic Cop:** You were doing forty-two.
>
> **Me:** Oh.
>
> **Florida City Traffic Cop:** Well, this time I'm just going to give you a warning.
>
> **Me:** Cool, thanks!
>
> **Florida City Traffic Cop:** Where are you headed?
>
> **Me:** Key West.
>
> **Florida City Traffic Cop:** Then I'll give you some advice, too: Be careful in Key West. The cops down there love handing out traffic tickets.
>
> **Me:** Thanks!

The third time was in Key West.

> **Me:** What's up?
>
> **Key West Traffic Cop:** You ran a red light.

103

Me: I did?

Key West Traffic Cop: Yes.

Me: Really?

Key West Traffic Cop: Yes.

Me: Are you sure?

Key West Traffic Cop: *(Again I get that "You're actually asking me that?" look)*

Me: Uh, okay. Where?

Key West Traffic Cop: Back at that intersection.

Me: Oh.

Key West Traffic Cop: Did you see the light?

Me: No.

Key West Traffic Cop: Did you see me parked at the side?

Me: No.

Key West Traffic Cop: What were you looking at?

Me: The white car in front of me.

Key West Traffic Cop: Are they friends of yours?

Me: No.

Key West Traffic Cop: Well, I'm just gonna give you a warning this time.

Me: Cool, thanks!

Key West Traffic Cop: I'll also give you some advice: Don't follow that car any more. They ran the red light, too.

Last, I thought it'd be helpful to include some minutiae about the flat-n-straight state of Florida.

- The stop lights in Key West are placed really high so it's easy to miss them.

- Rest areas in Florida are guarded at night by armed patrolmen.

- Florida City, Knight's Inn on US Highway 1, Room 122. The sink faucet doesn't work.

- The McDonald's on Southeast 1st Avenue in Florida City

replaced their Muzak soundtrack with Jazz. Real Jazz. While sitting for a long time under an air conditioning vent, I heard Ella Fitzgerald's *It Don't Mean a Thing* and Sarah Vaughn's *Lullaby of Birdland*. Love Ella and Sarah.

- The Coronet Motel in Scottsmoor. Delightful little place! There's nothing fancy about the ten small rooms, but they're all clean and everything works. In the morning you can watch cardinals, blue jays, woodpeckers, cats and squirrels all enjoying themselves. And all of that for an agreeably low price. Even better is that the owner, Theresa, is a delightful conversationalist, a big fan of muscle cars, and a savior of lost animals.

- Okeechobee (fun to say!) is one of the few words in the English language that rhymes with itself and that alone is a good reason to go there. And so is Lake Okeechobee. If you happen to spend the night at the Flamingo Motel and come across a frog in the pool, say "Hi!" for me. We had a good time swimming laps.

- The traffic in South, West, North, or Whatever Miami is as bad as Bitch Flies.

20

LAWS AND CUSTOMS

Before I go any further (huh?), here's an important travel tip: When you're in the South, be sure to order PEE-can pie, not peh-CAWN pie. Trust me, you want the real thing. And while you're at it, do yourself another favor and wash it down with a tall, cold glass of sweet tea.

Although Florida is geographically in the South, most people don't consider it a southern state. It's easy to understand why because culturally it's so different from all the other states in the South. So when I cross its northern border, it's like going into a different country.

It's my first time in Georgia and I end my day at a funky Travel Lodge in Cordele. I still need to ride somewhere to get dinner and at times like this, I like to leave the helmet off and go au naturel from the neck on up. I mean, it's been hot, I've been wearing the thing all day, and the cool evening breeze slapping my hair around feels good. But because different states have different helmet laws, the issue that needs resolving is the legality of it.

I've a couple of hours before dinner so I gather up my dirty laundry, which is all the clothes I brought with me except for swim trunks, and walk out the door to the lone washing machine. On the way, I see three construction workers sitting on the sidewalk in front of their rooms listening to music booming out of a boom box and drinking beer.

It's a common sight: construction workers, after a day of constructing whatever they construct, sitting around drinking beer. They're usually good candidates for knowing helmet laws, so with my arms full of dirty laundry and wearing nothing but flip-flops and flowered swim trunks, I pop the question. It is then that I learn another important fact about life: When three guys are drinking beer, never try to get an answer about legal matters from the one in the middle.

Me: (*Loudly because of the booming music*) Say, you fellas know if there's a helmet law in Georgia?

Drunk Guy in the Middle: (*More loudly because of the booming music*) Wadyoo say?

Me: Is there a helmet law in Georgia?

Drunk Guy in the Middle: A horny what?

Me: No, a helmet law.

Drunk Guy in the Middle: A horny broad? Shit, if I had a horny broad, I wouldn't be sittin' out here talkin' to these two idiots.

Guy on the Left: (*Turns down the music*) No, he wansta know if you hafta wear a helmet on a motorcycle in Georgia.

Drunk Guy in the Middle: A motorcycle?

Guy on the Left: Yeah.

Drunk Guy in the Middle: I drive a pickup.

Guy on the Left: I know. But he wansta know if he hasta wear a helmet in Georgia?

Drunk Guy in the Middle: To drive a pickup?

Guy on the Left: No, a motorcycle.

Drunk Guy in the Middle: How th' hell should I know?! I'm from North Carolina anyways. (*Looks back at me*) Where you from?

Me: Southern California.

Drunk Guy in the Middle: Southern What?

Me: California.

Drunk Guy in the Middle: *(Big sigh)* It's not Southern Carolina, it's *South* Carolina and I'm from *North* Carolina. Them's two diff'rent states.

The reason I'm headed the way I'm headed is that my Georgia friend, Paige, had invited me to a pig roast, which sounds like a significant event. I've never been to one and as the miles go by, the possible significance of it grows and grows in my mind, and I begin to imagine it as some sort of religious celebration, which makes me wonder if I'm dressed nicely enough.

I've a ways to go and don't want to be late because, for all I know, that might be an unforgivable Pig-Roasting sin and I could maybe get into a lot of trouble. So I'm hurrying along despite the rain, which thankfully, stops just before I jump off Interstate 75 and go east on the two-lane Highway 16. And what am I greeted with?

Miles and miles of Pretty. Puffy white clouds prop up the grayish blue sky, lakes and ponds sprinkle the land with teal, and dark green trees and grasses mantle the easily sloping hills. As with New England, to my west coast eyes it looks like it would be an unpopulated or sparsely populated area, but it's not. Hidden amid all that foliage are shops, restaurants, school bus stops, satellite dishes and every other neighborly item.

The smaller houses are clean and pretty, and the big ones, too, and they're all on big lots. And all the lawns are perfectly manicured. Really. Perfectly manicured lawns are everywhere. Along with peaches, homemade wine and pig roasts, perfect lawns are evidently an essential part of the Georgia culture.

One more thing. Once the rain stops, it never starts up again, the temperature is in the 80s and the humidity is down in the 60s. Tell ya what, after riding for a week in Florida those numbers are downright comfy!

Anyway, back to the Pig Roast. I know I'm close, but none of the street signs are the one I'm looking for. So I'm riding back and forth and forth and back when I notice that one street doesn't have a sign so it must be the one I'm looking for, right? I check it out.

It's a narrow road that comfortably bends this way and that between more pretty homes and perfect lawns then deadends. I make a left, ride a quarter mile on a gravel road that's even more narrow and, voila, there it is! My very first pig roast!

It's wonderful! Kids laughing and running around, adults playing cornhole and getting as excited as the kids, and lively conversations everywhere. And the roasted pig meat? Damn tasty is all I can say. Tell ya what, if this is a religious celebration, count me in as a convert.

I've just finished my second helping when Paige brings me a mason jar full of homemade moonshine with cherries at the bottom. I look at it. I'm afraid. I smell it. I'm more afraid and wonder if this is a good idea. I ask Paige if it's okay and she nods. So I take a big breath for courage and take a swallow. I swear, within seconds my head is being unscrewed, my stomach has been thrown into the pits of a bonfire, and my perception of reality has become altered forever.

Good, good times.

∞

Paige lives in the Georgia town of Senoia, population 3,587 and one stoplight. I'm curious about the pronunciation so I do what I always do and ask a local resident, in this case Paige herself. According to her, it's officially seh-NOY, but almost everyone pronounces it seh-NOI-ya, which makes sense to me so that's what I go with.

Paige wants to show off the town so we climb into her car, drive past the Senoia Raceway, get onto Highway 16, turn left at the light, cross over some railroad tracks a quarter mile later, and boom, we're in the middle of downtown, all two or three blocks of it.

Looking around, I'm thinking that this is the kind of place you'd love to call home. I mean, it's so picturesque—the main street is actually called Main Street—so it's not surprising that a dozen and a half movies have been filmed here including *Driving Miss Daisy, Fried Green Tomatoes, Pet Sematary II,* and the remake of *Footloose.* It's also where the current TV show *The Walking Dead* is filmed, which is pretty funny because the Senoia town motto is THE PERFECT SETTING FOR LIFE.

Zac Brown (love ZB!) is a Georgia native and his terrific restaurant/ bar, The Southern Ground Social Club, is right there on Main Street. We walk in and see some bikers wearing leather vests each with a "Southies" patch on the back. So we're standing there wondering who they are when Kenny, a friendly Southie, walks up and tells us they're a biker club that raises money to help kids with cancer.

A few other Southies join the conversation and one lady says that they just came back from throwing an enormous birthday party for one of the kids and during their last poker run they raised $9,000. And one other time they raised $14,000. Twenty-three thousand bucks on only two poker runs in small Georgia towns?! Are you kidding? The Southies are awesome! And to top it off, friendly Kenny buys us drinks!

I get a room at the Sleep Inn in Peachtree City, a clean and somewhat upscale motel with a moderate price. (Nothing's expensive in Georgia.) While riding around, I see a lot of people driving golf carts, which are officially known as Low Speed Vehicles or LSVs, and it turns out Peachtree has over a hundred miles of LSV roadways.

Then I find out that twelve-year-olds can legally drive them when accompanied with a licensed adult, and fifteen-year-olds with a driver's permit can drive them alone. Sounds like a good gradient to driving a car.

The following day, Paige, the Beast and I go for a ride. With lazy curves, the road flows up and down a few low-lying hills through a prettiness that never ends, like a gently weaving ribbon on rich green velvet.

One place we go to is the very old Starr's Mill. It's next to a seven-foot waterfall, right below which a couple of guys are fishing in the pond. The mill itself was recently painted bright red, but if your peek through the windows, you can see much of the original milling equipment. It's idyllic.

We end our ride back in downtown Senoia at a pub called Maguire's. There's a large display case in one of the corners so I walk on over and see a Samurai suit of armor that was used in the film *The Last Samurai*. Why there's a Samurai suit of armor in an Irish pub in a small Georgia town, I have no idea, so I'll leave it at that.

I leave late the following morning and decide to ride around the bucolic countryside. I'm headed in a northerly direction but definitely staying enough miles east of Atlanta to avoid anything like big city traffic. In addition to some cows swimming in a pond, I come across several instances of Georgia-specific graffiti, all of them expressing a young man's love for a young lady. Like this one that was spray-painted on the back of a sign that's on the banks of a river.

Caitlane,
I love you with
all of me. Forever.
Don't forget that.

I spend the night in Dalton and the next day head east on a few country roads, then end up for the longest time on that loop that goes around Athens. Building a freeway loop around a big city is a good idea, many cities do it, but for some reason, this particular one gets me disoriented. I get off it several times, try to orient myself, get back on and, just like that, I'm lost again. In fact, I end up going around it for so long I'm getting dizzy.

Somehow, I finally extricate myself and get into some easy cruising on Highway 78 heading east. As the miles, one after another, pass under my boots, I think about the people I met in this friendly state.

I think about hard-working men and women who sit around together to share stories after a long day; about young people who use graffiti to express love; about friends who go out fishing on a warm Sunday afternoon; about a town that allows twelve-year-old kids the excitement of driving their own vehicles; about bikers who spend their weekends raising money for kids who've come into some bad times. And I think about families getting together on a summer's afternoon for no other reason than getting together and having fun.

How many Georgia folks nodded and smiled? How many shook my hand and wished me a safe journey? How many waved from atop their bikes *and* from inside their cars? It seems like all of them.

21

STORYTELLING

(Or Will Someone *Please* Tell Me Where I Am!)

One thing you encounter when riding long distances is people at gas stations asking for money. It's a common occurrence, especially in higher population areas, and I've gotten to the point where I can spot a panhandler before getting to the gas pump.

Most give you the usual, "Hey, can you spare a little?" Some are forlorn with drooping eyes and shuffling feet who meekly ask, "Think you could help me out?" There are the more direct ones who say, "I just need a buck, man." There are conversational ones who say something like, "Boy, the economy's really bad around here, went fishing yesterday, hey, you like college football?"

There are the proud ones who say, "I got a job, I got money, I'm just in a pinch." There are those who act like your best friend, tell you what a nice bike you have and giggle like you're sharing an inside joke. And then, once in every other blue moon, you meet someone like Skeetz.

I'm at a fairly large gas station/convenience store somewhere around Columbia, the capital of South Carolina, sitting next to the plastic jugs of blue windshield washer, checking the map and trying to figure out if my exit is a left or a right turn when Skeetz plops down next to me and starts his spiel. And what a spiel it is! (I *am not* making any of this up.)

His family is stranded in a motel room but can't leave because they can't pay the bill because they lost all their money when his wife's purse was stolen. He can't get any money from home (he definitely has the money to pay for everything) because the money transfer computers at WalMart and CVS Pharmacy have broken down.

To make matters worse, his wife is pregnant, has a broken leg and is in deep despair from her sister dying last week; and that's why he needs the money, so they can leave the motel room and get to the funeral. They have four kids ("the youngest one's got that autism thing, y'know") and he just wants to be a daddy they can rely on and be proud of.

The travails of this poor man!

The thing is, Skeetz's diction is perfect, there's no hesitation in his delivery, his hand gestures classic and, oh my!, the worry in his eyes, the anguish in his voice! He's not asking for money, he's the Anthony Hopkins of the panhandling world giving an Oscar-worthy performance of a narrative so creative it would humble Shakespeare. He's so good that I couldn't stop myself from giving him cash!

—⟡—

If you've read anything I've written, you know I've always been pretty good at getting lost. But that skill rises to a whole new level in South Carolina. I try and try but cannot figure out why it is that I cannot, in the least, find a sense of direction here. I mean, sure, not knowing east, west, north and south is one thing, but I'm usually pretty good at knowing if I should go left or right. What the heck is going on?

I've just checked out of my motel somewhere in Columbia. It's my first morning in the state and I'm getting ready to visit my friend Chip. Chip and I have never met in person, just a bunch of back and forth emails and a few phone calls, and I told him I'd be at his place around noon-ish. I have two and a half hours to get there and I'm confident I'll be on time because the directions are easy, about as direct as you can get.

So I take off, get on Highway 378, or so I think, and there I am scooting along as smooth as you please, enjoying the superb riding weather and wending my way through low mountains covered with pretty trees. Feeling good and looking cool. And sure as shootin', I'm headed in the wrong direction. To make matters worse, it takes me forty miles to realize it. Now I have to call Chip and tell him I'm going to be over an hour late.

This is embarrassing. Really embarrassing. You see, Chip's been riding forever and he's ridden everywhere and knows every pebble and pothole between the Pacific and Pawtucket, and now I have to tell him that of only two directions, I chose the wrong one.

In fact, this is so embarrassing that I'm thinking of coming up with a good lie. A really good one. Like I took a bullet in the shoulder when I stopped three guys from kidnapping a litter of kittens. Or NASA called and needed some help with their mathematical calculations. Or I went for a short jog and ended up doing twenty miles. Something like that.

But I don't. Instead, I man up, suck in the proverbial gut, make the call and tell the painful truth. Luckily, Chip is understanding and tells me that whenever I arrive is fine. Cool! So I take off in the right direction and get there straightaway. (Well, except for that one time when I come out of a gas station and turn left instead of right.)

After I arrive, we hang at a local deli/gas station for maybe two or three hours and it's the best. I drink about three gallons of sweet tea and eat this pork chop something or other that is seriously delicious. And Chip takes care of the bill!

The reward for all this is the conversation with Chip. He's not a native of South Carolina, but he's lived here for fourteen years and though he's never adopted a southern drawl, he *has* mastered the fine Southern art of storytelling. Man, oh man! Guys like Chip can combine adventure, ribaldry and philosophy in ways you could never imagine. Tell ya what, my friends, if you ever get a chance to sit down with an old school biker, do it. You'll laugh and learn and hate to leave.

Alas, we do eventually leave and as we're saddling up, Chip tells me that one of the cops in the area likes to give tickets to bikers. And because of that, he'll ride with me through town to make sure I don't get pulled over for breaking the twenty-five mile-per-hour speed limit. Good man.

~~∝~~

Storms are coming in and coming in fast and from looking at the swiftly moving clouds, I figure they're coming from the northeast. But then, maybe it's the southwest, I don't know. Either way, I figure I'll zoom over to the coast and wait 'em out.

I've gotten pretty good at predicting when and where the cloudbursts will happen, so my trip there is a stop-n-hide/get-on-n-ride journey. It's exactly like my friend Geoff, who did a Southern tour not too long ago, told me it would be. You stand under something while the clouds burst, wait for the rain to let up, then get back on the bike and with temperatures in the 90s, everything dries up in twenty minutes.

One of my stop-n-hide stops is at a convenience store in Gresham. I'm standing under the eve, eating a snack, and reading the signs and advertisements taped to the windows. The one that especially grabs my attention is a legal notice about the town's Sagging Pants Law. According to it, if you're in Gresham and your pants are three or more inches below your waist, or if your underwear is showing, you can get fined. The first offense is $25, the second is $150, the third is $400, and the fourth is, well trust me, you don't want to know.

It's nighttime when I get to Conway, which is on the outskirts of Myrtle Beach, and have a double cheeseburger for dinner. While eating, I consult with Mr. Google and discover that the Super 8 on Highway 17 is the best motel in Myrtle Beach (i.e. cheapest) so I call them and make a reservation because I don't want to be riding around in the rain looking for a place.

I get to downtown Myrtle Beach and it reminds me a lot of an amusement park, with a talking-fest of tourists tromping by, gift shops, fried food, a Ferris wheel, and a Ripley's Believe It or Not Museum.

I keep riding, eventually find myself out of town, consult my map and realize I'm going in the wrong direction. So I backtrack and there it is, the Super 8 Motel! Alas, there are two of them in the town and this is the wrong one. The chatty fellow at the desk empathizes with my confusion and gives me directions to the other one: Get on Highway 17 and go that way. (He points.)

So I do that, but when I get past the other side of town never seeing another Super 8, I pull over in a fancy neighborhood to look at my map again. Well, I assume it's a fancy neighborhood. I actually never make it into where the homes are, but I figure with a name like Briarcliff Acres it must be fancy. Anyway, an armed neighborhood patrolman pulls up next to me and wants to know what a biker clad in soaking wet black clothes is doing in his fancy neighborhood. Understandable.

I tell him what's going on and he says the problem is that there are two different Highway 17s and I've been on the wrong one. He gives me directions and I'm off again. But again and again, I ride the wrong way after making wrong turns and don't get to my room until after 11 P.M.

The next day I ride around the beach area between storms and that evening head out to do the town. Chip had recommended two bars: the Rat Hole (which I can't find) and the Suck Bang Blow, which is where I end up.

Now you might think there's a sexual reference with the name Suck Bang Blow—well okay, there is—but what I mean to say is that it's actually a description of how a motorcycle engine works. Most any engine, for that matter. The whole term, however, is Suck, *Squeeze*, Bang and Blow, and why the owners decided to leave out the Squeeze part is a mystery. Who knows, maybe they're not big on foreplay.

Getting back to the bar itself. What a great place! A beer is only two bucks, there's a damn good live band, and when she's not pouring shots, the bartender swings on a trapeze. Another thing that makes it special is that they have Pabst Blue Ribbon (PBR) in a bottle. Tell ya what, nothing will bring out the hick, redneck and cowboy in you like a cold bottle of PBR.

I find out from some other patrons that not long ago, another place opened up called the Beaver Bar and it's just down the street. Now if you think there's a sexual innuendo with that name, well duh! I go there (when a bar is named Beaver ya gotta go, right?) and the food is excellent, there's an excellent live band, beer is also only two bucks, and there's a huge alligator on the wall. And they, too, have PBR in a bottle!

Afterward, it takes a long time to get back to my motel room. Riding eighteen miles in the wrong direction will do that.

On my way out of South Carolina, I stop on a bridge that spans the Great Pee Dee River. It's dusk and as the sun and low-lying clouds conspire to create a comfortable sunset, I get to thinking about my time here.

Much of my riding in the state has been out in the countryside, and the small towns were pleasant and clean. Many of the homes are unique and well kept, all the way down to painted fences, sprawling lawns and short bridges that lead to one-of-a-kind mailboxes. The roads are easy to negotiate and would have been boring if not for the forested views, which are smile-inducing. The people I met were relaxed and smile-inducing as well and I never had a problem getting directions or having an easy conversation. South Carolina, an easy place to feel good.

22

LOST AND FOUND

I continue riding on or near the Atlantic coast and into North Carolina. The intermittent storms are vicious and three times I pull over to find cover. One of those times I sit under an awning outside a coffee shop for two hours listening to the rhythmic waves of raindrops hitting the pavement and watch people half-run to their cars, most holding a purse or magazine above their heads. It puts me in a contemplative mood so I take out my little notebook and begin writing whatever poetical and philosophical lines come to me.

They're brilliant. Genius! Philosophy at its best. Then, after some long and contemplative minutes, I go back and reread them, realize they're mostly immature junk and think, "Boy, am I glad no one else will ever see these!" It is true that a fundamental skill of a writer, any artist, or anyone living life, is weeding out the chaff.

Some time later, I get my first North Carolina motel room in Wilmington. After a day of wet roads and humidity, I understandably fall asleep almost immediately. I continue north the next day and it isn't until late morning when I discover that I no longer have that little notebook. That little notebook with everything in it. Names of people I met, conversations I had, roads I took, locations of photos, random and not so random thoughts, a few poems, everything. Including that immature junk.

I'm in a funk. It's useless to go back and look for it so there is only one thing to do and that's keep riding. It's a beautiful day, pretty much ideal, so it could be worse, I suppose. But it's interesting how the loss of that notebook changes my perspective because I'm now seeing things differently, as if the air itself has dreary tint. In a detached way I also notice that my northerly route is more aimless than usual.

I think it's around Hampstead where I pull over for gas. I walk into the convenience store where there's an excited conversation going about the largest sinkhole in North Carolina history having appeared last night. It's across from a golf course, which is not a mile down the next side road.

Caught up in the excitement a little, I get on the bike, ride around the road barriers, and a half-mile later, park at the very end of the country club parking lot. I walk down the street a bit and, sure enough, there it is. One of the workers comes over and says exactly what I'm thinking. "Yep, it's a big ol' hole in the ground, ain't it." And it is just that.

Still in an aimless frame of mind, I visit the coast, weave my way in and around several small towns, through grass covered hollows and over forest covered hills. I pull over often, sometimes to just look, sometimes to walk along a path through thick groves of pine, willow and cedar, and other times I wend my way around the cottonwoods on the fringes of small swamps where the only sound is bullfrogs plopping into the still waters.

One interesting thing about this area is the many family cemeteries, and I'm struck by their sweetness and the care with which they're maintained.

My day ends in Elizabeth City, which is in the northeast corner of the state. After getting a room and unloading, I ride over the Pasquotank River, pull into a turnout, walk a hundred or so yards on a wooden walkway, then watch a spectacular sunset blaze through an infinite spectrum.

The next day, my meandering mindset has me going west and the farther I get from the coast, the hotter it is. The views, however, are similar to yesterday's. Between the old and abandoned houses and the not-so-old houses in excellent condition, are woodlands of huddled pines alternating with rich fields of corn and soybean. And it seems like every several miles there's another family cemetery.

Norlina is a small town at the junction of Highway 158 and Highway 401 and it is here that I decide to start taking notes again. So I rummage through my big bag and pull out another small notebook, pleased with myself for packing a few extras. Now that I'm again chronicling my wandering ways, the dreary air lightens a little along with my spirits, but I still have a nagging notion that I'm missing something. But what?

I ride to Henderson for some food, and end up going to a McDonald's only because they always have excellent air conditioning. The long line isn't moving at all, and the reason is a loud customer who is finding everything wrong with the food and the service. She even questions the intelligence and parentage of the people working there. After she finally leaves, the patient lady behind the counter says out loud, "Hallelujah, praise the Lord and see ya later!" We all laugh.

To avoid the traffic of downtown Durham, I stay on tree-entwined side roads and end up spending the night at a Scottish Inn. Now, I've never been in a Scottish Inn that wasn't at least somewhat funky, but this one has a unique feature. When you open the door to the office, instead of a ding-a-ling or a buzzer, Beethoven's *5th Symphony* blares out of some cheap speakers.

It gives me a smile. I ask the owner for some paper and write down for him the best recorded performance of that masterwork: Carlos Kleiber conducting the Vienna Philharmonic. It's on a Deutsche Grammophon CD, which also contains what might be the best recording of Beethoven's *7th Symphony*. At a mere ten bucks, it might be the best musical deal on the planet.

The following morning, I'm still lazily going this way and that through the North Carolina countryside. The heat's seriously getting to me so I go to a grocery store and buy a lemon, the reason being something I recently learned from my son. Eating a half of a lemon is one of the best ways to steel your mind and body against oppressive heat. (It works! I'm not kidding!) My mind brightens up (you're right, it's not saying much) and I start thinking that maybe what I'm looking for is some good old-fashioned velocity so I jump on Interstate 40.

Speeding along is good, I like it, but I'm still looking for that elusive something, something that's missing in my road life. I look around at the few hills and compare them to the last five weeks of flat-and-straight. Even the few curves had been nothing I needed to brake for and the low hills were just that, low hills. This train of thought wakes up my inner biker and he soon starts screaming, "TWISTIES! S-CURVES! ALTITUDE!"

This makes sense. Twisties, s-curves and altitude *are* what I've been looking for and what I've been sorely missing. I guess growing up at the foot of the Sierra Nevada Mountains will make you feel like you need those in your life. Well, I'm going in the right direction (west) because somewhere up ahead are the Great Smoky Mountains, a place that everyone says is jam-packed with great roads.

As I get close to Hickory, I realize that that half lemon is the only thing I've eaten all day, so when I see a billboard for the Blue Ridge Harley dealership, I figure I'll go there, have a fine meal of popcorn and coffee, and buy a t-shirt.

While I'm paying for the t-shirt, I see a coupon on the counter with a deal that's too good to believe: Buy one tire and get the second one for a dollar. What?! I ask the cashier if it's a legitimate offer and she assures me it is. But it still sounds too good to be true, so I walk over to the service department and show the coupon to the manager. He tells me it is indeed valid, but he won't be able to put on the tires until tomorrow morning.

Okay, now I'm in a quandary. Do I keep streamlining it to the Smokys (they're only a hundred miles away) or take advantage of the best tire deal in the history of best tire deals? Decisions, decisions....

I go out and look at my tires and figure they have about a thousand more miles on them, so they'll need to be replaced long before I get home, anyway. Plus, money is a concern (hate that) and I'll never see another deal like this. True, the Smokys are just over those hills, but they'll still be there tomorrow while this tire deal is good only now, so I decide to spend the night.

The next morning, I've gone from eager to anxious. I mean, the twisties, s-curves and altitude of the Smokys are less than a half-day away! Around 11 A.M., the new tires are finally on the Beast and with a belly full of lemon, popcorn and coffee, I get back to cranking it on the superslab and it's not long before I see the promised land in the hazy distance. My inner biker is singing, "Hallelujah!"

23

MAGGIE AND THE DRAGON

I have discovered Biker Paradise. It is called The Great Smoky Mountains. The Beast, my inner biker and I are so, so relieved when we get to Waynesville at the eastern end of the Smokys. I stop at a convenience store for some water and trail mix, and to answer some phone calls and texts. It's a couple of hours before my normal find-a-room time but figure I'll get one anyway. You know, have a good night's sleep before attacking the legendary roads around here.

So I'm riding around looking for a cheap motel when I see a sign for a place called Maggie Valley. Well, that's one of the cutest names in the history of cutest names so that's where I decide to go. At a stoplight, I pull alongside another biker and ask if there are any cheap motels in Maggie Valley. He tells me it's the best place for them and if I turn left when the road deadends, I'll see a bunch.

Before I go any further, I must admit that I have an emotional attachment to correct spelling and grammar. Really. I'm an unapologetic word-nerd-grammar-geek who takes satisfaction when everything is spelled (or spelt) and written correctly. In fact, when diners and stores have incorrect spelling or grammar on their signs, including those damned unnecessary apostrophes, I withhold my business whenever possible.

Because of that, there is a small apprehension in my gut due to the spelling of Smoky and Smokys. By all logic, they should be spelled Smokey and Smokeys, maybe even Smokies, right? But when I finally start riding in them, the beauty, luxuriance and grandeur of these ancient marvels are so impressive that I gladly abandon my spelling and grammar proclivities. Truly, Beauty trumps all.

Back to the ride.

It turns out that Maggie Valley, home to several good-sized fishing streams, is biker-ideal because it has eye-catching views, friendly people, inexpensive but delicious food, no downtown area, and great riding no matter which way you point your front tire.

As the biker in Waynesville said, there are dozens of roadside motels, which are interspersed with sports grills, pizza and barbecue joints, diners, steak and seafood restaurants, and an honest to goodness trading post. There are a bunch of other cool places around here, too, like the Wheels Through Time Museum, the Soco Falls, walking trails along the Soco River, the Oconaluftee Indian Village, and the Road to Nowhere. And if you're so inclined, Harrah's Cherokee Casino is only fifteen miles west.

The first order of business is to find a room, and I gotta tell ya, I love roadside motels. You pull in, pay for your room and, boom, fifty feet later you're parked in front of your own doorway. And at night, you sit under the outside awning chatting with your neighbors and you all pitch in for pizza and beer.

The motel I choose, Laurel Park Inn, is perfect except they don't have a laundry room and with a bag full of sweat-soaked clothes, I'm definitely in need of one. Take it from me, it's hard to make friends and easy to lose them when your clothes smell like a dead frog left in a puddle of rainwater for a week.

But it's not a problem because Gina (she and her husband are ex-military and own the place) tells me to go across the street to the Valley Inn and use theirs. She even calls the owner there to let him know I'm on my way. And he's thrilled to have me spend a handful of quarters.

On one hand, however, my arrival here is an unfortunate one. While checking in, I discover my phone is missing. I must have left it on top of my bag at that convenience store and when I rode away, it flew off into the wind. I've done it before and, well, what can you do except get another one? But I've already decided to end my riding for the day so it's something to do tomorrow.

On the other hand, my arrival in Maggie Valley is a delightfully serendipitous one because I unknowingly arrive the day before the very weekend of the Maggie Valley Bike Rally, maybe the only rally in the world with a name that rhymes with itself.

Later, another serendipitous thing happens. I get an email from my daughter telling me she got a call from a guy who found my phone and wants to return it. Wonderful! He gave her his number so I borrow my neighbor's phone, call him, and he says that since I'm a visitor from California, he'll bring it over himself. More wonderful!

A half hour later he and his fiancée arrive and with big smiles hand me my phone. While they hang around and chat for a bit, I notice that even though their Toyota is clean it's really old and the tires are bald. Their clothes are old, too, but clean as well. I also notice they never say anything about a reward and never comment on their lack-of-money condition. They're all about good manners and good-natured conversation and nothing else.

When they go to leave, I offer a reward, but they refuse saying they just wanted to do something neighborly for a stranger. Nevertheless, I reach into my pocket and give them all my cash.

The next day, Saturday, I ride on over to the Maggie Valley Festival Grounds to enjoy the rally for a few hours and what a fun rally it is! There looks to be about a thousand bikers, half of whom are out riding at any one time, several local motorcycle clubs, a terrific live band, cheap jewelry, cheap leather, cheap t-shirts (I buy one), lots of red meat, some chicken and, as you would expect, an endless supply of beer. (You'd need a specialized GPS app to find a vegetable.)

It's early in the afternoon when I head west on Highway 19 to explore the Smokys. It's a pretty route that doesn't require much in the way of riding skills until five miles later when it starts wigwagging a good deal. The curves aren't *that* extreme, but they're windy enough to let me know that after five-plus weeks of nothing but flat and straight, my twisty skills need some work and a lot of it.

A few miles after the wigwagging starts, there's a traffic stoppage and whatever is the cause is around a bend and out of eyesight. All of us bikers cut off our engines and begin chatting, mostly worried if another biker went down, so we walk up to the bend and see the reason for the delay: two deer taking their time crossing and re-crossing the road while showing off their enormous antlers.

After the deer decide to hike up the hillside to the left and the traffic gets moving again, I ride another twenty or so miles, turn around and go back a ways to one of the truly legendary roads in the United States.

The National Scenic Byways Program was created by the U.S. Congress in 1991 and the 150 or so roads it administers are among the most beautiful in the United States. The U.S. Department of Transportation maintains these roads, and I've never been on one that wasn't in excellent condition. Because of that, my recommendation is this: If you ever see a sign for a Scenic Byway, take it. You'll be glad you did.

Many say the Blue Ridge Parkway is the best and most beautiful of these byways and when you're riding it, you can't imagine it otherwise. The southern end starts about eighteen miles west of Maggie Valley at Highway 441, another fabulous route, then goes east and south for a while before twisting its way northeast to Waynesboro, Virginia.

I've not yet ridden the whole thing but three times have experienced long stretches of it. No stop lights, no stop signs, no places of commerce, no billboards, very little traffic, and a perfect road surface that takes you on a route that could not have been better chosen or designed. If biker-heaven could be packed into 469 miles, this is it.

I jump on the Blue Ridge and ride the short distance between Highway 19 and the southern end, and even though it's only thirteen miles, the sheer quantity of Beauty would make the most hardened man drop to his knees in reverence. At each turnout, and there are a number of them, you stand in awe at how the mist covered, serrated mountaintops stair-step their way into the distant clouds. And below those mountains, shrouded in mystery and lost to time, is a riot of beast and brush entwined by Mother Nature herself.

After a Sunday filled with more good times at the rally and good conversations with my neighbors, it's time to head on out. But which road to take? The area in and around the Smokys is crisscrossed with so many awesome roads with awesome views that it would be impossible to choose a bad direction. In addition to the Blue Ridge Parkway, there's Diamondback, The Devil's Triangle, SixGap and Moonshiner 28. Even the ones without exotic names are a dream, like Highways 165, 360, 68 and 30.

Well, despite the superabundance of great routes to choose from, my next destination is an easy decision. It's one that most every biker knows or knows about and it's at or near the top of every list of legendary motorcycle roads anywhere. Yep, you know it, I'm talking about the Tail of the Dragon.

When I first heard about the Dragon I figured that it was just another great road to ride. In Southern California (where I live) there are dozens of great riding roads, a few of them world class, and what could be better than them? Some years later while in Sturgis, I saw a guy wearing a t-shirt that said, "318 Curves in 11 Miles." What?! I couldn't get close enough to ask him about it, but when he turned around and walked away, I read Tail of the Dragon.

Imagine that: 318 curves in 11 miles. Now, the twistiest road in Southern California may be my beloved Little Tujunga Canyon, which I've ridden maybe a hundred times. On one of those rides I counted the curves from the stop sign at the southern end to where it becomes Sand Canyon, which is twelve or so miles, and came up with 225 curves. That means that the Tail of the Dragon is about 35% more twisty than Little Tujunga. Whoa!

Off I go! West on Highway 19, right on Moonshiner 28 (officially State Highway 28 and sometimes called HellBender 28), which leads directly— well, directly in a winding way—to Highway 129 and Deal's Gap, which is at the eastern end of the Dragon. It's a total of 73 miles of excellent road conditions, righteous curves, and constant growth so vibrant it makes you tingle.

Moonshiner 28 is by far the twistiest road I've encountered in a long time. And let's face it, when you see those yellow diamond-shaped road signs, one after another, that tell you to slow down to 5 or 10 MPH, you know you're in twisty land.

The only problem, and it's noticeable, is that my twisty skills, such as they are, still aren't quite up to par. Add to it the fact that I've slowed a bit because of the light rain and I'm sure that a better rider familiar with the road would have made much better time. Nevertheless, by early afternoon I'm in Deals Gap.

How cool is this place! Dragon statues, the Tree of Shame from which hang various motorcycle parts from crashes on the Dragon, a bar with fried food, and two stores where you can easily spend a thousand bucks on Dragon t-shirts, patches, stickers and shot glasses. They even have little cottages you can rent for a night or two.

For an hour or so, I walk around, talk with some folks, drink lemonade, take photos, and spend what seems like a thousand bucks on t-shirts.

To be honest, though, the real reason I'm hanging around so long is that I'm nervous. I mean, this is THEE Tail of the Dragon, right? The one I've been fantasizing about for years, right? A skillion curves in only eleven miles, right? And I don't want to ride it like a twisty-challenged newbie, right?

I amble over to the Beast and he's a little nervous, too, even though it's no longer raining, the temperature is in the high 60s, the air is crystal clear, the road is in perfect condition, and all the rainwater has dried up. We talk about it for a minute and finally come to a sedate, scholarly agreement by saying, "Oh, what the hell," and we're off. The first 150 yards are not a problem, there being just one slight curve. After that?

It's everything you heard it was, everything you hope it is. Really. If you're a biker or drive a sports car, the Dragon is a grand gift. With a mountainside on one side and thick trees and vegetation on the other, it's not a sight-seeing route, but it wouldn't matter if it was because you don't have time to see anything but the next curve. Heck, it's so intense that you barely notice the sign for the Tennessee state boundary.

The few straightaways are no longer than forty yards, and there are twisties, hairpins and s-curves galore. And they're not just a bunch of garden-variety curves, no sirree. The Dragon curves have personalities with names like Gravity Cavity, Grace's Esses, Brake or Bust Bend, Carousel

Corner, Shaw Grave Gap and the Pearly Gates. And get this: all the curves are *banked!* Yes, banked! Have you ever ridden banked s-curves? Better than any rollercoaster anywhere. Talk about riding with an "Oh Shit!" look on your face.

How'd my twisty skills serve me? Not bad. I got passed by one sports car, two cruisers and seven sports bikes. But! I passed two touring bikes and two cars, so at least I wasn't the slowest one there.

At the end of the Dragon, there are two turnouts opposite one another. One has a broad view of the Smokys, the other looks down over a lake. I pull into the one on the right, sit on the low brick fence, and with a goofy grin on my face think about the fact that after all these years, I finally rode the Dragon. No, I didn't tame it, but I *did* ride it. An old-timer sitting not far away looks over.

Dragon Old-Timer: First time?

Me: Yeah! How'd ya know?

Dragon Old-timer: That goofy grin on your face.

24

INSPIRATION

When my heart rate settles down to something akin to normal, I continue on Highway 129, the official name of the Dragon, and finally have a good look at the colorful countryside. On my left is the Little Tennessee River, which is scattered about with trees I don't know the names of and outdoorsy Tennessee folks enjoying the waters. At Highway 411, I make a right and end up getting a decent room in Maryville.

The Beast needs an oil change so the next morning I go over to Smoky Mountain Harley, tell the Beast I'll see him in an hour or so, then find about three hundred t-shirts to buy. I'm standing next to the cash register when I notice that the girl ringing up the purchases, Amanda, has a gorgeous right sleeve tattoo. I ask her about it—people love talking about their tattoos—and she tells me it was done by Joe at Chainlink Tattoo.

I'm inspired and decide to celebrate my Dragon ride with some ink, so the next day I go see Joe, a cool guy who rides an old Softail that's been mostly put together with parts from several different bikes. I ask if he's ever ridden the Dragon and he says, "Hell no! Too many curves!" Oh well, to each his own, I guess. Then we get to talking about a tattoo.

Now, my ancestry is Danish, which means, you know, I'm a Viking and that's why I have several Viking tats. Makes sense. One of them is a medallion with an ancient blessing written in Elder Futhark, the language of the Vikings. Translated into English it says, "Unharmed go forth / Unharmed return / Unharmed back home."

For years now, I've wanted to have that medallion made to look three-dimensional, but I've yet to find anyone who can do exactly what I want. I show it to Joe and tell him about the three dimensional thing. He's cool with doing it, but his enthusiasm level is, well, mediocre. Then I show him this photo of Odin, the top dog Norse god, that's been in my laptop for years.

Well, Cool Joe about jumps out of his skin with excitement and practically insists on inking Odin. What can I do? You can't refuse that kind of excitement, can you? When I show up the next day, Cool Joe has turned into Don't-Bother-Me-With-Small-Talk-I-Have-a-Masterpiece-to-Create Joe. And that's exactly what he does.

Afterward, I ride to the western end of another dream ride/Scenic Byway called the Cherohala Skyway, which connects the towns of Tellico Plains, Tennessee and Robbinsville, South Carolina. The name Cherohala comes from the combining of the two Native American tribe names Cherokee and Nantahala, which is why it's pronounced CHAIR-uh-HALL-uh.

Because the land is so rugged and the vegetation is so tangled around here, the planning for the road didn't even begin until 1958 and it wasn't until 1996, thirty-eight years and one hundred million dollars later, that it was finally completed and given its name. I'd been assured by many bikers that, like the Blue Ridge Parkway, it's non-stop perfection.

I have breakfast on the Cherohala a few miles east of Tellico Plains at a walk-up place that's next to the Tellico River. I talk with a local, another guy named Joe, and his main topic is the dangers of stepping on copperhead snakes in the river. The only other thing he tells me about is a side road off the Cherohala called Bald River Road that "Ya hafta take, ya jus' hafta take."

After we shake paws, I take off and not long afterward, following Joe's advice, I do ride up the one-lane Bald River Road to Bald River Falls and it is, without a doubt, one of the most enjoyable, beautiful, cozy and quiet side roads anywhere.

I get back on the Cherohala and soon realize that all the bikers who told me about it were right. It's one sweet sweeper after another, intermixed with half-twisties and paved turnouts with gawp-jawing views. When the name changes to Massey Branch, it remains a delightful route with scant traffic, though there are a few churches and other structures.

When I reach the deadend at Tapoco Road, I immediately turn around. I'd taken take my time riding the forty-three miles of the Cherohala, stopping at every turnout to take photos, but on the way back I cut loose and, dang, what a thrill!

There's a Harley store on the Cherohala not far from Tellico Plains. No bikes or service department, only, you guessed it, millions of t-shirts. I stop there for a rest and to buy a t-shirt, and end up sitting on the wooden veranda outside talking with six other bikers. After a while, an older couple pulls up on an old Electra Glide and joins us.

The old-timer tells us that he's lived in this area his whole life and goes into a bit of personal history. When he was a kid, back in the 50s, his grandpa would take him and his brothers and sisters into the wilderness to camp. At night he'd tell them stories about the Indians and early settlers and before sunup, would nudge them awake and tell them, "Go down to the creek and fish us up some breakfast."

While they were gone, his grandpa would bake batches of homemade butter biscuits in a portable cast-iron stove over an open fire. When they came back, he'd let them eat as many biscuits as they wanted while he fried the fish they'd just caught. The old-timer gets a sweet smile on his face and says, "Fish frying in butter along with the early morning pines is the most wonderful smell. I'll never forget it."

Coming out of Tellico Plains, I meander around for a while and end up taking Highway 30, one my better decisions. It's another banked and sweeping route in excellent condition surrounded by the seductive splendor of the Smokys—is there no end to spectacular roads in Tennessee?—and I follow it all the way to McMinnville.

Along the way I stop, park on the narrow, grass-covered shoulder next to a driveway, walk across the road and take some photos of a gently sloped countryside covered with a quilt of multi-colored greens that reaches up to a crystalline blue horizon. As I walk back to my bike, there's this older guy standing in the driveway staring at me. I say, "How do?" and he nods.

I'm putting away my camera when he walks up and says, "Pretty out here, ain't it?" "Sure is!" I say. Then he asks if I want to photograph some real beauty, something more amazing than what's "over there." I tell him I'd love to. (I know what you're thinking, but he's unarmed and I'm bigger and stronger, so if he has something weird on his mind, I've nothing to worry about. Besides, I'm still wearing my helmet.)

So I get my camera back out, follow Lewis (that's his name) to behind his house and see his idea of beauty: two spotted horses just standing there as content as can be. He explains that his two beauties are gaited horses, which is why they're called spotted. If they were quarter horses, they'd be called painted. Who knew?

Mama is close to thirty years old and Big Boy, her offspring, is the friendliest fellow. Lewis was there when Mama was born and years later when she birthed Big Boy. When she was younger, Mama was "somethin' else" and won a bunch of show awards.

I take a bunch of photos and ask Lewis for his email address so I can send him some. He says he doesn't own a computer, but maybe I can send them to his daughter and she can print them out, so I give him my address to give to her.

Lewis and I share stories for an hour. I find out that he has lived and worked all over, from California to New York to England to Italy. Now, with his wife having passed, he lives alone in this picture-perfect part of Tennessee. I'm glad we met.

I've come to think of Tennessee like that quiet kid in grammar school, skinny and not too tall. You don't think about him much until you hook up in a one-on-one basketball game and he whips your butt. After that, you're friends forever. Like that kid, I truly like Tennessee and its citizens. They're quiet when you first meet them, but the moment you speak up, they're like an old pal. Two instances in particular stand out.

In Maryville, I had some stuff to mail home so I go down to the post office and park next to another biker, a tough looking guy in, I'd say, his mid-40s.

Me: How do?

Tough-Looking Tennessean Biker: 'M aright. Havin' fun ridin'?

Me: Oh yeah. It's a pretty day.

Tough-Looking Tennessean Biker: Wish I was, but I hafta run errands for my mama all day.

Me: Well, ya gotta do what mama says.

Tough-Looking Tennessean Biker: Yeah, 'at's right. If ya don't she'll put ya over her knee an' give ya a spanking, y'know.

Me: And it doesn't matter how old she is.

Tough-Looking Tennessean Biker: Or how old you are.

Another example of the friendly Tennessean temperament happens one afternoon as I'm standing outside a Sonic Drive-In waiting for my lunch. A mother is walking toward me with her four-year-old daughter, who's carrying a big stuffed animal. When the girl first sees the Beast, she freezes with a startled look. But then she cocks her head slightly, calmly walks right up to him, and looks him over with eyes as big as a harvest moon.

Tennessean Four-Year-Old: *(With perfect manners)* Is this your motorcycle?

Me: Yes, it is.

Tennessean Four-Year-Old: It's pretty.

Me: Thank you.

Tennessean Four-Year-Old: May I come over to your house and play with your daughter sometime in the next two weeks?

25

LAYERS

In solitude,
I am visited by the River Mississippi.

There, the maelstroms of misery, wreckage and death;
There, the wellsprings of elation, bounty and living;
There, the blood and bloodlust of generations;
There, in the sun-flamed waves, the longings of daughters and sons.

Hear in the ripples the rhymes of Faulkner and Hughes,
Hear in the shadows the eulogies of Williams and Chopin;
Hear in the currents the songs of Welty and Twain.

There, the choruses of desire and despair;
There, the melodies of cries and ecstasy;
There, the rhythms of losing and love;
All suspended in forever-flowing escape.

db Mikkelsen

I cannot grasp Louisiana, Mississippi or Alabama. It's not that I'm uncomfortable here, I'm not, but while riding throughout these three states, I get the feeling that there are histories and layers of histories that we outsiders

137

will never know. Anywhere I look, there's an unavailable past and I can't help wondering what happened, how did it all get this way.

∝

Coming southwest out of Tellico Plains, I ride a wide arc around Huntsville in north central Alabama, cross the Tennessee River, then make two more wide arcs around Birmingham and Montgomery. After that, I stay on the county roads and find myself in areas that are cloaked with the hypnotizing deceptions of living green and dark shadows, the blue sky disconnected and inert. There are some houses made of brick, some of brick and wood, and abandoned houses of only wood, and it's these that most fetch my attention.

I'm going in a southerly direction and when I get close to Opp in the southern part of the state, I head northwest, weaving around Highway 84. Still scattered among the newer, lived-in homes are the abandoned ones along with former places of commerce that have long since become hopeless for prosperity. None have been occupied or used for decades and I wonder why they're still standing. Beacons of contentment in years past, perhaps? Reminders that failure is a forever possibility?

As the billowing, wet heat surrounds me, I remember a scene in a story I once read. A young girl and her kind uncle, impoverished and traveling on foot, were in desperate need of shelter when they came upon a large abandoned house. The girl was afraid to go inside because of the possibility of ghosts. Her uncle told her not to worry because "ghosts hate dust and spiders more than you and me."

At Monroeville I get onto Highway 84 heading west. Normally, I would be highly entertained by a somewhat secluded and hilly road like this, but because my mind is preoccupied with the mysteries that lie all around, it feels more like I'm riding by a giant mural instead of being in the environment.

I continue seeing abandoned homes all along and every now and again, in the darker shadows farther away, I catch a glimpse of yet another. I'm drawn to the warm mysteries and several times turn onto narrow dirt roads that are more like footpaths.

It's interesting. Here I am, an outsider on a loud motorcycle, but the reactions of the people living there are no more noticeable than their reac-

138

tions to the detached, passionless sky. Those walking never slow their pace, those raking leaves never hesitate, and the one on a front porch rocking chair continues her back and forth pilgrimage without pause as if she's going back in time. But they all watch, following me with only their eyes.

There's more and more traffic as I get farther and farther into Mississippi, but despite that, the feeling of hidden histories expands and the air itself becomes a riddle. The winds unfurl to their own rhythms, the trees and grasses whisper in their own language, the clouds wander to their own whims, and the songs of the cicadas and katydids are filled with enigmas. Again, as I weave around a main highway, I wonder what's *really* here, what it is I'm missing.

I skirt around Meridian and the closer I get to Highway 19 and Kosciusko, the more those shadowy mysteries fade into the background of new pavement, clean commercial buildings, and the methodical traffic of working men and women.

I see a sign for another Scenic Byway called the Natchez Trace. You gotta love the name because you can't help but sound like an old-timer when you say it. I stop at the information center and learn that this was originally a 440 mile trail that was used by Native Americans, mainly Choctaw and Chickasaw, and later by white traders going home to Nashville, Tennessee after delivering their goods down the Mississippi River. (The traders used it because before steam engines, it was too difficult to travel back up the Mississippi against the current.) So with a map and information pamphlet in hand, I head on up the fabled route.

If there was ever a road that welcomed you, this is it. It's new, wide and elevated from the surrounding area, and the brown of the asphalt color-coordinates with the broad and clean landscape like it was all created by a master set designer. The speed limit is fifty miles-per-hour, but with its wide angled turns and lack of traffic you could easily ride it at twice that. But you don't. You don't speed up because fifty seems just right.

The Natchez Trace has a colorful history that includes highwaymen, church missionaries, gamblers and prostitutes. In fact, this is where Meriwether Lewis of the famous Lewis and Clark Expedition died in 1809. The official story is that, faced with a huge, looming debt and possibly being saddled with a morphine/opium addiction, he committed suicide. However, at the time many believed he was murdered and the exact cause of his death has never been determined with one hundred percent certainty. Another Mississippi mystery.

26

FORTY-EIGHT

After my Natchez Trace jaunt, I head west, jump onto Interstate 55 North for a bit then head west again, and soon find myself again crossing the Mississippi River, this time on the Helena Bridge. In the middle of it is the Mississippi/Arkansas border and when I see the sign for it, a smile of satisfaction crosses my face. Arkansas is the forty-eighth of the forty-eight contiguous states that the Beast and I have ridden in. Cool!

The clouds are beginning to glow with the sunset when I come to a town called Helena-West Helena. It's an odd name so, you know, I have to find out about it and the explanation turns out to be as straightforward as it could be. Back in 2006, the cities of Helena and West Helena incorporated into one city and the government types decided to call it Helena-West Helena. The creativity!

I find myself over on the West Helena side and get a room at a place called Crown Inn & Suites. It's not the worst place I've stayed at but close to it. But hey! It's cheap and the amenities are amazing: If you turn on the hot water and leave the cold water off, you can take a lukewarm shower!

After unloading, I take off to photograph the sunset and on the way notice my headlight has burned out. No big deal, bulbs don't last forever. I don't have a spare one with me, but figure I'm only going a couple of miles and on the way back, when it'll be dark, I can use the streetlights and cars' headlights to see where I'm going. Besides, what are the chances a cop will see me and give me a ticket? It's worth the risk because this sunset looks like it'll be legendary.

I get to the western outskirts of town, turn right on a side road, and as I'm standing next to it photographing a sunset that is, indeed, legendary, a biker couple drive up in their 4X4 to make sure my bike and I are okay. (Bikers are just the best, aren't they?)

It's Wild Bill and Danylle (dan-YELL) and they are a hoot. Wild Bill is the only mechanic at the local airport and says that we should go there because the sunset views are better. So I follow them and we park right there in the middle of the runway. It *is* a better spot, but unfortunately, most of the colors have already faded to dark.

We start chatting away, and I find out that years ago Danylle's dad worked in Milwaukee for Harley-Davidson and that Wild Bill has two bikes, an old Knucklehead in his garage and a twenty-eight-year-old Electra Glide that he keeps in his living room. (Gotta love bikers.) Also, from his stories and knowledge of the lifestyle, it seems like Wild Bill has been riding since the company was actually run by Misters Harley and Davidson.

After a while, we all agree we're hungry so they invite me to dinner at a place called Bistro Bar & Grill. Sounds good, so I follow them to their place, and while we're waiting for Wild Bill to "dress up," Danylle tells me that he's the vice president of the local chapter of ABATE, which is one of the many State Motorcyclists' Rights Organizations (SMROs). I'm in the front seat next to Wild Bill (Danylle insisted) and on the way there, I start up a conversation.

> **Me:** So Bill, you're the vice president of ABATE?
>
> **Wild Bill:** Used to be president, but it was too much work.
>
> **Danylle:** See, he says it uh-BAH-tay.
>
> **Wild Bill:** It's not uh-BAH-tay, it's AY-bate.
>
> **Danylle:** I think you could say it either way.
>
> **Wild Bill:** It's AY-bate.
>
> **Danylle:** But uh-BAH-tay sounds better.
>
> **Wild Bill:** It's AY-bate.
>
> **Danylle:** Well, okay. It stands for American Bikers Aimed Toward Education.

Me: I thought it was American Bikers for Awareness, Training and Education.

Wild Bill: What it really stands for is A Brotherhood Against Totalitarian Enactments.

If you make a trip to the University of Google, you'll find out that all three monikers are used along with a few others. And the proper pronunciation of ABATE? Well, you can say it however you wish, but I'm going with Wild Bill.

We get our food to go and when we get back to Wild Bill and Danylle's place, I meet their dog, Chewie, and that old Electra Glide. After dinner, Wild Bill gives me four locks for my bike because according to both him and Danylle, I'm staying at the worst motel in the worst part of town. Wild Bill also insists that I follow them back to my motel and to stay close so if there are any cops around, they won't notice my lack of a headlight.

Well, evidently I wasn't following close enough because we do get pulled over. Wild Bill immediately jumps out of his car and starts giving an impassioned spiel to the officer, much of which is true. I'm an old friend from out of town and they were just helping me get back to my motel by having me closely follow them because my headlight just burned out.

The officer asks me where I'm staying and I tell him. He says, "The Crown Inn? Sheeit, that's the worst motel in the worst part of town." Thanks to Wild Bill, I get off with only a warning. "I don't ever want to see you without a headlight in my town again."

Before we say goodnight, Danylle tells me that she works at Mary J's Country Cafe in Ethel and they have the best peach cobbler in the country and that I should come by for lunch. That sounds like a fine idea because if I had unlimited access to cobbler I'd be an incurable cobbler addict and weigh five hundred pounds, so I head on over there the next morning. It's about forty miles away and though I get lost a few times, it's enjoyable because I'm smack dab in the middle of some amazingly fertile farmlands.

When I get to Ethel, I find out that it's not a town or even a village in the normal sense, just a one-room post office and the Ethel Country Store, which is a problem because I see no sign of Mary J or her cafe. No one is working at the post office so I walk into the store to ask for directions and, whaddya know!, Mary J's is right inside!

What a wonderful place! It's exactly what you'd want a country cafe to be. It's decorated with old photos, old toys, old farm implements; and at tables covered with gingham tablecloths, several local folks are dispensing old-time wisdom. And the peach cobbler? I had three helpings and I'm ready to admit that it *is* the best in the country. I just might end up weighing five hundred pounds after all.

That afternoon, I get a replacement bulb at the dealership in Little Rock, decide to spend the night (there are a couple of motels within walking distance) and get an oil change the following day. Later the next morning, as the Beast is getting his infusion of 20W-50, I walk around a bit, unsure of what to do next. Well, I know I'm going to ride, but ride where? I've no ideas. I don't even bother taking out a map. So I walk a bit more and, with a tinge of melancholy, come to realize that it is time to leave the South and head on home.

As I ride west on Interstate 40, I reflect back on the past six weeks and of all the things I've seen, the one that haunts me the most is the Mississippi River.

To this outsider, the Mississippi River is something alive.

Throughout my rides in this part of the South, it has been the ever-present overlord—everything either flows to it or comes from it. I think about its place in American history and the incalculable commerce and fortune it has carried in the past three centuries. I think about that enormous earthquake in 1812 when its waters ran north instead of south and about the fact that today it actually runs uphill.

I think about the Curse of Kaskaskia that turned a hub of culture and commerce into a ghost town; about Mark Twain, glass of bourbon in hand, piloting his riverboat on a muggy afternoon as the sun sets; about cold-eyed river gamblers bluffing an all-in bet on nothing but ten-high; about the Piasa, a monster-bird that was so big it devoured full-grown men; about the Muscogee Tie-Snake, that maybe it did exist and, still today, slithers deep in the bottom muds looking for humans to snare.

I think about moonshiners and French pirates; about voodoo priestesses, vampires and readers of bones; about money-hungry preachers, prostitutes

144

and profiteers; and about Robert Johnson, the blues guitarist who sold his soul to the devil.

I think about the river's influence on the Battle of New Orleans, about the Siege of Corinth during the Civil War and the more than 8,000 casualties at the Battle of Vicksburg; about the explosion aboard the steamship *Sultana* in 1865 that killed 1700, all but one hundred of them Union soldiers, just days after the most destructive war in American history ended.

I think about the never-counted dead from the Trail of Tears as it crossed its waters in 1838 and 1839.

How much blood has the Mighty Mississippi consumed? How many bones has it buried? How many tales of triumph and tragedy has it witnessed? How many nightmares and dreams has it spawned? How many mysteries and layers of mysteries does that giant ribbon of history forever hold within?

PART IV

THE ALASKA HIGHWAY—
BEFORE, DURING AND BEYOND

The desire for safety
stands against every great and noble enterprise.

Tacitus

SERENDIPITY

May you live every day of your life.

Jonathan Swift

Man, am I feeling good! Not only did I take off early enough to escape the punishing Mojave Desert sun, my socks are brand new. Add to it the fact that I got a new patch vest only six months ago, my jeans are only a year old, my t-shirts only two, three or four years old and my boots, well, I don't know how old my boots are, but they look like they were worn during a cattle drive in the 1870s. But it doesn't matter because, hey, my socks have no holes in them!

The idea is to get in enough miles on Day One so I can make a side trip to the Arches National Park on Day Two, and on Day Three make it to Denver to watch Holly and Marco, two good friends, take their wedding vows.

The Beast and I zoom east on the I-210 then up the I-15 past Victorville, Barstow, Zzyzx (yeah, there's actually a place called Zzyzx, though I don't know anyone who's ever been there), Baker, Las Vegas, Mesquite, across the northwestern tip of Arizona, then past St. George and Cedar City. Not long after that, I'm blessed with a fine bit of serendipity that gets filed under What Are the Chances?

I pull off the I-15 for some gas and as I'm filling the tank, I notice a woman walking out of the convenience store to her bike. Nothing unusual with that, I always notice women walking to and from their bikes. However, there's something familiar with this one, but I can't get a good enough look to see if I know her or not.

I park a ways away and as I'm walking toward the front door I realize that, by pure happenstance, I have run into my good friend, Lisa, the Beemer Biker Babe, in Beaver, Utah. (Now hold on guys, before you start with the jokes, I should tell you she's happily married to another biker named Rick, the lucky bastard.)

Amazed at running into each other like this, we talk for the longest time about, well, all the things bikers talk about. (Except we don't talk about *that* biker stuff because, you know, she's a married woman.) Anyway, it's a real life proof that even if you have no riding partners, you're never far away from a friend.

I continue up the I-15 and make a right onto the I-70, which is an interchange that has always perplexed me because right here in Utah is the meeting point of two national thoroughfares, but there are no places of commerce; nothing but some cows and a bunch of low-lying plants leading up to low mountains.

It's all fine by me, though, because this section of the I-70 is almost void of traffic, the road is in excellent shape, the sun is at my back, cool summer breezes brush my face, and the clouds are in crisp outline above mountains colored mauve, charcoal and ivory. A perfect setting for sixty miles of curves so perfectly designed that you never have to slow down from the 80 MPH speed limit.

I end my day at the Rodeway Inn in Salina (suh-LIE-nuh) and the following morning, I'm loading up at the same time as a bunch of others. The conversation veers toward mileage and it turns out that three of them are Iron Butt guys who rode 1100 miles the day before. Then there're a biker and his lady who rode two-up for 800 and four Bandidos who each rode 750. My 600 miles puts me at the bottom of the heap and I'm too embarrassed to mention it.

Arches National Park is a place I'd wanted to visit for some time because I enjoy finding faces and animal shapes in wind-sculpted rocks, a sort of cousin to cloud watching, and I want to see some of those towering, gravity-defying rock columns which have one of the coolest names ever invented: Hoodoos. And arches. Real eager to see some arches.

The fellow manning the Arches entrance gate tells me that if I buy one of those National Parks passes that are good for a lifetime for any park in the United States, in a very short time I'll save money. I tell him I do like saving money and would love to buy one but have only enough cash for this one entrance. I also promise to buy one of those passes when I go to the next national park. He says okay and lets me in for free. I like that guy.

A good rule to keep in mind about riding a motorcycle or doing anything in hot weather is this: You'll need more water than you think you'll need. In fact, a good policy is to figure out how much water you'll need and pack twice that amount. And if the temperature is in triple digits, triple the amount. The good Arches folks know all about this so right outside the Visitor's Center they installed two faucets where you can fill up all your containers with purified water au gratis.

When starting out this morning, however, I didn't follow that packing-twice-as-much-water policy so I have only two water bottles. So I drink as much as I can drink without running back to the bathroom, then fill each one to the brim, hoping it'll be enough.

I ride up the main road nestled between tour buses and tourists. The sky is a profound blue, the few clouds a blinding white, and the surrounding scrublands stretch all the way to the horizon where the mountains mingle with the sky in a diaphanous haze.

The dominant denizens, however, are these enormous, vertically etched, salmon-red monoliths that sit mute and immutable. As you begin to spot those human-like faces hidden in them, you wonder if they're oracles with secrets to reveal or guardians with secrets to keep. I've seen similar wind-chiseled rock structures in New Mexico, but there they each stand alone; here, they've gathered together like a grand council of knights-errant for Mother Earth herself.

It's so hot and dry that it's not long before I'm "sweating like a sumo wrestler running a marathon in the Sahara." (That's my favorite line from

151

the first Freedom's Rush book.) I'm hydrating every time I stop for photos, which is a lot, and after about forty-five minutes I'm out of water.

Soon, my thoughts and perceptions are a little hazy, but I keep riding because I've yet to see any arches. I mean, this is the Arches National Park, right? Where are they? But then, maybe arches experts consider those holes in the rock formations as arches, I don't know. But dammit, I want to see some *real* arches, the kind that gracefully go up and over like they were designed by a legendary sculptor. So I keep riding and riding and getting more in need of water and finally see a sign for something called Delicate Arch. Sounds good!

To actually see Delicate Arch, you have to walk up a trail, half of which is stone steps. I'm not feeling well and should turn back to drink some of that water at the Visitor's Center, but it's a long ways down and I want to see that arch *now*. To make matters worse, not long after starting out, I twist my hip and my sciatica has decided to punish me every step of the way.

Three hundred miles later (okay, I'm exaggerating) I reach the top and, boy, am I disappointed. The lookout is about a fifty yards away from an arch that's fifteen feet tall at the most. So there I am, disappointed, in pain and water deprived with fuzzy eyesight, when I hear a conversation between a boy and his Dad.

Boy: Dad, what are those things?
Dad: What things?
Boy: Those things under the arch.
Dad: Oh, those are people, son.
Boy: Really? They're people?
Dad: Yeah!
Boy: They're really small.
Dad: They just look small because they're so far away.

Huh? I shake the sweat out of my eyes, focus and, whaddya know!, Dad's right, those *are* people! Dehydration must have screwed up my depth perception because those people look to be a half-mile away and that ol' Arch named Delicate is enormous!

One last item. The Arches is close to the picturesque town of Moab. I'd always pronounced it MOW-awb but was never certain that that was right, and I've found many others who wonder the same thing. So I ask Missy at

Walker's Drug and General Store, and she clears it all up by telling me that Moab rhymes with Snow Crab. So if you're ever in Moab, walk into Walker's and say "Hi!" to Missy for me. She won't remember me, I'm sure, but hers is a good conversation and she will appreciate your company.

I want to make it to Grand Junction for the night, which means I need to get back onto Interstate 70. The two routes to choose from are northwest on the quicker but rather boring Highway 191, or northeast on Highway 128, which veers and flexes in concert with the Colorado River. Not much of a choice.

Highway 128 and the Colorado River cut through steep and high mountains and any biker will agree that riding alongside a river is a rush. The traffic is scant and fishermen, hikers, campers and boaters are enjoying the waters all along. The only possible issue is that the road surface is riddled with tar snakes, but I've never been bothered by them as much as some other riders so I'm ripsnortin' hard.

As the 128 gets close to the I-70, I see a sign for a place called Cisco. I decide to go take a look (it's not far) and find out that it comprises only three streets that form a narrow right triangle a couple of hundred yards long. The interesting thing is that no one is there. Not a soul. The place looks completely abandoned and every structure appears to be rotting to the ground, including the old post office that's the size of a small bedroom. Great place for photos, but at night it's got to be spooky.

The one possible exception is the old Cisco Landing Store. In front of it is a rickety wire gate that's chain locked, to the right side is a tall, white crane, and lying in the weeds in front of the wooden porch is a stop sign that reads, "Please leave animals in car."

The more I look at it, the more interesting it is. Much of the building, like everything else, is falling apart, but I notice it has a new electric meter, new windows and a new door. I'm no carpenter, but aren't doors and windows among the last things you'd install? At any rate, it seems like someone is trying to bring back the glory days of Cisco and I wish them luck.

I head out of Grand Junction pretty late, but with the way the traffic is flowing, it looks like I'll get to Denver long before sunset. But the moment I begin to think, "Heck, why not take a Helluvit or two," I run into a seventy-five mile long traffic jam that, at best, is averaging two miles-per-hour. (This time I'm not exaggerating.) What makes it more frustrating is that lane splitting is illegal in Colorado. (What's up with that, Colorado?)

It's brutal. The Beast is overheating and so is yours truly so we pull onto the shoulder for fifteen minutes to cool off. I look around and start to think this shoulder would make a fine motorcycle-only lane because it's four to five feet wide and there are no traffic-jammed cars on it. So when I get back on the Beast that's exactly where I ride.

This is seriously illegal but so is lane splitting. I don't know which infraction would cost more, but I do know that riding on the shoulder is faster and safer, and the Beast won't get overheated. Pretty soon, a couple riding two-up start following me and then four other couples and two solo riders join in. Here we are, a merry band of biker renegades enjoying an unencumbered ride through the glorious Rockies. Despite all that, it takes six hours to go those seventy-five miles.

I make it to Denver well after sunset but still enjoy the conversations of a wonderful family for hours. The following morning, Holly and Marco's wedding is the best. But then I say that about every wedding I go to. Two people pledging their hearts to one another and all their family and friends wishing them everlasting happiness. Makes me tear up every time. In honor of the newlyweds, next time you're having a round of drinks, raise your glasses to Holly and Marco. Good and beautiful folks.

28

YA GOTTA LOVE IT

It is respectable to have no illusions;
and safe, and profitable.
And dull.

Joseph Conrad

One of the rewards of riding around the country is visiting family and friends and that's exactly what I do for a couple of days. Also, one of the Beast's light bulbs has burned out (it happens every six months or so) so I get a replacement from Sun Harley before heading north on Interstate 25. I ride through Laramie, Wyoming, take Interstate 80 west, have a late lunch in Wamsutter, one legitimately odd place, and finally head north on Highway 191.

I spend the night in a place called Farson, population 313. There's one gas station, one snack shop, one lawyer, one hairstylist, one diner that closes at 6pm, and I'm the only guest staying at the only motel, Sitzman's. The building is made of red brick, the rooms are tiny, and right outside those six rooms are hitching posts for horses. Gotta love Wyoming.

The woman who owns the place, Micki, has a bunch of cats, one of them a Siamese with crossed blue eyes who looks to weigh about twenty pounds. Siamese cats love to talk and this one is no exception. She immediately jumps up on the desk and tells me her two complaints. First, all the mice are too fast to catch and, second, she has to eat the same food as the other cats, which is at odds with the royalty she most definitely is.

I leave the following morning continuing north on Highway 191. The blazing blue sky is crisscrossed with white clouds and the rich, undulating fields, left and right, are like great seas of light green and dark green that peacefully stretch to slate gray mountains I don't know how many miles away. The air is crisp and the Beast and I are rumbling down the road like we own it all. Ya know, there's a whole lot of something special about Wyoming because it always makes me feel that way.

I pull into a turnout to take a few photos and a few minutes later five friendly, helmet-less riders from Illinois pull over as well, and the first thing each one does is pull out a cold can of beer and drink it. I wish I could do that. I mean, I could, of course, but if I did, with the way alcohol affects me, I'd have trouble getting back on the bike and even more trouble staying on it.

I ride with them a while as we merge onto Highway 189, which slithers alongside the Snake River, and eventually stop at Obo's in Pinedale (cool place!) for gas and lunch. While they each down another beer, I, in manly biker fashion, drink a tall, cold lemonade.

After shaking paws and wishing each other well, they take off fifteen minutes before I do, so again I'm riding alone. It's along here that I realize one of the many commonalities we all share and I can't recall ever hearing anyone mention it. At least once every day, even if only for a moment with an under-consciousness level of thinking, we each decide where we're going to wind up. Well, today is my day to wind up in a small valley between angular peaks of the Tetons on one side and the Snake River on the other. Tell ya what, Jackson Hole is one of the better places to wind up.

For years, I've wondered why it's sometimes referred to as Jackson and other times as Jackson Hole, so I ask one of the Jackson/Jackson Hole residents working at the Maverik Car Corner. She tells me that Jackson is the name of the town, Jackson Hole is the name of the valley. Mystery solved!

I've never been to Jackson Hole before but have often heard about how awesomely beautiful it is. It's early afternoon so I decide to ride around a bit, see what all the dang-it's-beautiful-there fuss is all about. I turn left on

State Highway 22 for no other reason than I see the sign and end up riding a 110-mile mountain loop that I'll never forget.

Highway 22 (Highway 33 in Idaho) winds its way up the mountainside giving you a physically and spiritually elevated view of the valley resting under an exquisitely blue sky that's held in place by a dozen white clouds. And the higher the road goes, the more elevated my emotions become.

In a way, a great ride is like reading a great book. There are times you stop reading to pause and reflect, partly because you want to and partly because the story and the writing are so good that they deserve some moments of respect. It's like a silent, personal homage to a writer who pulled off something incredibly unique.

It's in the same spirit that I pull over at a place in Victor, Idaho; to give a nod of approval to a superior road that's flat out fun. I'm sitting at a picnic table outside when three riders, a dad, a mom and a son, roll up with ear-to-ear grins.

Dad is a talkative sort and as is sometimes the case—okay, many times—the conversation veers into the realm of just plain silly.

Dad: Pretty day, ain't it.

Me: It is that!

Dad: That 33 sure is a great road.

Me: I'll say!

Dad: You headin' back soon?

Me: Well, I was thinking of making my way over to Highway 26 and into Swan Valley.

Dad: Swan Lake? Ain't that a ballet?

Me: Uh yeah, but this is Swan Valley. But there might be a lake there, I don't know.

Dad: *(Looks over at his wife and son)* Hey, you guys wanna go to a ballet?

Mom: You want us to go to a ballet?

Dad: Yeah! This here fella says it's over on Highway 26.

Mom: There's a ballet on Highway 26?

Dad: Yeah!

Son: I dunno, that sounds weird.

Dad: They even have a real lake.

Mom: Yeah, it sounds weird.

Son: I'd rather ride back the way we came.

And ride back the way they came is exactly what they do.

After Highway 33, I follow Highways 31, 26, 89, and finally the 191 and back into Jackson. The traffic is such that no one makes me slow down, though the route itself has a fair amount of curves that do. Most of the time the sun is soft on my face, but there are stretches where I pass through shadows dappled with sunlight where the mountain pines give off their unique, scented chill.

Then there's the Snake River. Much of the route has the Snake by its side and I'm going to make a suggestion right now. If anyone ever asks if you want to ride along the Snake River, say yes.

Being that Jackson is a famous destination, you'd think it'd be an upscale place with upscale prices and, sure enough, it is. The cheapest room I can find is at the Virginian Lodge (at $116 a night it's $13 less than the Motel 6), but even though it's the cheapest or one of the cheapest places, there's a big laundromat that's clean and filled with a bunch of washers and dryers that actually work. There's also a liquor store that sells deli sandwiches, a restaurant, a heated pool, a Jacuzzi, a tanning salon and a lively saloon.

Regrettably, I can't join any of the fun stuff because tonight is my night to do laundry. Life on the road. Just like Wyoming, ya gotta love it.

29

NEW WAYS OF SEEING

My destination is no longer a place,
rather a new way of seeing.

Proust

You can either see what's there
or see only what you've been told to see.

db Mikkelsen

I was born and raised in Visalia, which is in the middle of the San Joaquin Valley in California. Above and to the east of us were two national parks, Sequoia and Kings Canyon. When I was young, I loved camping, hiking and fishing in those mountains, especially the area nestled between the two, Mineral King. (Get a shot of Jack and few beers in me and I'll tell you about the time I wrestled Big Foot.) However, north of Sequoia, Kings and Big Foot is the big name national park in California, Yosemite, a place that deserves every bit of praise it has gotten over the years, and it's gotten a lot.

A couple of years after learning the alphabet, I found out that Sequoia is one of the few words in the English language that contains all the regular vowels. (If you're in the Los Angeles area, you'll recognize Figueroa as another one.) Then I figured out *on my own* that if you combine it with the Y in Yosemite, you'd have *all* the vowels because Y, as you know, is sometimes a vowel. Cool! One of my first word game triumphs! Also around that time, after seeing some Ansel Adams photos, I became infatuated with Yosemite, proud that it was in my home state.

I was still a little kid when I learned of Yellowstone in Wyoming and I remember being annoyed that there was another national park beginning with the letter Y. I mean, Yosemite is a special place, Y *belongs* to Yosemite and Yosemite belongs to California and I'm a Californian and, darn it, they should change the name of Yellowstone so it doesn't start with a Y. (I would have said dammit, but you know, I was a little kid.) What about Lemonstone or Goldstone? Or Mustardstone or Saffronstone or Fulvousstone? They'd all work just as well, right? (Yeah, I looked up Yellow in a thesaurus.)

I don't know, but perhaps I've unknowingly carried that childhood annoyance with me all these years and that's the reason why, of all the times I'd been to Wyoming, I never visited Yellowstone. Until today.

～∞～

Back in 1872, President Grant and the U.S. Congress made Yellowstone the first national park in the United States and what a damn good idea that was. If you're riding north toward this grandfather of national parks on Highway 191, you first go through the Grand Tetons National Park, but don't even begin to think this is just a passing-through place. Really. It butts right up against Yellowstone and the only way you know you're going from one to the other is the man-made entrance gate.

In places as naturally aesthetic as the Tetons and Yellowstone, all you need to do is look and it will awaken a rich and deep awe that is freedom-giving and energizing. And you soon get to the point where you just want to sit for the longest time and look at it and admire it and be it.

The winding roads that reveal breathtaking vistas at every turn, steeply walled ravines, V-shaped valleys that reach far into the earth, secluded hollows of Mother Nature's perfection, trees and bushes that defy the seasons, zigzagging streams and rivers that cut through time and soil. Your senses flow out so wide and far that there is no periphery, no "over there," no inkling of any kind of boundary or demarcation whatsoever.

When riding through wilderness like this, you feel like you're going home, that "civilization," with its flat screen TVs and cell phones and government regulations, is a temporary stopping point, worthy of nothing more than a brief looky-loo.

The thing with Mother Nature is that she never stops. She constantly evolves and grows, never looks back, never regrets the setbacks she endures, and I wonder how many of us, if any, can keep up. Take that raging wildfire that destroyed one-third of Yosemite in 1988. I see very little evidence of it. It is true that the very moment a calamity happens, Mother Nature begins coming back. Simply put, she allows no hesitation. Wouldn't it be something if we were all like that?

Alas, there are bison. Twice, the traffic stops because of those guys. Now, I've never seen a bison do anything unexpected or show any kind of hostility, but you know, they can weigh up to 1500 pounds (more than twice the Beast's weight) so even when they're in a playful mood, which they sometimes are, they can do a lot of damage.

So the first thing I always do when the traffic flow stops because of bison is work out an exit strategy. Or at least find a place to hide, like squeezing between a pickup and a motorhome. But I've got to say that if I'm going to be hung up in traffic, I'd rather it be because of wildlife than automobiles.

I pull over at the upscale Jackson Lake Lodge for gas and an early lunch. It's a big place with several eateries and the cheapest looking one is the packed-to-the-brim Pioneer Grill, so I go there and have a tasty chili cheeseburger with no bun and good conversations with the two food servers, Kent and Mallory.

Later, I pull over at Lewis Falls because I couldn't stop myself from enjoying the area and taking photos. After that, I get onto Highway 20 at the West Thumb of Yellowstone Lake. From what I read, it's called West Thumb simply because it resembles a big thumb, but whoever came up with the name must have a better imagination than me because it doesn't look at all like any hand-bound extremity I've ever seen.

As I wind around that watery thumb, I stop several times on the banks of the lake itself and realize that there is no better place to be right now. The only other place I walk around is Brink Upper Falls where the Yellowstone River proves that, just like any good woman, she can be as powerful and wild as she is sweet and caring.

As it sometimes happens during a superior day of riding, I do come across a disappointment. It's at the Canyon Village General Store in the form of an egg salad sandwich. First, it's nine bucks (seriously pricey) and second, it has about as much appeal and flavor as an old mechanic's work shirt. Even after I smother it with salt and pepper.

Nevertheless, as I get onto Highway 212, I reflect on the enjoyment of a perfect day of riding and it puts me in a philosophical frame of mind. Again, I come to the conclusion, like we all have at some point, that there are simple wisdoms to life and they can most easily be found in places like the Tetons and Yellowstone.

30

QUIRKS

What gives value to travel is fear.

Camus

Beartooth. Say the word to any biker who's ridden it and his eyes will light up, he'll look into the distance, shake his head slightly, exhale, and most likely say one word: Yeah.

The Beartooth Highway (or Bear's Tooth or Beartooth Mountain Pass) is sixty-nine miles long and connects the towns of Cooke City at the northeastern tip of Yellowstone to Red Lodge in Montana.

Sixty-nine miles doesn't sound like much. You could ride sixty-nine miles in less than an hour, even ten times sixty-nine miles in less than a day. The thing is, miles is a quantitative term, but when you're talking about Beartooth, you're talking quality.

I arrive in Cooke City just before sunset and the first thing I see is one of those temporary, diamond shaped orange road signs that reads INCIDENT AHEAD. Probably an accident, I figure, but as I follow the directions of a guy with a beer bottle in his hand and go to the left side of the road, I see it's a Cooke City street party. My kind of incident!

After getting a room, I walk back to join in the fun and fun it is with people milling about and talking and laughing. There are bales of hay to sit on and a dance floor where little boys are dancing with their mommas

163

and little girls are dancing with their daddies. The music is courtesy of a five-piece Country and Country Rock band (three guitars, bass and drums) with excellent three- and four-part vocal harmonies. And they're seriously kicking it.

The band takes a break so I go over and talk to Rich, one of the guitar players. He tells me he's the one who does the bookings and also tells me their name was chosen by Johnny, their first drummer. And what is it? The Bucky Beaver Ground Grippers. Uhhh, okay. You hear a name like that and you have to ask, right?

The story is that Johnny and the lead guitar player, Joe, are big fans of golf and golf history. Well, Joe owns a golf course outside of Billings, Montana and Bucky Beaver Ground Grippers were the very first golf shoe that had spikes. I guess it makes sense. Sort of. But hey, it does make for one helluva band name.

So why the festivities? The party is called *Save the Peaks* and was put together in conjunction with a hospital in Billings to raise money for breast cancer awareness. I don't know how much money they raised altogether, but I do know that a painstakingly hand-carved wooden table lamp auctioned off for $2000. (Two thousand bucks?!) In a small town (fewer than 200) in a small valley surrounded by high mountains under a pale pink sunset, good-hearted Montana folks are doing it right.

Cooke City is at the western end of the Beartooth Highway, and in the morning I'm buzzing with excitement as I head east on the legendary route. There's no precipitation, the road is mostly in excellent condition, half of the sparse traffic is motorcycles, and we're all happy-drunk with the wind in our faces. It's like the street party in Cooke City moved to the open road.

Beartooth is like a good friend's hospitality, like it wants to indulge you with a bacchanalia of winds and curves and mountains views. It takes you through a vast, towering area where the lakes and rivers are a crystalline dark blue (the water is co-o-old) and the acutely angled peaks are in perfect focus against the distinctively huge Montana sky.

It starts out at around 5200 feet, switchbacks its way up to almost 11,000 feet, then zigzags all the way back down with most of the curvy stuff in the middle. When the weather's agreeable, like it is today, the route is as enjoyable as a piece of freshly baked apple pie. And when you come to the many curves, you experience the full thrill of riding, whatever that means for you, from cruising at a moderate speed with a good woman on the back to hitting the curves like they were meant to be chewed up and spit out. For me, I sort of split the two approaches except, alas, I have no woman on the back.

The first part of the route is rather mild with only a few broad sweepers and sweeping views of the lower Absaroka Mountains. About six or seven miles before Beartooth Lake is when you run into the first of a series of curves that lead up to the Top of the World Store, where I hang out for a while and talk with bikers from all over, east coast to west coast. The conversations are as brisk as the air and the smiles as big as the sky.

After another seven or eight miles and a group of titillating switchbacks I pull over and catch a view that's the grandest I've seen in a very long time. Man, is it huge. Below an infinite white and blue sky, the road weaves along a carefree path and looks like something we would have built for our slot cars when we were kids if only only we'd had an unlimited supply of tracks.

I'm stopping often to take photos and take another long-ish, walk-about stop at Rock Creek Vista, where hundreds of little squirrels have learned that their finest meals are brought to them by two- and four-wheeled travelers. After that, the road drops back down about four thousand feet in the span of seven or so miles with more and more unblemished curves. Dang this is fun!

Ride a motorcycle for even a short period of time and freaky things will happen. A scorpion sunbathing on your gas tank, insects stuck inside your pant leg, a skunk that sits and stares as you're coming right at him, a swarm of wasps coming to visit while you're at a stop sign.

Non-living freaky things, too. Like plastic bags sticking to your windshield, a balloon popping on your pipes, oil covered tollgates, loose manhole covers, a tree branch flying off a truck and any of dozens more. We've all experienced things like that, but something happens on the Beartooth that's the freakiest thing in the history of freakiest things. For me, anyway.

I'm toward the end of the ride, within twenty minutes of Red Lodge, when I negotiate a hairpin and in front of me is almost a mile of straight-away. I hear tires screeching, look in my rearview mirror and going way wide around that hairpin is a brand new Corvette with a custom paint job. Tan with gold flames. Yeah, you read that right. Tan with gold flames. Sigh. Allow me a rant.

It's a special kind of oblivious mind that will cause someone to spend thousands of dollars to paint what is possibly the most American of badass American cars tan and gold. Corvettes should be bloodthirsty red. Or cold-blooded black or shark gray. Dark blue, even white and yellow will work sometimes. Maybe a ruthless racing green.

But tan? A *tan* Corvette? Really? That's like Dracula wearing a Hawaiian shirt, plaid shorts and ballet slippers. Anyway, the driver stomps on the gas so I pull over to let him pass and it's like I'm at a carnival freak show while I watch a style-deprived boob and his equally clueless silicon girlfriend.

Okay, rant over.

So I'm alone. Minding my own business. Not a care. La-di-da, la-di-da. Then, right out of the blue, no warning whatsoever, bang, just like that, an enormous spider is crawling across my sunglasses. I squeal and scream like a little girl, bat the thing away and frantically scrape my glasses with both hands. The Beast is veering all over the road and by sheer luck I end up in a turnout.

Hopping around like I'm covered with fire ants, I jerk off my helmet, jacket, flannel and gloves and violently shake them out. I check my boots, all the pockets and folds in my jeans and t-shirt, and every nook and cranny on the bike, and finally conclude that that eight-legged monstrosity is finally gone. I've narrowly escaped a painful demise. Hands on knees, breathing heavily, sweat dripping off my nose, whimpering like a cocker spaniel left out in the rain.

A couple riding two-up on a Honda Goldwing ride by and I just know what the lady is saying. "What'd I tell you, Harry, Harley riders are nuts."

31

GETTIN' ON

The great affair is to move;
To feel the needs and hitches of our life more dearly;
To come down off this feather-bed of civilization
And find the globe granite underfoot,
And strewn with cutting flints.

Robert Louis Stevenson

Eleven hundred miles. That's how far it is to Mile 0 of the Alaska Highway in Dawson Creek, which sits on the eastern border of British Columbia. To get there, I have to ride through Alberta, but first I need a good night's sleep in Red Lodge, which is easy to come by after the near-death experience I had with that spider.

After a good, early morning breakfast, I head north and cross the border at Sweetwater, which turns out to be the easiest and quickest border crossing I've ever done to any country. Earlier, I'd hooked up with three other riders and it took only a few minutes to get to the border guard, who had only one question for me: Any contraband? (No.) He didn't even check my bags.

After the mountains of the Tetons and Yellowstone, it's soul-settling to ride through the sprawling farmlands of Alberta. Little ponds here and there, and plants, planted by humans and not, growing without pause.

Because of the harsh winters up here, the roads are in only okay shape and the speed limits of 50-100 KM/H (30-62 MPH) are appropriate. (I'm in Canada now so the kilometers thing makes sense.) It's interesting because in Utah and Texas when you settle into the speed limit of eighty miles-per-hour it seems right as well. Yep, the mindset *does* match the road.

Despite the on-and-off rain, I'm merrily going along, pass through Lethbridge and eighty kilometers (fifty miles) later pull over for gas and a snack in Claresholm. I'm sitting on a bench under an eave outside the convenience store eating some jerky, when a guy in a pickup pulls in and excitedly announces to everyone that a quarter of a meter (ten inches) of hail just descended on Calgary and the national weather bureau has issued tornado warnings. Well, to bikers, tornado warnings mean only one of two things: go back or get a motel room. I get a room.

I had intended to get a new set of tires on this trip, but the type I wanted (Michelin Commander II) are a new product and motorcycle tire places aren't yet stocking any because they don't know if riders will want them. So instead of waiting a few days for a delivery in Billings, I had ordered them through Redline Motorsports in Calgary and Rick, the owner, assures me they'll be there when I arrive.

The tornado never materialized, but there's still a lot of wind and rain when I take off the next day. Despite that and getting a little lost, I get to Redline at 11 A.M., but the delivery truck is late. So I go have lunch at Tim Hortons (damn, that missing possessive apostrophe riles me up!) and get cookies for the Redline guys. The delivery guy doesn't show up until 1:30, but wouldn't you know it, my tires were put on the wrong truck so I have to wait until tomorrow.

Tomorrow shows up, as it always does, and so does the delivery guy with my tires. Again, despite the wind and rain, I show up as well with more cookies and Rick gives me a long-sleeved Redline Motorsports undershirt. He says it'll come in handy when I get into the Northern Rockies and he's giving it to me because I had to wait an extra day, but I'm thinking the cookies had something to do with it as well.

Prices are higher in Canada and when I get the bill for $547 Canadian, I remark that were I smart I would have gotten the tires in the United States. But then Rick does some quick calculations.

There's a tax in Canada called GST, which stands for Goods and Services Tax. (Canadians like to call it the Getting Screwed Tax.) Rick tells me that when you're a visitor, you can get a refund for all your GSTs when you leave the country. Factor in the exchange rate ($1.31 Canadian = $1.00 American) and the real cost for my tires is only about $355.00. Excellent price! Sometimes my mis-planning ways pay off.

[Side note. Getting a GST refund from Canada has become a near-impossible task and there are many items for which you can't get a refund. I ended up not even trying.]

A little backstory. I once got into a one-bike accident just fifty yards after getting two new tires. Broke my right leg and a finger and thoroughly busted up my right knee. Got a little road rash, too.

The reason had to do with this sexy woman (I'd never seen her before) who was sitting on a wall being as sexy as a woman could be so, you know, I had to show off, which means the accident was her fault, right? (Please say yes.) But does she come over with tears in her eyes and comfort me? Tell me everything is going to be okay? Offer to have my children? No, she doesn't. I swear, some people can be so ungrateful.

Anyway, ever since then, I've been extra careful, probably too careful, when I get new tires. They *are* slippery and depending on whom you listen to, it takes fifty to five hundred miles to dry out all that greasy petrochemical stuff. Also, when you first take off, they're cold, which is another reason they're slippery.

So here I am in Calgary with two new tires, trying to enjoy the rain while slowly making my way out of the city. I get honked at twice, but it's not a bother—my only concern is staying upright—and, as I expected, get lost. But because I have no actual schedule and no particular route in mind, that's not a bother, either.

The main thing on my mind is that not long after rolling out of Red Lodge, the Beast started having little electrical issues. Lights flickering now and again, bulbs going out, stuff like that. None of these is affecting the engine so I keep riding, but I *am* getting a little concerned. I get new bulbs at Heritage Harley in Edmonton, but after that, my speedometer and odometer stop working intermittently.

The engine is still unaffected so I decide to keep going and have the guys at the Harley dealership in Grand Prairie check it out. Pretty soon, the odometer and speedometer are rarely working and it's a disappointment because I need fewer than five hundred miles for the odometer to turn over to 100,000, which is a big deal for the Beast and me.

I make it to the dealership in Grand Prairie and discover it's called Mighty Peace Harley. I like the name but chuckle a little thinking about a Harley dealership gone Hippie. But it turns out to be typically well-run: friendly, helpful and efficient. (By the bye, the whole region up there is called Mighty Peace Country, the center point of which is the Peace River.)

I tell Rick, the service crew chief, what's been going on. Rick is one of those mechanics who zeroes in on a problem like he's reeling in an eighty-pound largemouth bass. Love that. He doesn't even bother rolling the bike into the service bay. Instead, he gets down on his back on the dirt and gravel parking area, checks out the alternator and finds the connection a little loose and corroded.

He scrapes off the corrosion, tightens the connection with a zip tie, refuses to charge me anything (good man!), and tells me to ride around for a while and make sure nothing else is wrong. (Zip ties. You don't need them often, but when you do, you give props to whoever invented them.)

Everything's perfect until an hour or so later when the speedometer and odometer quit working again. So I head back to Mighty Peace Harley, but don't get there until after hours, and tomorrow's Sunday and they're closed, so I'm back in Grand Prairie for two more nights.

Monday rolls around, Rick takes another look and finds that the grounding wire to the battery is frayed and oxidized. So he puts on a new one and I'm good to go again. Everything is working perfectly for much of the day, but when I'm only 135 miles away from 100,000, the speedometer and odometer go back to their on-but-mostly-off dance. But as before, the engine is sounding and running like it should so the Beast and I continue our foray to British Columbia.

Finally, I make it to Mile 0 in Dawson Creek with a big, big smile on my face. This is it! The start of the Alaska Highway! To make the occasion even more festive, the good Dawson Creek folks put up a big sign along with several small markers celebrating the fact.

ACHIEVEMENTS

It's the great, big, broad land 'way up yonder,
It's the forests where silence has lease;
It's the beauty that thrills me with wonder,
It's the stillness that fills me with peace.

Robert Service

The official name of this road is the Alaska Highway, at least that's what all the road signs and maps say. But I like calling it by its nickname, the Alcan (from ALaska, CANada), because there's an adventurous, faraway ring to it, like it has a tough and challenging personality, which it definitely does.

It was built by the United States Army in 1942 and connects Dawson Creek in British Columbia with Delta Junction in Alaska. The original length was about 1,700 miles, but over the years, the road construction guys and gals have straightened it out a lot so that it's now just under 1,400 miles. The reason it originally had so many twists and turns has to do with the reason it was built.

The plans for it were drawn up just after the Japanese attack on Pearl Harbor in December 1941. The military intelligence people in the United States figured that the Japanese would most likely invade the United States from the north, coming down from Alaska and through British Columbia. (Turns out they reckoned it right.)

Alaska was pretty much isolated back then (much of it still is) so the military needed a road so they could get up there and defend it. Well, airplanes fly in straight lines, which means their bombs and machine gun fire also come down in straight lines, so the Alcan was built with all those twists and turns in order to lessen fatalities. Makes sense.

Building the Alcan was an amazing feat. The actual construction was begun on March 8th, 1942 and completed on October 28th that same year, which means they built 1700 miles of road in just 235 days. That comes out to 7.23 miles per day. I mean, wow!

Sure, it wasn't paved, but how many trees had to be cut down? How many bridges built? How many lakes and ponds did they have to curve around? How many injuries and illnesses did they have to deal with? And how'd they get all the supplies to the guys constructing it? Then there was the bad weather to contend with. I swear, when we humans decide to do something, we get it done.

The Alcan out of Dawson Creek is pretty much like any unremarkable highway running out of a hearty and off-the-crossroads-of-the-world town with a population of 12,000. Expansive farms left and right, moderate truck traffic and clean air, though a constant rain gives the views an unhappy hue. Plus my speedometer and odometer still aren't working, but no matter, I'm thoroughly amped up and for good reason: I'm finally riding the Alcan.

The stops along the Alcan are small, most couldn't even be called towns (more like hamlets), and the "big" ones might have a population of 300. And there aren't many, but they all have gas pumps. I knew this all along, even made a list, but still manage to do something epically stupid.

I'd filled up the tank some ways before Dawson Creek and when I get to Wonowon, I see only one gas station with only four gas pumps and about ten big trucks waiting in line. Plus, it's surrounded by mud. I don't feel like being a part of that and figure the tank has enough gas to get to the next stop. Yeah, you know what happens next.

My mechanical gas gauge is unreliable and because the odometer isn't working and my attention has been mostly on the surroundings, I mis-figure my mileage and run out of gas, coasting to about a hundred meters from the top of a hill.

I open the reserve tank and figure that if I coast down all the hills, keep my RPMs low and do a few other hypermiling things, I can make it to the next stop, which according to my list is about twenty miles away. Well, I guess my reserve tank is smaller than I thought because I only make it another couple of miles, again within a hundred meters of the top of a hill.

I'm in trouble and the only obvious option is to hitch a ride to a gas station eighteen miles away then hitch a ride back. Nevertheless, I rock the bike back and forth to try and coalesce a drop or two of gas into the carburetor. It works, the bike starts, I get over the hill, coast down a bit, follow the road to the right and, whaddya know!, there are two gas pumps within walking distance!

I continue to coast down to the bottom, do some more rocking, and finally run out of fumes thirty yards in front of a place called Pink Mountain, which somehow didn't make it onto my list. (I gotta say that, as a guy, it's tough to admit getting my butt saved by a place called Pink Mountain.)

If you're ever up this way, heed this vital Alcan lesson: When you see a gas pump, fill up the damn tank!

After a nice chat with the owner and her dog, I take off and soon come across the most talked about item on the Alcan: road construction and repair.

The first two aren't that bad (lots of gravel and thick, orange-ish dust), but the third one is tough, it being covered with mud. I talk with the stop sign girl, Chantal, and she tells me all sorts of stuff about the road construction here, only one of which is good news, which is when the mud is deep, there's usually a flatbed truck that'll take your bike across. Then she tells me the bad news: No one is providing that service this year.

Twenty minutes after I arrive, Chantal turns around the stop sign so it reads SLOW, and I venture forth, staying as close as possible to the pilot car. It's about a two miles long and the middle half-mile is rocks mixed with thick, gooey mud. (One of the other bikers describes it as baby shit mud.) The Beast almost never voices a consideration about the conditions he endures, but on this occasion he tells me, "Dude, I'm a cruiser not a dirt bike. This could be considered abusive." Nevertheless he boldly goes forward with his rider in a state of shock.

The pilot car is going fifteen miles-per-hour, oftentimes slower, so it's a first and second gear affair, and with all the little slips and slides and my heart pumping full force, my feet are off the pegs much of the time like I'm the biker version of an outrigger canoe. I make it to the end, wobbling but upright all the way and feel like I deserve a medal.

Soon, I'm riding along as relaxed as you please, stopping often to take photos, and thrilled to be riding the Alcan. Other than the occasional road construction (yes, it's often called road destruction), the ride is unencumbered. True, probably half the traffic is large trucks, but there're just not that many of them. You can often ride ten to twenty miles without seeing anyone else.

After crossing over the Peace River and passing through Fort St. John, the farms give way to a bit of wilderness and I begin to see mountains to my left. Though it's still raining, the only disappointment, and it's minuscule, is that the only wildlife I've seen have been bison (stopped twice to let them cross the road), a porcupine, some rabbits and squirrels, and a lone, adolescent moose that looked like he was lost. No bears, wolves or mountain goats.

∽∝∽

The Beast's speedometer and odometer have been pretty much non-existent for hundreds of miles when Miss Serendipity comes to visit. Right out of the proverbial blue, both of them come on like they just came from the factory and the odometer is only twenty-five miles from 100,000.

I'm watching the numbers go by, hoping they don't disappear altogether, and calculating the remaining mileage with every change. 25-24-23 ... 4-3-2. Finally, about twenty miles south of Prophet River, the odometer reads 99,999. I take a bunch of photos, ride another mile and take a bunch more. Of course, the real 100,000 miles happened 5-600 miles ago, but now the Beast and I have proof. Yes!

I spend the night in Fort Nelson and when I continue the next morning, the rain has stopped and it's not long before I'm surrounded by the spectacular mountains of the Northern Rockies. Yep, civilization has finally disappeared behind me. For a while, there's no road repair and it seems like the Beast and I are stopping every five miles to take photos. And we are feeling fine, carefree almost.

However, when we come alongside the Tetsa River, the Alcan lets us know that she's still in charge as we're confronted with a punishing stretch of road repair that just goes on and on and on, maybe for twenty miles. (I would have checked, but the odometer stopped working again.)

Rocks, puddles and mud as slippery as oil-covered ball bearings. There are spots where the ground is so uneven that I have to duck-walk the bike, and the whole crossing lasts as long as a slow moving baseball game. (Okay, I'm exaggerating. But only a little.)

We get through it without going down (amazing!) and despite being covered with mud and it's raining again, the exhiliration hasn't diminished in the least. Why? The sweeping, incomparable views.

Man, oh man! You're never far from a bewitching river or lake and the trees cluster together in great and primeval patterns and wedged between them are flawless, light green meadows, and as the mountains grow higher, the valleys deepen and they seduce you into joining them as they wend their way between the those towering, hard cut giants eventually disappearing into a distant, mythical haze.

Though the Beast and I covered only a little over hundred miles, we feel as if we've had a productive day, so when the Toad River Lodge appears on the left, we decide to spend the night.

It's a quaint place, with a restaurant (decent food), a gift and souvenir section, and 10,095 caps hanging from the ceiling. Next to it are a bunch of cabins that face the peaceful Reflection Lake, which is bordered by a gently sloping, placid and green mountain on the other side.

33

MUD, MUD AND, WELL, MORE MUD

Few places in this world are more dangerous than home.
Fear not, therefore, to try the mountain passes.
They will kill care, save you from deadly apathy,
set you free, and call forth every faculty
into vigorous, enthusiastic action.

John Muir

After dinner that evening, an almost midnight sun evening, I wonder why there's so much road construction and repair on the Alcan so I use my allotted two hours of internet time to find the reason. (Two hours of Wi-Fi is all you get at the Toad River Lodge, and you have to pay for it.) Well, it has to do with something called chipseal and here's a kindergarten-type explanation of it.

Chipseal and asphalt are the two most common ways to pave a road. They use the same ingredients but are made differently. Chipseal is cheaper (about 1/5th the cost) and a quicker fix, which is important because the weather up here allows road crews to work only two or three months a year. The problem with chipseal is that it doesn't last nearly as long.

There are five stages to chipsealing.

1. Dig up one to two feet of the road and remove all of it. (This is when you get to ride through deep mud behind the pilot car.)

2. Mix it with water then heat all of it in a big heater/mixer alongside the road. (Yep, you still have that deep mud.)

3. Spray the heated mixture back down on the road. (This is where you chat with the stop sign girl and the other bikers. Maybe eat a sandwich.)

4. Put a layer of dirt and gravel on it then steam roller it. (Keep talking and eating.)

5. Ready to roll! (If it's dry, you'll kick up a little dust, but when big trucks are around, the dust is as thick as old axel grease. If it's raining, you get to ride on a thin layer of slimy mud.)

Pleased with learning all about chipsealing, I head back to my 8X10-with-a-small-bathroom room. With pure mountain air to breathe, a full gas tank, a full stomach, weary muscles and bones, and proud proof of 100,000 miles, I easily slip into a deep sleep.

I wake up around 10 A.M. not feeling well. Thick head (jokes accepted), no appetite and so on. I go for a walk, but it doesn't do any good. I try to eat but really can't. Around noon, I finally pack up, load up, and take off into a robust rain. I ride through two short slimy mud stretches then come to a long stretch of road repair. The deep mud kind.

I ride to the front of the line, the accepted protocol on the Alcan, and chat with the stop sign lady, Amanda. She says it's a long stretch and will be about forty minutes before the pilot car finishes leading the vehicles coming from the opposite direction, so we talk about kids, grandkids, taxes, old Shovelheads, MotoGP and so on. She also tells me a bunch of stories about the stupid things people do when riding through road repair sites.

Like this guy in a Ferrari, or something like it, who zoomed past the pilot car, thereby chewing up the underside of his $200,000 car. He landed in jail. And the two dirt bikers who did the same thing. They didn't ruin the underside of anything, but they also ended up in jail. How were these guys caught? Well, Amanda explains, there are these things called license plates, the workers have radios to call the police, and there's only one road up here, no alternate routes at all, no places to hide.

Amanda and I have been chatting for a half hour when it starts raining really hard. My physical and mental states have come to match the miserable weather so I head back to the Toad River Lodge, decide to get my room back for another night, and begin to seriously consider giving up on my Alcan adventure.

I mean, I've already had a great Summer's ride, I can come up to Alaska a month and a half earlier next summer during the no-to-little rain season (mid-June to early August) and get here via the shorter and safer Interstate 5. Besides, the Beast is still having electrical issues, the idea of food makes me want to vomit, and my innards are shaking.

After walking around a while, I figure I'll have another go at eating and the only unoccupied chair is at a table where a lady is sitting alone. She says it's okay if I join her so we shake paws and have a nice conversation.

Jaq teaches nursing at a college in Anchorage and knows a lot about the area up here so I mention my surprise at having seen only one moose so far. She tells me it's because moose like to find shelter when it's raining and that if it wasn't raining, I'd be fighting mosquitos, which is a much worse fate than a lack of wildlife sightings.

I mention that the one moose I saw seemed to have no clue whatsoever as to where he was or which way to go, which seems contrary to what wildlife should act like. She tells me the reason moose appear crazy is because of all the mosquito bites they get and when it gets really bad, they've been known to jump off of cliffs just to get some relief. I'm thinking that if death is preferable to mosquito bites, the mosquitos up here must be evil incarnate.

I do manage to keep down a bit of food, walk around some more then go to my room. I sleep a bit, wake up still miserable, then remember I have some garlic tabs. I take some, sleep some, take some more garlic and so on like that into the night, still thinking I might head on back the way I came.

Sometime during the night, I wake up and can't get back to sleep so I reread some emails. One is from my friend, Jaume, who just finished riding the Dalton Highway, which is that near-impossible road that goes from Fairbanks up to Deadhorse in Prudhoe Bay, which is on the north shore of Alaska. That's right, the *north* shore, right on the edge of the Arctic Ocean.

The road is 414 miles long and very little of it is paved. And there are 16% grades. And rain. And snow. And mud. Lots of mud. And big trucks. And no amenities, not even an outhouse. You even have to carry your own gas. Thankfully, it's not part of the Alcan.

On Jaume's ride back to Fairbanks, the temperature gets below freezing, the precipitation is alternating between sleet and snow, and so as not to get stuck, he's having to ride through "slush mud" at fifty miles-per-hour through low clouds with a visibility of maybe ten feet. Everything is going along fine until his carburetor float bowl freezes open and drowns the engine with gas, resulting in an empty gas tank.

So as not to get plowed over by a big truck, he pushes his bike to the side of the road. He said it was funny, being dressed in leather and armor, doing jumping jacks to try and not freeze to death. Though he eventually gets a ride from a father and son who were hauling timber, he will always be part of that small percentage of bikers who can say, "I rode the Dalton."

Reading Jaume's email reminds me of Carl Stearns Clancy, one of my motorcycle heroes. Carl is recognized as being the first person to "girdle the globe" on a motorcycle. He did it on a seven horsepower Henderson (*yes, only seven horsepower!*) in only eleven months, from October 1912 to August 1913. His route covered four continents (Europe, Asia, Africa and North America) for a total of 18,000 miles.

What he must have gone through! Sure, he averaged only 51 miles a day, but where did he get gas and oil? (Were there even gas stations back then?) How did he get parts for repairs? And tires? Where did he get food and how did he access his money? He tented it much of the way and most of the roads had to be dirt or mud, right?

And he did it over a hundred years ago, way before Alaska became our 49th state, way before the Alcan was built, way before motels on the Alcan were built, way before chipseal, pilot cars and stop sign girls were invented. I don't have an internet connection, but there is a quote of his in a folder on my desktop.

One must die sometime
and to die with one's boots on
is very noble.

I like that, always have. As I think about Mr. Clancy's globe-trotting, I come to the conclusion that all these thoughts about cutting short my trip is me just being a wimp and I need to cut it out. So I take some more garlic, sleep for a long time and in the morning I am completely energized. I mean, I am feeling goo-oo-ood!

It's still raining when I take off after breakfast and the first patch of slimy mud I come to gives me a thrill. It's not long, about thirty yards, so I slow down to about twenty miles-per-hour, but as soon as I get on it, the whole bike starts slowly sliding toward the right, where there's a couple of feet of grass then a five foot drop into the Toad River. I put my feet down, but they're sliding along with the bike. I keep going forward and to the right, and just as I'm a foot from the grass, I reach the end of the mud and stop sliding.

I'm laughing. Sure, dropping into an ice-cold river would be bad enough but not nearly as bad as the tombstone I'd get.

FOSTER KINN
WITH THE BEAST HERE LIES
A RIVER CALLED TOAD
HIS SORRY DEMISE

I won't bore you with all the mud patch thrills, but one thing I will mention is the eye-dazzling Muncho Lake where the water is colored a phosphorescent aquamarine that lights up the air and stretches to distant dark mountains where it looks like a giant hand had carved out a huge chunk of the mountainside leaving a cut in the shape of a butterfly that glows amber in the afternoon sun.

As things are going (i.e. slowly), I figure I'll stay in Liard Hot Springs, but when I get there and gas up (remember to gas up!), the motel desk ladies tell me they have no rooms left and the closest motel is in Watson Lake, 210 kilometers (129 miles) away. Well, I'm tired but have no choice, so off I go.

Then, maybe an hour later, I see a place called the Coal River Lodge. This is weird because I seem to remember another Coal River Something-or-Other way back before Liard Hot Springs and I know I'm going in the right direction. At least I *think* I'm going in the right direction. Anyway, I don't recall seeing this place on the map so maybe it's new, I don't know. But I *do know* it's there!

What a cool place Brent and Donna, his daughter, have created! It's a family and friends operation with cute and clean rooms and behind the place is a large meadow with a gaggle of Canada Geese going for a stroll.

Even though it's dinnertime, Donna makes me a huge, tasty omelet then Brent invites me out to his garage office for a beer. A Coal River friend named Roger joins us and we talk and talk for the longest time about whatever. Pensions, moose season coming up, hustling darts, working with the Canadian Army and on and on.

True, I may not have gotten in a whole lot of miles today, but man, am I glad to still be going forward.

34

HEROES

Security is mostly a superstition. It does not exist in nature.
Avoiding danger is no safer in the long run than outright exposure.
Life is either a daring adventure or nothing at all.

Helen Keller

The next day I get to the famous Signpost Forest in Watson Lake (population a whopping 1500) where there are over 100,000 signposts from around the world. Travelers are allowed to put up their own signs and there's even a small building where you can get a personalized wooden one made. The hours of operation are Alcan unique and handwritten on the door. OPEN WHEN I'M HERE, CLOSED WHEN I'M GONE. But if you really need that sign right now, John left his phone number.

Before leaving, I take one last look and right there at the top of the front wall is a sign from my hometown: Visalia, Pop 62,245, elve 300. I'm figuring the sign was made long after I moved south (the population was 12-15,000 when I was a kid) and the sign itself was probably a throwaway because of the misspelling. (It should be elev, not elve.) Nevertheless, seeing it gives me a big smile.

Beginning with Watson Lake, the Alcan sneaks into the Yukon, squiggles its way back into British Columbia for a bit, then goes back into the Yukon as it boldly tracks its way to the Alaska border. There are several road repair stops along the way so I'm not eating up a whole lot of miles, but I don't mind. I love the land and people up here and am taking an inordinate amount of photos, though I doubt any will be worthwhile because of the rain and low clouds.

I've been riding alone for a while, no other travelers around, when I come upon a marvel of Alcan engineering. The right side of the road is covered with a pile of dirt about five meters (16.5 feet) high and fifteen meters (fifty feet) long. On the left side of the road is a hole the same size as that pile of dirt, and at the bottom of it is sizeable layer of sloshy mud. Not only that, the slopes leading down to the bottom are angled at around forty degrees.

There are four guys working this section (one on a bulldozer, one on a backhoe and two with shovels), and they're frantically trying to get it filled and firm enough for vehicles before the next pilot car comes along. How I missed my pilot car and came to be alone, I don't know, but here I am. And they're all looking at me like, "Where the hell did you come from and what the hell are you going to do?"

It's a dilemma. I need to make a decision and it's the type of decision that men, and only men, have faced since the beginning of time. Do you do the smart thing, or do you do the guy thing?

In this case, the smart thing to do is watch the workers fill up the hole and wait for the next pilot car, even if it takes an hour. But being a guy, I decide to do the guy thing and negotiate that hole because, you know, you have to secure your place in guy-hood by engaging in some badass-ery now and again, right? It has to do with pride and honor, right?

So I think, "Just relax (yeah, right), sit up straight (good posture!), trust the bike (better at this than me), look straight ahead (the least frightening view), and don't go too fast or too slow."

And I make it. I actually avoid going down or getting stuck. (I was going to say that I didn't waver in the least, but honestly, I was so terrified I can't remember any details.) More importantly, I avoid embarrassing myself in front of four fellow guys. And to make it even better, I give them a pfft-it-ain't-nothin' smile as I ride off. Of course, in my own mind I'm wondering if I need to find a secluded spot to change my underwear.

Around 5 P.M., I cross over the Teslin Lake on the longest metal bridge on the Alcan. Right past it is a settlement called Teslin where there's a restaurant, a small general store and the Yukon Motel. It's a friendly looking place so I decide to spend the night.

The following morning, I pack up, load up and check out, but when I go to start the Beast, all I get is a rapid clicketa-clicketa-clicketa. Yep, dead battery. I'm hoping all the battery needs is a jump start and figure the best way to find a person who can do that is to give the bike a whore's bath. (No, there's no logic to it, but it's a good idea, anyway.)

So I get a bucket and fill it with water, get a bunch of paper towels, sit down next to the Beast and commence cleaning off layers and layers of mud.

Then the electricity goes out in the entire area. Electricity runs everything up here, gas pumps and water faucets included, which means no one can fill their gas tank or even flush a toilet. The guy who's going to fix the contraption that creates all that electricity has a two-hour drive to get here, and all the while, the big parking area fills up with trucks, motorhomes, cars and motorcycles, all with empty gas tanks.

During those two-hours, a wonderful aspect of the Alcan becomes clearly evident. Because of the heartiness of the travelers up here, not only is no one complaining, there's a bit of a party atmosphere to it all.

So there I am, wiping down the Beast with a bunch of increasingly muddy paper towels when Trucker Mark walks up. We get into a conversation and I tell him about the dead battery. He commiserates and apologizes for not having a way to help, but he does give me an apple, two bananas and a bottle of water to make my situation more tolerable. Good guy.

The water in the bucket is now dark brown, but I go back to "cleaning" the Beast anyway. A shadow falls over me so I look up and see two jovial fellows wearing blue and red, full body rain gear. It's BMW riders Jerry and his son Sid from Ontario, who are waiting for the electricity to come back on so they can gas up and continue northwest to see their daughter/sister. They ask what's up and I tell them about the dead battery. That's when their smiles get real big.

It turns out that Jerry and Sid are certified master electricians (what are the chances?) and brimming with eagerness to fix my problem, which means they're certified heroes, too.

Sid immediately gets his bike and rolls it next to mine so we can recharge the battery. He unwinds a heavy gauged wire that's holding up something on his bike while Jerry unwinds a heavy gauged wire that's wrapped around his belly. I look at him quizzically and he says, "It stops the wind from blowing in under my shirt." (Makes sense.) Then he says to Sid that while they're at it, they should check the alternator, so he goes to his bike and gets a voltmeter.

Now, how many bikers in the world carry heavy gauge wires and voltmeters with them? Yeah, I'd say a total of two, Jerry and Sid. I mean, talk about Boy Scout prepared. Well, the alternator is working as it should so the logical next step is to recharge the battery.

Before I go any further, I should admit something. If you read the first Freedom's Rush book, you know I'm terrified of vegetables (they *are* scary if you think about it), but something else that terrifies me just as much is electricity. I mean, it's like voodoo magic, you never know what it's going to do.

Sure, somebody somehow throws a bunch of volt and watt things into a wire and, boom, your computer fires up, I get that. But what about the times those volt and watt things jump into the air and zap you between the eyes, turning your eyebrows into a raging inferno? See what I mean? They're unpredictable. And dangerous.

Anyway, Sid is able to easily attach his wires to the bolts on his battery, but the bolts on my battery are hard to get to, so Jerry holds the bare wires against the positive and negative terminals with his bare thumbs for a full five minutes.

Now, I'm an electricity imbecile, but I'm pretty sure that should hurt. That's what electricity does, it hurts, right? So I ask him, "Jerry, I'm an idiot when it comes to electricity, but aren't you getting electrocuted?" He says, "Oh yeah, but it's only twelve volts."

Only twelve volts?! Twelve volts for a solid five minutes?! Are you freakin' kidding me?! If I got electrocuted with twelve volts for only five seconds I'd swear I passed through the portals of Hell!

To not make a long story any longer, I'll just say the battery is a goner and needs to be replaced. I make some calls. Whitehorse, the closest town, is two hours northwest, but there are no Harley places there and no batteries that'll fit. Same with Watson Lake and Fort Nelson ten hours back down the Alcan.

The closest one is in Fairbanks, Alaska, 1125 kilometers (700 miles) away, but if I get it from there, it would have to be shipped across an international border and who knows how much extra that would cost. And having to go through customs could take weeks and there's no guarantee it would even get through. Heck, it might even be illegal.

The next closest one is at Mighty Peace Harley in Grand Prairie, 1350 kilometers (840 miles) away. But how do I get it here? This is Teslin, population 122. No FedEx, no UPS, and according to the manager of the restaurant, the mail gets delivered "whenever." I need someone who knows the ins and outs of delivering things in the Yukon and figure the best way to find that person is to have some lunch. And that's when another hero shows up: Lois, the waitress.

When you eat in diners, cafes and restaurants a lot, one of the things you learn is that waitresses know everything there is to know and Lois is no exception. She gets on the phone with another hero, Jennifer the parts gal at Mighty Peace Harley, and they figure out the best way to send the battery is via Greyhound. So Greyhound it is! But there are other issues.

Today's Saturday and it's past the cutoff time to drop off a package, but Jennifer-the-Parts-Gal-Hero says she'll take it to the Greyhound office tomorrow (Sunday), her only day off. Then, because Greyhound has a new policy of not delivering auto or motorcycle parts, she'll wrap the box to make it look like a present for her friend, Foster Kinn, who lives in Teslin. What a sweetie!

Another thing. Greyhound Buses come up this way on only Mondays, Wednesdays and Fridays. After dropping off the package, Jennifer-the-Parts-Gal-Hero calls and says that the Greyhound Bus lady said my battery won't make it to the terminal in Fort Nelson in time for the Monday bus, so it'll be on the Wednesday bus.

Still another thing is that the bus doesn't stop in Teslin, it only passes through. So Lois-the-Waitress-Hero gets on the phone with the Greyhound Bus lady in Fort Nelson (another hero) and gets her to persuade the bus driver to stop in Teslin. Whew!

189

The end result? I become a resident of Teslin for five days. When you're on the road, five days in one place is a long time, so by the end of the second day I'm thinking I should fill out some employment applications and get a job. Maybe get a Canadian passport and phone number, too. Learn to ice fish and ride a snowmobile. Start saying "eh" after every sentence. Eat poutine instead of chili cheese fries. So much to learn!

On the third night, I wake up around 3 A.M.—no particular reason, it happens now and again—and open the door to get some fresh air. I'm looking at the twinkling and pulsating stars and how they cluster together in cryptic patterns when, without warning, an enormous broadsword of luminous green explodes into view and slashes the entire sky in half. I stand and watch, mesmerized, as it evolves to an even brighter green then slowly fades to nothingness as if it had never been. It's the first time I've seen the northern lights, the aurora borealis.

I get dressed then walk away from the motel until I'm alone next to a sparse copse of pine. It's here, away from all man-made lights, that I get to see them in their unadulterated glory.

Sometimes, they erupt into a vast, incandescent blaze and other times gradually glow bright and brighter and they swell and swivel and swirl like great celestial serpents covering the entire sky in wild and unpredictable patterns and sometimes a million shards shoot up and out of them cutting the night like daggers and it reminds me of how the Vikings described the teeth of the Midgard Serpent, then they slowly fade into gray and black while others begin their cycles of light and death.

How magical it is to be alone in the Yukon night and see this with not a sound, not even a rustling leaf.

In addition to the northern lights, there are many other things that make my time in Teslin special. I keep meeting fabulous people and get to share road stories from all the bikers who stop by. I have a chat with two women who are bicycling the entire Alaska Highway, and a fellow named Andy who is trying to break his own record for riding it on a bicycle. And the guy from Georgia with long white hair and a long white beard whose baseball cap said, "Santa Claus on Vacation." And the six-year-old girl who thinks bison are the cutest animal there is.

On her day off, I climb into the passenger seat of Lois's car and she gives me a tour of the area around Teslin Lake. Pristinely beautiful places I never would have seen otherwise.

I get up at 2 A.M. on my last night, walk over to the general store and wait for the Greyhound Bus. It rolls in forty minutes later and the bus driver and I have a lively chat. He tells me that because it's so beautiful up here, he has the best driving gig in the world and I tell him there's no way anyone would argue the point.

Later that morning I install the new battery, the Beast starts right up and we finally continue northwest around 11 A.M. with good memories of heroes, fellow travelers and northern lights, the kind of memories that brighten your days, soften your nights and make your loads lighter. What a rich world this is, even in places with a population of 122.

35

FORTY-NINE

I'd rather sing one wild song and burst my heart with it,
than live a thousand years watching my digestion
and being afraid of the wet.

Jack London

Whitehorse is the capitol of Yukon Territory and with a population of around 23,000, it is by far the largest settlement on the Alcan. There's even a McDonald's there. And a WalMart. And a Starbucks. And stoplights, streetlights and sidewalks. And automobile dealerships, movie theaters, chain restaurants, big name hotels, and gas stations with the names of big oil companies.

It's weird because every other place of commerce on the Alcan is mom-and-pop owned, even the gas stations. Honestly, I don't know what to make of it or how to act and can't tell if Whitehorse wants to be more Alcan-like or more big city-like. Nevertheless, despite the quasi-big city trappings, after only a few miles of continuing west, I'm back in the Alcan environment that I've come to love.

Really. The views up here are flat out stunning and I can't write about all of them because this book would end up with ten thousand pages. Nevertheless, I've already mentioned a few and will mention a few more including the one I come across the next day, sixty kilometers (thirty-seven miles) after Haines Junction where the Alcan cozies up to the shores of Kluane Lake.

I pull over at the southern end and in the distance, a dominating mountain on the left cuts a jagged profile against the dust-free sky, and then, like an architectural wonder, angles steeply down and seamlessly melds into the emerald waters that stretch into forever. Above, the clouds are sculpted into patterned bunches or into long, narrow wisps that create their own infinite perspective.

I cross over a two-mile bridge, which is more like a causeway, and once on the western side, look out at an island, but because I'm standing under that infinite perspective, there's no way to tell how far away it is. It's perfectly reflected in the lake, and with its caramel-colored soil and residents of dark foliage and a few naked trees, it looks a 16th Century Flemish master painted it.

I continue along the shore and come to Destruction Bay, which got its name back in 1942 when strong winds kept blowing down the structures built during the Alcan's construction. Despite a population of only thirty-five, the motel and restaurant are pretty big and there's a neat souvenir section in the place where you pay for gas.

I get a room and after unloading, go outside to watch the goings-on and this is when I put my full attention on ravens, the official bird of the Yukon. I'd been seeing them all along and really like how they look, all shiny black with a slightly hooked beak and black eyes that see everything. And they're smart, too, always working together as a pair, one as a sort of scout and the other as the gatherer.

Here, however, there's a whole gaggle of them, but they still seem to operate in pairs and each pair has staked out its own territory and they stay there, never crossing into another pair's space.

The next day I run into the most exhausting stretch of the ride: the 185 kilometers (115 miles) to Beaver Creek, which is the longest distance without a gas station. There's a small museum in Burwash five minutes outside of Destruction Bay, but other than that, the only structures that offer seating are two port-a-potties at a turnout. It's raining off and on, but the real challenge is that three quarters of the road is covered with that slimy mud. Yeah, 145 kilometers (90 miles) of mud.

After a particularly long, mud-covered stretch, I come to some chipseal and it's like shaking paws with an old friend so I pull over to rest and stretch. A minute or so later, Ty from Texas pulls up on his '08 Harley Rocker, parks behind me and I get to shake paws with a new friend. Ty's a typical Texan, friendly and a good storyteller, and we talk for a while about all sorts of things, including family, friends, bacon and beer.

He's ready to get moving before me so he puts on his helmet, gets on his bike, pulls up next to me and says, "I'd tell you to keep the shiny side up, but on a road like this there ain't no such thing."

I arrive in Beaver Creek a full seven hours after leaving Destruction Bay, not tired but exhausted.

While checking into one of the two motels, I meet Javier, a fellow with a big and ready smile. Javier is one of those adventure bikers like Jaume I mentioned earlier, except he's riding all the way from Santiago, Chile to Deadhorse, Alaska. He's been on the road nine months, has tented it the entire way, and is doing it all on a Suzuki DR650.

For money, gas and food, he does odd jobs and sells these stickers a friend of his made. On them is a fully packed motorcycle with the words, "Ida y Vuelta en Moto." Roughly translated, it means "Going out and returning (or round-trip) on a motorcycle." I give him five bucks for one.

Sometimes people will buy him a meal or a tank of gas, sometimes they let him stay in their homes or motorhomes, and sometimes in the back room of a restaurant. The rest of the time, he sleeps wherever, occasionally sharing his accommodations with small wildlife. Much of the time, personal hygiene is accomplished by washing his clothes and himself in the ice-cold rivers and lakes he comes across.

I found out later that his Suzuki broke down two weeks after we met and he had to finish his ride on a 200cc Chinese motorcycle. Javier: one tough man.

Then I meet Tsai from Taiwan, who figured a good vacation would be to drive his family (wife, mother, son and two daughters) over the entire

Alcan then over to Anchorage in his brand new, pure black BMW X5. When I first see him, he's vigorously washing the mud off his car. I'm thinking, "Why?" But he's determined to get it looking showroom new and because there's no hose outside, he keeps retrieving fresh paper towels and filling up a bucket with clean water from the shower in his room.

I feel sorry for Tsai—a beautiful, expensive new car and he made the mistake of taking it up here—so I keep going outside to try and cheer him up but never quite get there.

It's cold, gray and wet when I leave Beaver Creek. Nevertheless, it's exciting because in fewer than thirty miles I'll be in Alaska, the forty-ninth state the Beast and I have visited. It's been a long time coming.

The road has a lot of rough patches, more than what I've seen so far, but at least there are no stretches of mud. I get to the border station and have to wait for only one car. But then the border guard decides to ask a million questions. Maybe he's lonely and looking for a friend, I don't know, but I'm antsy and have that will-you-puh-leese-hurry-up tone in my voice. I mean, Alaska is right there!

He keeps asking more questions, most of them he's already asked (how many times did I tell him my zip code?), and after a couple of eons is finally convinced I'm hauling nothing illegal or dangerous and I am, indeed, the person in the photo on my passport. I put on my face wraps, helmet and gloves, and off we go.

We're finally, *finally*, in Alaska! Yes!

Once you enter Alaska, the Alcan turns from chipseal to asphalt and I gotta say that of the two, asphalt is noticeably more comfortable. And you can quote me.

As I said, it's gray and wet and so overcast that I can barely see a half-mile. I stop to take photos anyway because even if they're not worth showing anyone else, I enjoy looking at them because they take me back to time and place. But the things I tend to remember are odd little details. It's funny. I can't remember the names of streets or towns, but I can remember what the gravel felt like under my boots or how difficult it was to remove my gloves or which way the rain slanted, stuff like that.

It's cold as well and a recent addition to my bundling-up technique is to put newspaper between the layers of clothes and paper towels between the cloth and wool face guards. It works. Not totally, of course, but I am more comfy temperature-wise.

Other than a pleasant conversation with a local gal at the Naabia Niign (NAW-bee-uh NIN) Gas and Food Store, nothing much happens until I stop for lunch in Tok (pronounced Toke), which is about ninety miles inside the border.

I'm in Fast Eddie's Restaurant when Paul comes over, sits right down, and we end up talking for so long we each have to order another piece of pie. I like Paul. For instance, his response when people warn him of the dangers of riding a motorcycle. "A motorcycle is just a motorcycle, and a road is just a road."

He's another adventure guy like Jaume and Javier and he's on his way home to Idaho after riding the Dalton with a buddy of his. (This is the same Dalton Highway I mentioned earlier.) He's riding alone now, however, because his buddy had to sell his bike in Deadhorse after it broke down.

The thing is, Paul is so energetic you'd think he just spent the weekend at a spa in the Bahamas getting B-12 shots. The other thing is that he's totally prepared for weather like this. I mean, he's wearing so many layers of clothes that even though he's a slender guy, his outerwear is XXL.

The truly wonderful thing Paul does, however, is spend half of every year in Peru where he founded a large non-profit organization, The People of Peru Project, that takes care of under-aged girls who have been abused. And when people come down for a winter of volunteer work, he treats the bikers with a motorcycle tour of Machu Picchu. Good biker, good man.

It's well into the afternoon when he rides away on his mud-covered, perfectly packed KLR, so I decide to get a room and ride to the end of the Alcan tomorrow. Besides, the Beast and I are feeling a little mellow, like we deserve a good, sweet rest, a sort of reward for having ridden together in forty-nine states.

In the morning, it's still cold, gray and wet, and I immediately wish I had on as many layers as Paul. (He's definitely smarter than me.) The rain comes and goes, and a half hour later, when strips and patches of blue sky begin to wiggle their way into the clouds, it warms up to the mid-40s (7°C), so it's rather peachy.

You know, it's funny. Were I back home in Southern California in weather like this, the Beast would be in the garage and I'd be inside bundled up in layers of quilts. I guess the mindset matches the temperature as well as the road.

Speaking of the road, it's mostly straight, in decent condition and there are more and more dry patches. I'm getting some decent photos (I hope) and making good time and the closer the Beast and I get to the end of the Alcan, the more excited we get.

It's mid-afternoon when I finally see Delta Junction (population 948) and the Beast and I, sporting loud pipes and big smiles, proudly rumble into town.

And ride right past the world famous, end-of-the-Alcan monument.

Tell ya what. If I ever do a mistake-free ride I'll probably have a heart attack. Anyway, I U-turn the Beast and, dang it! We made it!

36

A SINCERE WORD

As is a tale, so is life;
not how long it is, but how good it is,
is what matters.

Seneca

Was the Alcan a tough ride? For me, sure. Take all that mud, for instance, which accounted for about 150 of the 1400 miles. I live in the Los Angeles area and hardly ever ride through mud so when I first saw those road construction spots I was stunned. "I'm supposed to ride across *that?*"

Or that time I was sliding sideways toward the Toad River. For a few seconds, it was scary, but then what flashed through my mind was that old Laugh-In TV show where a guy with crazy hair and thick glasses would ride out on a tricycle and fall over. That's why I laughed afterward.

I'd gotten used to riding on mud about a quarter of the way through the Alcan, but that's not to say I came to like it, only that it was no longer a heart-crimping experience. The thing is, you have to be constantly alert and aware of the road so you can't ever sit back without a worry. On a road like this, the concept of relaxation is like a distant, foggy memory of something you once read about in a fairytale.

There are places in these chapters where I made it seem like this was a stress-filled, even treacherous, ride and, indeed, there were times it was. And let's face it, the fact I was on a seven hundred pound cruiser with street tires and not on some sort of adventure/enduro bike with mud tires didn't make it any easier. So yeah, it was tough. But that's me.

On the other hand, consider adventure bikers like the ones I wrote about: Jaume, Javier and Paul. Now, those guys are fearless. They'll jump into the maws of impossible terrain just for the heck of it, as if it's nothing more than a comfortable hobby, and won't even begin to get happy until they're being chased by a starving mama grizzly with rabies. Really. I mean, they're so good they could do the Alcan riding backward with flat tires.

So to all the adventure guys and gals around the world, all I did was get a little wet and dirty. As it is with most things, it's all relative.

The truth is that I'm a good to very good rider, sometimes excellent. I'm not great and not an expert nor do I pretend to be. It's also true that a good number of the bikers reading this can handle a motorcycle better than I can. The point I'm getting to is that if I can ride the Alcan, you can. And my recommendation is that you do just that.

This is marvelous country up here. Sure, a lot of other places are beautiful. The Rockies, the Great Smokys, Michigan's Upper Peninsula, Yosemite and Yellowstone, the Acadian Forest, oh there's no end to the beauty in this world. But to paraphrase my author-friend Jefe, an Alaska native, it's definitely gorgeous up here, but it's the sheer magnitude of it that sets it apart.

Back to my recommendation.

Ride the Alcan. If your sweetheart doesn't want to go with you, give him or her a good, long hug, say you love them and you'll be back. If you have kids, hug them and tell them you love them, too, and let them know they'll be getting some of the coolest t-shirts around. Then roll on over to Dawson Creek and start that trek to Delta Junction.

Create the time and find the money. Quit your job and sell your stuff if you have to. Get the bike you want and the gear you need. Travel a road you've never seen, breathe a different air, feel the waters of a river you never knew existed. Shake paws with that stranger, leave the waitress a big tip (she works hard), and make extraordinary memories for yourself and everyone you meet.

Handle whatever comes up, help others and accept help when you need it, because we all do at some point. Relish your highs and never regret your lows—we all experience them. Push yourself but stop and look around now and again. Laugh at others' one-liners, tell your own tales (you'll have them), heed the wisdom of those who've been there, and be sure to pass on what you've learned.

And always, always, always stay true to the person you create yourself to be.

37

PURGATORY

*A bend in the road
is not the end of the road.
Unless you fail to make the turn.*

Helen Keller

First, I have to give props to the Beast. When we left Grand Prairie (seems like a year ago), I promised him that I'd get all of his electrical issues fixed if he would just get us to Fairbanks. And he did just that, rumbling all the way like a champ and handling all the adversities a helluva lot better than me.

I take him to Outpost Harley in Fairbanks (the northernmost Harley dealership in the world) the morning after I arrive and the first thing Art, the repair guy, notices is that the ignition coil housing on the Beast's left side is being held up by only the spark plug wires. This is amazing because that coil is supposed to be held in place by two steel brackets. That's right, the bumps on the Alcan *broke* two steel brackets on my bike.

I realize immediately that the final blow was delivered just before the Alaska border. At the far side of a short bridge was nothing but water-filled chuckholes, but I couldn't see them until the last moment and there was no way to avoid them because of a car coming the other way. I remember it well because it felt like my spine poked through the top of my skull.

Art gets the welding done and the next day, I tell him about all the electrical anomalies and he decides to check out the electronic MAP sensor, which is cuddled up against the carburetor. The MAP sensor on the Beast is just a basic one, but some of these sensor things that motorcycles have (cars and trucks, too) are amazing. And I'm not talking about run-o'-the-mill, wow-the-thermostat-turns-off-at-72° type of amazing. No sirree.

The fancy MAP sensors monitor and adjust all sorts of things based on all sorts of variables, like air temperature, oxygen level and barometric pressure. (There's a rumor that the new Honda Goldwings will have one that monitors the commodities market in Singapore.) Anyway, Art does some Sherlock Holmes work and finds twelve error codes. That's right, the Beast kept on running *despite twelve error codes*. What a machine!

The result? Even though Marcus, the repair write-up guy, gets a new sensor from Milwaukee (the home of Harley) as fast as possible, there was the welding, an oil change, and a weekend in the middle of it, so I get to spend five days in Fairbanks with no transportation.

The good news is that I again meet up with friendly Ty from Texas, the very same Ty I met on that muddy 115 miles between Destruction Bay and Beaver Creek. And here we are a week or so later, each renting a room in the same motel in Fairbanks waiting for our bikes to be serviced by the same Harley dealership. Great guy, great conversations, including a lesson for yours truly about the technology behind horseshoeing nails. I swear, riding a motorcycle may be the best education around.

However, the most important thing I do with my time is figure out how to visit some friends in Washington before getting back home for an event of utmost importance: my twin granddaughters' first birthday party. No way am I going to miss that.

I look at the days I have remaining, check the mileage to Vancouver (2,100 miles, 3,350 kilometers), look at the weather forecasts (snow in the Northern Rockies), make some calls, and come to the conclusion that shipping the bike from Anchorage to Seattle and me flying there would not only be faster, it'd probably save me some money. So that's what I decide to do.

The Beast's fixits are done in the afternoon so I ride around Fairbanks for a while then go to an outfitters store where I get some new glove liners and a new thermal top. The primary reason for riding around, however, is to check how the Beast is doing and, tell ya what, he's feeling as good as ever, which is damn good. And the price for all this? All I can say is big time thanks to Art and Marcus at Outpost Harley for doing right by the Beast and me.

I have two days to make it to the shipping place in Anchorage. It's only 365 miles, but the real problem is the two hundred miles to the other side of the Denali Pass, which promises to *not* be a cozy ride in the park. It's early in the morning when I bundle up as well as I can and leave Fairbanks into hard rain, howling wind, and a temperature of 38° (3°C).

After a brunch of beef jerky in Nenana, I head up the Denali Pass while the temperature drops in inverse proportion. A while later, the rain turns into hail then snow then hail then snow again. Nothing heavy, but still it's snow and hail, know what I mean? (Just an aside here. I gotta say that hail defies physics. I don't care how well you're bundled up and protected, some of those little hail guys will find a way to zap you right on your eyelids.)

I pull over for lunch at Rose's Cafe in Healy and the parking lot is the same as all the parking lots up here. Nothing but gravel and mud with chuckholes big enough to swallow zeppelins, and there's really no way to squiggle through them without splashing in a few.

I pause in front of a thermometer that's on the outside wall next to the front door, and it shows 26° (-3°C). I'm too cold to mentally process what that means.

I go inside, sit at the counter, order my entrée of choice for this trip (double chili cheeseburger, no bun) and go about trying to get warm, but it's not going well because, being a fairly busy Sunday afternoon, people keep leaving and coming in and every time the door opens, a cold draft shoots right at my head. After an hour, I'm as warm as I'm going to get and the wind and precipitation have let up a bit, so I get back on the road.

The clouds have lifted some, which is good, but it starts sleeting when I come across an upscale lodge in McKinley Park. I decide to not go inside, however, because I'm wet, cold, and pretty much all things not upscale. Nevertheless, it's exciting to walk around and warm up a bit, but also because with the higher clouds, this is my first opportunity in a long time for a decent photo. I mean, most of what I've seen of beautiful Alaska has been cloudbanks.

When I get close to Cantwell, the precipitation mercifully stops for good and I actually see the fuzzy outline of the sun and I'm thinking it's the most hospitable thing I've seen in weeks. I still have about eighty miles of the Denali Pass to get through, but it's now in the low 40s (5-6°C) and the road's drying up so it's not bad at all.

Pretty soon, however, the temperature starts dropping again and so do the clouds, so all I see of Denali are more cloudbanks. I don't bother stopping. I keep riding and riding, the clouds keep getting lower and lower, it keeps getting colder and colder (down to the low 20s, -6°C), and I'm in desperate need of a room, but all there is, is fog filled forest that goes on forever.

After a freezing eternity, I turn a corner and, boom, right there, in the middle of the cloud-shrouded forest is a place that's all lit up. Whaddya know! It's the Trapper Creek Trading Post and tonight is Jam Night. Six guitar players (one doubling on harmonica), no bass, no drums, no keyboards, and they're all singing. It's a toe-tapping time and I'm loving it.

For the second time today, I order a chili cheeseburger, no bun, and ask the kid behind the cash register if they have any rooms for rent. He asks Cylla if their cabins can be rented, but she has to check with Jennifer. (A cabin sounds expensive, but I'm cold and tired and don't care what it costs.)

Five minutes later Jennifer comes back, hands me the key to Cabin A and says she already turned on the heater. Excellent! I ask how much it is and even though she manages the place, she doesn't know what to charge because the cabins are brand new and have never been rented before. Neither Cylla nor the cash register kid have any idea so she says, "Would fifty dollars be okay?" Fifty bucks? Are you kidding me? That's the cheapest lodging I've come across since Wyoming!

I unload everything into my warm cabin, go back to the cafe, get into a conversation with some toe-tapping locals, and enjoy my chili cheeseburger along with the music. The most interesting thing about all this is that I never actually check in. In fact, the cash register kid puts the charge for the cabin on the same handwritten bill as my chili cheeseburger. How cool is that?

One more thing. Next time you're in Trapper Creek, take note that Bingo Night has been moved to Fridays at 6 P.M. in the park.

Anchorage is only 120 miles away so with an easy day in front of me, I decide to make a fourteen-mile side trip to Talkeetna, which I've heard is a fabulous place and, sure enough, it's just that. Along with historical landmarks, there are unique eateries, pubs and gift shops all over, and a healthy amount of healthy tourists walking about. There's even a lake outside of town where you can go for rides on what are called pontoon or float planes. And the mayor is a cat named Stubbs.

It's early in the afternoon when, laden with t-shirts and souvenirs, I'm again heading toward Anchorage. It's nice because, unlike yesterday, the weather is lovely (in the 40s and 50s) and with not very far to go, I can lean back and relax. Sure, I run into some traffic in Wasilla, but right after crossing the Mantanuska River, it becomes a relaxing ride again. Until I get close to Anchorage, which is a big city and, well, big city traffic and roads are what they are.

I find a motel, go to dinner, have a decent night's sleep and the following morning get the Beast to the shipping guy on time. Now I get to spend four days and five nights in Anchorage, again with no transportation.

Being on the road is, among many other things, a constant learning experience, and it's right after I come back to my motel that I learn still yet another important lesson about traveling: A cheap motel in a big city is a completely different experience from one in a small town or out in the country.

The cheapest place I could find, and the one I checked into, is called the Arctic Tern Inn. It sounds quaintly Alaska-ish, I guess, but I swear, in my entire life I have never been surrounded by so many people drinking prodigious amounts of cheap alcohol at all hours of day and night, people selling drugs, people taking drugs, hookers offering their services and people buying them, and yes, abusive arguments, fist fights, knife fights and gunshots. How often do I think to myself, "What in tarnation am I doing here?!"

Nevertheless, with some luck and hiding in my room a lot, I manage to get out alive and somewhat mentally intact.

38

A WHOLE LOT OF CUTE

Say what you like,
to get its joy, to breathe its peace, to face its truth,
one must return with a clear conscience.

Joseph Conrad

Take care with the end
as you do with the beginning.

Lao Tzu

After escaping the Arctic Train Wreck, I mean Arctic Tern, I land in Seattle to wait for the Beast and where am I waiting? In a place that is, thankfully, the complete opposite of that motel: Wayne and Frances's house.

What wonderful people! Their hospitality and humor is remarkable—they're bikers originally from Canada so it makes sense—especially considering the fact that we've never actually met in person. Wayne and I have emailed each other a lot, sure, but I'm basically a stranger. Nevertheless, they welcome me into their home and I gotta say that staying here is a complete pleasure.

For instance, Frances, a nurse by heart and profession, is the equivalent of a walking Wikipedia so a conversation with her is like a miniature TedTalk.

Then there's Wayne. Now, it's common knowledge that Canadians like to say "eh" at the end of sentences. It rhymes with "say" so, going along with his roots, Wayne named his Road King The Eh Team. Even his license plate says EH TEAM.

Also, the Canadian sense of humor is similar to the Danish sense of humor—I'm a Dane—so when Wayne says something that on the surface, or logically, isn't funny I still laugh. Like, "Got you some coffee, but you'll have to drink it first." I cannot for the life of me explain why that made me laugh, but it did every time. (He tells me later that what he really said was "... you'll have to heat it first," but I always heard it as I wrote above. Besides, a laugh is a laugh so it doesn't really matter.)

Wayne graciously gives me access to his bike ("Why don't you take it for a ride, eh?"), so one gorgeous day I get onto Highway 410 and ride into Mt. Ranier National Park. Once you get into the mountains, it's a pretty and enjoyable route, though not particularly challenging. Tree-lined, not much traffic, clean and crisp air, and a pretty darn good road surface that follows the White River much of the way.

Once you get into the park itself, you begin to catch glimpses of Mt. Ranier and it's reminiscent of Mt. Shasta in that everything else around it is snow-less, but the famous mountain itself sits right there with a year round overcoat of white.

I get out and about another day courtesy of my writer-friend, Gary. Even though he picks me up in his Hummer, he's an honest-to-goodness long distance biker. He once said something like, "I've ridden in forty-eight states, but some of 'em I've just pounded the shit out of." (Apologies for the misquote, my friend.)

Gary decides to take me to a place called XXX. Sounds a lot like that motel in Anchorage, but what it really is, is one of the better diners in existence anywhere, decorated wall-to-wall and inch-to-inch with 50s memorabilia. Not only that, in the parking lot is Buddy Holly's original tour bus. With a posted notice next to the front door that says, "Warning—nothing that you eat or drink here is good for you," I figure this is my kind of place.

There's another notice that says, "Note: Diet Coke does not stand a chance against our calories, so have a famous root beer!" And that's exactly what I do. Now, I'm particular about my root beer and I gotta say, this homemade version is outstanding, well worth a second and third trip to fill up your cup.

The chili is also homemade so I get my usual chili cheeseburger, no bun. I always get nervous at times like this because I'm almost always disappointed with homemade chili, being that most of the time it's too sweet. I mean, I like my chili with a no nonsense spicy kick and my taste buds tell me that the XXX chili (recipe by the owner, Jose) is legitimately awesome.

The Beast arrives after a three-day delay that'll make it harder to get to the twins' birthday on time. With a tinge of melancholy, I say goodbye to the good Seattle folks and head south to the land of t-shirt weather.

It's when I stop in Tacoma for a late breakfast that I start getting sick. Fever, aching muscles and a puffed up face. Pretty soon, I'm really sick and the puffiness has nearly closed my right eye. In fact, my whole head is so swollen that I can barely get my helmet on and off, and it takes some real effort to make it to Vancouver where I spend the night. (That'd be the Vancouver in Washington, not Canada.)

I get in touch with Brett, another biker-friend and frequent Helluvit rider, tell him where I am and he suggests we meet for breakfast the following morning at a place across the street from my motel. I think that's a fine idea so that's what we do, and dang, he picks up the tab! Now that's a damn good man right there!

I've been taking generous amounts of garlic and oregano water so the swelling has gone down a bunch, but I'm still not feeling a hundred percent. Also, at every stop since Seattle, I would catch a faint, odd smell. Then, at my first stop after breakfast, there's a strong odor that's like an open septic tank for medium-sized wild animals. I pull off the seat to check the battery and, yeah, fluid is leaking out of it, which is probably the reason I was getting sick.

I'm hoping to make it to Medford, the home of the closest Harley dealership in a southerly direction. It's not out of the question. I mean, the bike starts immediately every time and there are no performance problems at all so I should make it, right? I keep riding.

I stop at the Motel 6 in Roseburg (terrific selection of pies at Shari's Restaurant next door), check in, go back out to the bike, and instead of hearing it fire up, I again hear that heart deflating clicketa-clicketa-clicketa.

Man, all I gotta say is that if there was a word that had the all-encompassing impact of Fuck, I'd use it.

The following morning I get it towed a hundred miles to D&S Harley in Medford, but as you might have anticipated, the tow truck is an hour and a half late. (Geez, how hard can it be to get to my twin granddaughters' birthday party?) We get there around noon and I tell Adam, the service manager, it'd be best if I talk with the guy who's going to do the work because I've so many electrical tales to tell that it'd take an hour to write them all down. He thinks it's a good idea, takes me to the back end of the work area and introduces me to EJ.

Now, there's a thing about electrical issues with motorcycles. Cars, too. Mechanics hate them. Really. Tell a mechanic you have an electrical issue and you'll see their eyes glaze over with a brief "aw, shit" look. Makes me feel bad. So bad that I've long since begun my explanations with an apology. "Sorry 'bout this, man, but the bike has some electrical issues." EJ's response? "Great! Electrical is my specialty!" My mouth drops open and I'm looking at him like he just dropped in from fantasyland on another planet.

But he's for real and finds out that my regulator somehow swallowed a load of steroids and was hyper-charging everything on the bike, which, of course, included the one-month-old, perfectly operating battery. Not to worry, though, because D&S has the three parts I need: battery, regulator and master circuit breaker. EJ installs them posthaste and I'm off just as the rain stops. Hallelujah!

Thankfully, all the Beast's electrical issues are finally, finally, *finally* handled for good and I am finally, finally, *finally* on my way to that birthday party. I spend the night in Weed and the following morning, continue getting warmer on Interstate 5 South.

It rains for half the day and the temperature is in the high 50s, but compared to the Alcan, it's like running though the sprinkler on a hot summer's afternoon when I was a kid. I'm making good time and make only one stop longer than twenty minutes and that's to see an old friend in my hometown, Visalia. (Hi Kathryn Ann!)

The ride home from Visalia to Southern California is trouble free. I take the time to reflect on the last seven weeks, all that bad weather, bad traffic, bad roads, mud and other obstacles. It truly is an odd thing that we bikers do, riding through conditions like that. You wonder why. We don't invite them or look for them, surely, but when they are upon us we relish the challenge and silently claim the superiority of adventure over comfort, wilderness over warmth, discovery over certainty.

I do make it to my twin granddaughters' first birthday party on time (a promise kept) and to celebrate the occasion I eat way too many cupcakes. The biggest reward, however, is hanging out with those two little girls. Tell ya what, Ana Lucia and Vienna Lyn are the biggest bundle of cute you'll ever see.

PART V

ANGELS AND GHOSTS

And when he shall die,
Take him and cut him out in little stars,
And he will make the face of heaven so fine
That all the world will be in love with night
And pay no worship to the garish sun.

Shakespeare

39

AN ANGEL GETS A RIDE

I forget things, always have, and my kids know it. My parents knew it, too. I'd take off for baseball practice and my dad would say, "Son, you might want to take your hat, bat and glove with you." Oh right, good idea! When I became a parent, it was my kids saying things like, "Dad, did you remember your wallet?" Oh right, good idea!

I'm wandering around Pennsylvania and just before noon, pull over for gas and a corn dog, check my phone and see that my son had called. He didn't leave a message, but that's the way my kids and I roll. We call, knowing that the other person will call back and then, instead of leaving a one-sided rambling, we have an actual conversation.

A phone conversation with my kids is in two parts. First, they ask if I'm remembering to do all the things a responsible adult should. Like pay my bills and make my mortgage payment (usually I've forgotten), eat healthily, not ride when I'm tired, stuff like that. Then they bring me up to date with all the family, national and international goings-on that a responsible adult should know about.

So I call my son and after all the boring responsibility stuff, he tells me that the 9/11 motorcycle memorial ride in Washington D.C. was not granted a permit by the National Parks Service, which riled up bikers from all over, and they decided to ride to Washington D.C. anyway. After all, they're public roads and anyone can ride on them, right? Then he tells me that they're expecting or hoping for a million bikers to show up. A million? Are you kidding me? That's twice as many as there were in Sturgis the last time I was there!

I look on my phone and check the date. September 10th. I immediately abandon my wandering ways, head toward the nation's capital via Interstates 76, 70 and 270, and get a room in Gaithersburg.

The beginning of the bikers' 9/11 ride is at the Harley dealership in Fort Washington, Maryland and with the directions firmly committed to memory, that's exactly where I'm headed early in the morning. I'm excited and having as much fun as you can have playing tag with the D.C. commuters during my first ride on the famous Beltway.

Along the way, I recite the streets and turns I need to take and, as usually happens, get mixed up. I mean, I remember all the street names, but it's their sequence and the sequence of left and right turns that get muddled up in my far from perfect memory.

Now I'm worried I'll miss the whole thing so I look around for some other bikers to follow. There are several, but I notice that one in particular keeps looking at his gas tank where I'm hoping there's a map or a GPS unit. I follow him onto a turnoff with an unfamiliar name but it's not a concern because the mere possibility of him knowing where to go and how to get there gives me more confidence than the mish-mash of street names and turns in my mind.

I pull up next to him at the stop sign at the end of the ramp, notice he does indeed have a GPS unit, ask if he's going to the 9/11 ride (he is), and if it's okay if I follow him. It's fine with him and we take off on a contorted tour of Washington D.C. neighborhoods courtesy of a GPS unit with a pretzel-like mindset.

My new riding partner is a jolly guy with an easy, hearty laugh and we're having fun. It's the first time either of us has been to our nation's capital and, in a way, it is a sight. We're in the neighborhood parts of D.C. and because we get to stop at every traffic light at least once, we get a thorough look at all the old and dirty brick buildings that mingle with new and dirty metal and glass buildings.

The roads are a potpourri of warped asphalt and chuckholes that are mind blowing, like a modern art masterpiece was laid to rest on the road. After a while, he apologizes for the slow and roundabout tour his GPS unit decided on, and I say it's all right, not to worry, we'll get there. Then he says, "We haven't seen any famous buildings yet, but just think, if we hadn't come this way we would've never seen that guy over there in the blue shirt!"

We finally arrive and there are so many bikers that we have to park next to a Shell gas station a quarter of a mile from the start of the ride. The first thing I do is ask my new friend his name and he says, "Terry from P.A." I like that, how Pennsylvanians commonly refer to their home state as P.A., and it always gives me a smile when they do.

The air is electric. People of all ages and nationalities have come from all over the world on every imaginable combination of two wheels, from huge Goldwing trikes (okay, that's three wheels) to 250cc street bikes to mopeds. Terry and I decide to walk down to the dealership and buy a souvenir or two, maybe a t-shirt, but when we get there, they've pretty much sold out of everything and have closed the cash registers.

It isn't a waste of energy, however, because we meet all sorts of people from all sorts of places, but as it often is with bikers, there's not a stranger in sight. We're like an enormous group of old friends, sharing trail mix and water along with high fives and hugs.

There is, however, one non-biker fellow who's walking around and handing out address labels. We get ours, and mine has on it the name Donald A. Robson. The address label guy tells us that each label has the name of someone who died in the 9/11 attacks and his idea is that all the bikers will put labels on their bikes as a sort of tribute.

Sounds like a good thing to do so I put mine toward the bottom of the Beast's tiny windshield. I figure that after what happened to him, Donald A. Robson might like a ride on a motorcycle. Besides, with my moderate motorcycle handling skills, I can benefit from having an angel nearby.

The ride finally begins, going past us from left to right, and it's as slow as refrigerated honey. And seemingly endless. It's interesting because I'm sure every biker here dislikes being in thick and slow traffic as much as me, but because of the reason we're here, the camaraderie, resolve and joy aren't diminished in the least. After a while, a few bikers stop to let us enter and Terry and I finally join the procession. However, we quickly become separated and I feel a bit of regret that I'll never see him again.

The National Parks Service may not have given us a permit, but the Washington D.C. cops do everything they can to help, so we all get to pass through several red lights and, let's face it, running through red lights with impunity in front of dozens of cops is fun. Soon, I'm amid hundreds of thousands of bikers defiantly riding into our nation's capital and what a glorious sight it is. We're covering two lanes of the freeway and all I can see in front of me and in my rearview mirrors are motorcycles.

As we get close to the capital, however, we have to meld in with the automobile and truck traffic and that's when about 150 of us get disconnected from the rest of the ride. I'm completely lost and I think everyone else is, too, except for this one guy on a dark blue Suzuki Boulevard, who makes his way to the front of the pack like he was born to lead.

We all follow him off the freeway and after not too long he makes a left, a right and another left, then parks on a wide walkway next to a grassy area across from the National Mall. We all do the same and have an impromptu meet-and-greet. Evidently, our leader just wanted to rest in the shade.

Other than riding with countless other bikers in a tribute to those killed on 9/11, I had also wanted to see all the "important" government places, including Capitol Hill and the White House. I don't have a set plan for any visits or tours, but figure I'll just follow the signs (there must be signs) or get a map if I need to. But for now, I'm content to just hang around here for a while, talk with a bunch of other bikers, and watch the traffic on Jefferson Drive.

After an hour or so, I get back on the Beast and start a very slow, very unplanned tour of the nation's capital looking for important buildings and signs pointing the way to them. I don't know which is more oppressive, the heat or the traffic, and within minutes I'm miserable. And going slow. But mostly just sitting, hoping for a breeze. I never do get close to the White

House or Capitol Hill, and after a couple of hours, find myself back where I started.

Hoping the traffic will soon clear out a bit, I get some lunch from a nearby food truck and hang out with a couple of bikers from Alabama. While we're standing in the shade talking about this and that, a TV reporter from Macedonia (yeah, Macedonia) walks up and asks if she can interviews us. We agree, and for the next ten minutes all I can think about is my bright future as a Macedonian TV star.

40

REMEMBER

After lunch I go for a walk because I want to see some monuments and walking appears to be faster than riding in this traffic. The World War II monument is the first I come to and it's impressively grand. With a clear view of the Washington and Lincoln monuments on opposite sides, there are fifty-six columns representing the forty-eight states, six U.S. territories, Washington D.C. and the Philippines. There are also fountains, memorial bricks, and engraved slabs of granite with dedications to all who served in the great battles.

There's a lot of information to take in, all of it interesting, but what connects with me the most is a quote by General Douglas MacArthur.

> *Today the guns are silent. A great tragedy*
> *has ended, a great victory has been won. The skies*
> *no longer rain death—the seas bear only commerce –*
> *men everywhere walk upright in the sunlight.*
> *The entire world is quietly at peace.*

Next, I walk over to the Korean War Memorial and it, too, is impressive but in a different way—here it gets a little personal. Looking at the nineteen stainless steel statues, I appreciate the fact that they're larger than life-sized, a metaphor for the need of soldiers in war to rise above, become bigger than life, so to speak.

Next to the statues is a black granite wall on, or in, which are the images of nurses, mechanics, chaplains, and other military support personnel. When you stand in front of it, your own insubstantial image is among them along with the translucent reflections of the nineteen stainless steel soldiers. It's humbling to see myself in such company.

My next stop is the Vietnam War Memorial, what has become known as simply The Wall.

Much has been made of the dishonesty that led to the Vietnam War and the corruption that continued it, and much should be made of those things, but the narrative is properly balanced with the courage and sacrifices of our soldiers. While the government may have had all the wrong reasons, our soldiers fought and died for all the right ones.

When you first hear or read about the Vietnam War Memorial, it doesn't sound like much. A slightly sunken walkway next to a granite wall with names engraved on it. And when you first see it, it doesn't look like much, either, especially compared to the other grandiose memorials around here. In fact, you almost can't see it from the street and as I stand next to it, I wonder how many of the people in those cars, if any, even know they're driving by a memorial.

I'm on the sidewalk just before the entrance when I see a man approaching from the opposite direction: middle aged, tall and broad shouldered, the sunlight bouncing off the muscles of his tank-top covered torso. He's partly supporting an elderly man, by appearances his father, who is somewhat hunched over but undoubtedly was once as strong and physically impressive as his son.

I pause to let them enter, then watch them go down about fifteen yards and stop and look. After some moments, the father points at a name and begins to cry, the son holding him in both arms. I stand back to allow them their moment of remembering and reflection, and the visitors on the other side of them do the same.

The Wall isn't that big so when I get onto the cement path in front of it, I do more standing than walking. For some minutes I casually look at the nicely trimmed grass on my left and scan the Wall itself, not resting on anything in particular. It's not until I'm close to halfway when I finally read a name. James S Graham. Then another. Emmett E Ballree. Then others. McArthur Coleman and Gerald L Gooden. Bobby Clyde Wood, John M Madden Jr, Dorse Riggs and Stanley R Lewter.

I go on and on like that, just reading names. Soon, what happens to me is what would happen to anyone with a conscience. That two-dimensional wall transforms into the multi-dimensional depth and breadth of human life.

I begin to think of living men and women who accomplished things and wanted to accomplish more. I think of their mothers and fathers who wanted nothing but the best for their children; of their wives and husbands who prayed for futures bright and long. And I think of their children who were proud of their mommies and daddies and waited every day for them to come home.

Last, I think of all the dreams that were cut short, the breathing and laughing and loving men and women who left those dreams behind to do what they felt in their hearts was the right thing to do.

My plan was to make another attempt at visiting the "important" buildings in Washington D.C., but after my visit to the Wall, they have lost their luster and draw. Instead, I sit on a bench in the partial shade for the longest time thinking of dreams forgotten and lives lost. Several passersby stop to ask if I'm okay and I nod once with a half smile. Physically I'm okay, but inside something has changed.

It's late afternoon when I make my way back to the Beast and look at the address label fixed to my windshield. Donald A Robson. I had originally thought to remove it after the ride, but instead, I decide to leave it there so he can ride with me as long as he wants, a riding partner and watchful angel, if you will.

It's a comfortable evening when I land on Interstate 270, the traffic moderate and sensible. A natural time and place to reflect. World War II, the Korean War, the Vietnam War and 9/11. Memorials and events that are now only memories.

But memories change us and whenever we think of them, the changes they made within us are amplified and, in turn, we think differently, act differently, treat others differently, and the relative importances we have assigned to the facets of our lives are forever altered.

I glance at my rearview mirrors. Washington D.C. has disappeared from view and now it, too, is nothing but a memory. I ride through the cool night, still with no regrets about not having seen its "important" buildings.

BLOOD

On the morning after my visit to the Wall, I check out of my motel room as late as possible and slowly eat a full breakfast before heading northwest, a while later crossing over the brown and slow moving Monocacy River on a steel-trellised bridge.

I come to a place called Point of Rocks, dismount, and wend my way down to the shores of the famous Potomac River. There is a tonic to the sound of a river so I sit for a while, listening, and think about its storied history and wonder if it has changed as much since the Revolutionary War as the United States has.

Afterward, I ride around a roundabout and end up on a pretty and well-maintained two-lane road with a fifty mile-per-hour speed limit. There's a broad countryside on my left as I ride past a few rail fences, some small cornfields, thick lawns, a periodic huddling of leaf-laden trees, and wooden one- and two-story houses, some with red brick foundations. I cross Catoctin Creek and later Little Catoctin Creek, which is so little it barely deserves a bridge. It's a tad on the warm side but comfortable enough and the rustic views, though not magnificent, would lend a calm to anyone traveling here.

Somehow, I end up on a road somewhere around Knoxville (the one in Maryland, not Tennessee) that runs alongside some old railroad tracks, on the other side of which is the Potomac River. But instead of taking another look at it, I start working my way north again. I come to a fork in the road, veer left onto Porterstown Road, its single lane intimate with exploding greenery that is as constant as the blue sky.

Highway 34 takes me through the Antietam (an-TEE-tum) Battlefield site, but the gas gauge needle is at the left side of empty, so I continue into Sharpsburg, fill up, and re-enter the site off of Highway 65.

It was just after I reached teenager-hood that I first read about Antietam. At the time, I'd had no concourse with life other than my family, friends, school activities, YMCA Camp, little league baseball, and trying to figure out girls. My only knowledge of war was from stories I'd read and movies I'd seen. In other words, I didn't personally know war, and still don't, but only knew *about* it. Nevertheless, reading about Antietam had a sobering effect. I've often thought to write a full piece about it, and still might, but for now here are a few data.

The Battle of Antietam, known in the South as the Battle of Sharpsburg, was between the Union Army under the command of General McClelland and General Lee's Army of Northern Virginia. The entire battle lasted only one day, September 17, 1862, which was exactly 75 years after the adoption of our Constitution on September 17, 1787. Militarily, the battle was a draw, but because General Lee's army ran out of ammunition and retreated, it was scored as a victory for the Union, albeit a technical one.

There's a good chance, however, that General Lee would have won had his Maryland campaign plans not been discovered by some Union soldiers a week or so prior to the battle. Believe it or not, they were wrapped around some cigars in an envelope that had been left in a campsite. It's incredible how significant events oftentimes pivot on insignificant happenings.

And the Battle of Antietam was a highly significant event not only because it was the first Civil War battle in a northern state, but also because the technical victory of the Union Army directly led to Lincoln feeling confident enough to issue the Emancipation Proclamation five days later.

The other reason it still has a prominent place in history books is that, even after all the wars since, the Battle of Antietam remains as the bloodiest day in the history of the United States.

Fighting began at dawn (around 5:30 A.M.) and by noon, only six and a half hours later, there were 13,000 casualties; by the time the last shot had been fired, the number had risen to almost 23,000. The fighting itself lasted about twelve hours, which means there were over 1,900 casualties an hour. Put another way, that's about one casualty every two seconds. All of that with no automatic firearms, no grenades, no bombs and no air strikes. After all these years, I still cannot comprehend the enormity of hand-to-hand carnage that was compressed into such a short time.

I browse the visitor's center for a bit, get a few pamphlets, then slowly ride around the former battlefield on a narrow road, often dismounting to look at one of the ninety-six monuments, included in which are monuments to each of the ten northern states that lost soldiers at Antietam.

There are also monuments to each of the six generals who died here; in the exact place where each one fell is what is called a mortuary cannon, which is an inverted cannon barrel in a block of stone. To me, the most poignant monument is a wounded lion carved out of a single block of white granite for the 15th Regiment Massachusetts Volunteers.

I continue my slow tour of Antietam, several times stopping to simply look over the grounds. Other visitors amble about. Birds chirp in the distance, others fly as nonchalant as the few clouds rolling by. Grasses flutter in the breeze. Trees sit like sentinels.

I come to the Roulette Farm, a modest wooden structure, which was used as a Union hospital after the battle. The rail fences around it have long since been mended and there is a small field of corn next to it. I wonder how it managed to survive that day in 1862.

Not far from the Roulette Farm is a sunken clay pathway with a small sign next to it that says, "Bloody Lane." The fighting on and near Bloody Lane lasted for four hours, resulting in about 5,000 casualties, with one contemporary account describing it as "a river of red mud."

Immersed in the quiet and peace, I close my eyes and try to imagine what it must have been like, twelve hours of directed violence amid the constant thunder of 5,000 cannons. I cannot.

There is one other monument that I'd like to mention and it's the one for New York's Irish Brigade. The story behind the Irish Brigade is beyond the scope of this book, but it's so damn interesting that I have to write about it.

The soldiers in the Irish Brigade were known equally as ferocious fighters and prodigious whisky drinkers, and their motto was "Never retreat from the clash of spears." (Today they would be bikers.) Despite repeatedly suffering enormous losses, they admirably proved themselves over and over in many battles, including both Antietam and Gettysburg. General Lee, who fought against them several times, once wrote,

> *The gallant stand which this bold brigade made on the heights of Fredericksburg is well known. Never were men so brave. They ennobled their race by their splendid gallantry on that desperate occasion. Their brilliant though hopeless assaults on our lines excited the hearty applause of our officers and soldiers.*

For much of the war, they were led by Brigadier General Thomas Meagher (pronounced "Mar"), an Irish Nationalist who had been born into a wealthy family. He had fought for Ireland's independence from Great Britain in the 1840s and in 1848 was captured by the British, tried for sedition, and sentenced to be "hanged, drawn and quartered." However, clemency prevailed and the sentence was commuted to life imprisonment in Tasmania, Australia.

After three years, he managed to escape to San Francisco and arrived in New York in 1852. At the start of the Civil War, he immediately began calling for the Irish to take up arms for the Union and they did so in big numbers. During the war, he was wounded a number of times, and during the Battle of Antietam fell off his horse and laid on the ground unconscious until his men carried him to safety.

After the war, in 1867, President Johnson appointed Meagher governor of the Montana Territory.

Boy, talk about a man who attacked life with passion. Definitely a biker. But after all that adventure, danger, fighting and intrigue, how does he die? By drowning in the Missouri River after falling off a boat. The cause for the fall has been attributed by various historians to either illness, drunkenness or murder. Who knows, it could have been all three.

42

WE PULL THROUGH

After a restless night in Sharpsburg, I take off on some country roads in the general direction of east and a little south. My emotions are rife with Antietam so I don't really notice much about the countryside or even which roads I'm on. I do, however, notice that I am now much more aware and appreciative of the relative stillness and peace around me.

My destination is Glen Burnie, Maryland and the reason I'm going there has to do with a woman I wrote about in the first Freedom's Rush book. Kathryn Ann is a bona fide angel who once went way out of her way to help me, and I'm now on my way to have lunch with her son, whom I've never met. We have no business to discuss, so I guess we'll just shake paws and be two guys hanging out, eating lunch and talking about whatever.

Jeff is a fine young man and he chooses the perfect place, a sports bar. We have a long conversation mostly about the crazy things we've done, the successes we've enjoyed and the plans we've made. I must say, seeing that chiseled, handsome face full of ambition and listening to that voice full of future triumph is a balm.

I'm deeply moved because, as it has happened many times before, I become cognizant that somehow, by many and varied means, certain and faulty, the citizens of the United States have always pulled forward and always will.

After lunch, I somehow make it through Baltimore and onto Interstate 95 without a hitch. A while later, I nip off the northwestern corner of Delaware, jump on Interstate 295 (going northeast now) then arrive in New Jersey via the wow-inspiring Delaware Memorial Bridge, figuring that the only reason New Jersey isn't part of the name is because Delaware must have paid for the whole thing.

I pull over at a Pilot Travel Center for some gas and a bite to eat, and while I'm sitting on a bench, an elderly gentleman walks over and starts a conversation. Dale is retired bank manager and says that after six months, he finally got the bandages from his eye surgery removed, and the first thing he's doing is driving down to Virginia to see his grandkids. I cannot think of a better way anyone could celebrate newly found eyesight.

The day is hurrying on so I'm in a bit of a hurry to get across New Jersey before the sun sets. Now, I'm not reluctant to ride in the dark (I rather enjoy it, actually), but I want to get to the Atlantic Ocean before nighttime because, being a life-long west-coast guy, I have never seen an ocean sunset without the sun.

Eventually, I get onto Interstate 195, which heads straight east. When the freeway ends, I don't know how far it is to the Atlantic Ocean, but figure if I keep going east, I have to run into it sooner or later, right? (I'm hoping it's sooner because the sun is close to the horizon.) My eastern vector ends at the Belmar Boardwalk, which, in case you're wondering, is a real boardwalk made out of real boards. And yes, I get to see my first ocean sunset without the sun, and yes, it *is* beautiful.

The following day, I head north to see my friends David and Tanya and their kids, who live in a fabulous house in West Orange. David tells me that when they first bought the house, they had one child and very little furniture, and that since then they've been hard at work filling up the place. He's thinking about furniture and furnishings; I'm thinking, "Yeah, you filled it up with three more kids!"

That night, David takes me and the two older kids into New York via the famous Holland Tunnel. It's great to see a place for the first time that you've heard about all your life, isn't it? It's also my first time in the City

234

and when I see the condition of the roads, I feel sorry for the bikers; even more so when I see the traffic.

We've all heard that in New York City, the right of way belongs to whomever gets there first, right? Well, from what I saw, you could be the second, third or fourth to arrive and *still* grab the right of way. Nevertheless, David is unconcerned by any of it and somehow manages to find a free parking space within minutes. I'm impressed.

The reason for our short trip is to see a Broadway musical. Ya know, it's an odd thing about Broadway shows and me. When I listen to *just* the music, I almost never enjoy it and it almost always drives me nuts, but when I see one performed live, I'm *there*, thoroughly enjoying every moment. As David says: it's two hours of marvelous escapism.

Anyway, here we are in New York eager to see a real Broadway musical performed by a real Broadway cast on the real Broadway. We try to get tickets for *Wicked*, but they're sold out, so we go to *Spiderman, Turn off the Dark* instead. With only two exceptions, I'm not at all taken with the music, but I have to say that David is right: the escapism is marvelous.

The next day I go with David and the kids to a block party (how cool!), and the following morning I ride down the eastern side of New Jersey on Highway 9 for a while, then head west and make another enjoyable crossing of the Delaware Memorial Bridge.

On Highways 13 and 113, I ride down the middle of the Delmarva Peninsula, the name of which comes from the three states it comprises: DELaware, MARyland and VirginiA. (If you're a word-nerd-grammar-geek like me, that kind of thing is called a portmanteau.)

It's interesting to ride through this countryside. Cut out of thick forests who knows how many decades or centuries ago, are numerous right angled farmlands worked by hard working folks. It's pleasant, weather-wise, view-wise, and people-wise, and I gladly join the steady, mellow rhythms of the broad and level countryside.

At the end of the Delmarva Peninsula I come to the twenty mile long Chesapeake Bay Bridge-Tunnel.

Wait. A bridge *and* a tunnel? Twenty miles of riding over *and* under water? Really?

The Chesapeake Bay Bridge-Tunnel is officially known as one of the Seven Engineering Marvels of the Modern World and I don't know anyone who wouldn't agree. Twice, the bridge slopes down into one-mile-long tunnels that, yes, go *under* the water and end up landing on man-made islands.

The road is in excellent shape, but I'm a bit worried that the road in those tunnels will be wet and slippery with moss or algae. But they're not. They're nice and dry and the lighting is excellent and, man, is this fun!

I pull over to walk around one of the small, narrow islands. Most of the people here are fishing and from the looks of it, several have gotten pretty lucky. I sit on a low wall at the edge of the ocean and reflect on the past few days.

Fishing, much of the time, is a relaxed sport and relaxed is the current mood, yet fewer than two hours away is the site of the bloodiest day in the history of the United States. I think about that. That maybe scenes of harmony and peace, like people fishing and block parties and filling up homes with kids and furnishings, like grandfathers visiting their grandkids, like young people planning bright futures, is what all those soldiers hoped would be the end result. I like to think so.

43

WHATEVER HAPPENS, HAPPENS

Virginia is in the South and when I cross the border into Chic's Beach, it's immediately noticeable, like a smack of ice-cold sweet tea on a hot summer's afternoon.

There's a steadiness to all the activity down here along with a charming vocabulary. Mom and Dad become Momma and Daddy, kids are Little Ones, strangers are Darlin' or Sweetie, and if you mind your manners, the ladies will call you Hon (pronounced Huhn, short for Honey) with a slight, demure angle of the head. If they're interested, they'll open their eyes a bit, drop their voices to a seductive pitch and slowly call you HUHnee.

Now, I should point out that not everyone here speaks with a Southern accent. Sure, many of the folks out in the countryside do, but as you get around more and more population, you hear it less and less. The reason why, I've read, is the recent migration of citizens from the North.

Moving to the South is understandable. The winters aren't as severe, the roads are in better condition, the folks are hospitable and the cost of living is lower. I and many others, however, hope that the distinctive Southern way of speaking withstands this northern onslaught and forever remains a cultural part of the United States.

I head east on Highway 60 because I want to get a good look at Virginia Beach's actual beach and when I get there, I'm impressed. According to the Guinness Book of Records, it's the longest pleasure beach in the world and I believe it. I mean, it's big. Really big. Where I am, it's about seventy yards wide and when I look left and right, I can't see the end of it either way.

The odd thing is that, despite a postcard-like day with the temperature in the mid-70s, there are no more than a dozen beach-goers, which is a big difference between the east coast and the west coast. On a day like this in Southern California, there'd be tens of thousands of people calling in sick to their employers so they can lie on the sand and for whatever reason try to get that forever desirable tan.

After lunch, I find some smaller roads going northwest to Richmond. Yeah, I'm headed toward a big city, the only reason being that the rock group Chicago is having a concert there tomorrow night and I don't want to miss it. I'd done a bunch of orchestral arrangements for them some years ago, which was one of the most fun gigs ever—great group of guys—and was offered a free ticket and backstage pass. There is, however, another very good reason to go: A backstage pass at a rock concert always means outstanding food.

Speaking of road conditions. (Huh?) Many of the roads in the Virginia countryside look bad, like they're rife with bumps, but they're not. It's a welcoming sensation to ride over a gnarly looking patch expecting to be bounced off your seat, but instead, you keep smoothly going along with your worries left in the lurch, which is a good place to leave them.

So there I am, smoothly riding along on a smooth Virginia road when out of the proverbial blue, I begin wondering if my tires have become too smooth and when that happens, the fun of riding leaks out of my soul just like I'm worried the air will leak out of my tires at any moment. It's time for an oil change and new back brake pads, too, so I decide to go over to Steel Horse Harley the morning after the concert.

Getting back to road conditions, I'd be remiss if I failed to point out that all this talk about excellent roads *does not* apply to the bigger cities. Really. I have come to believe that you can pretty much determine the population of a city by how bad the roads are, and this is true no matter what state you're in. I mean, who in Richmond thought it was a good idea to put manhole covers every forty feet, at every possible lane position, and sink each one *into* the asphalt two to three inches when the speed limit is fifty-five miles-per-hour?

Another thing about Richmond. It seems like every major road has three different names. For instance, Washington Highway is also Highway 1 and also Brook Road. For a direction-challenged guy like me, it makes simple directions complex and complex directions impossible. But then, there *is* an advantage to this, I guess, because if you're riding around in circles like I did for a while, you can easily get the illusion of getting somewhere.

I decide to spend the night at the Motel 8 on Highway 60 in Midlothian. The check-in gal is an elderly lady sitting in a chair fervently reading a book through thick wire-rimmed glasses. I respect readers' rights so don't say anything until she comes to a stopping point and looks up. She smiles, gets up out of her chair and walks to the counter. Typical of life-long readers, she is a combination of interest and angelic playfulness that dances out of sparkly eyes and half-smiles, so I decide to try one of my schticks.

Me: Say, may I get a discount if I have a Triple-A card?

Angelic Elderly Lady: You may! Five percent off, Hon.

Me: Cool! May I get a discount if I have a library card?

Angelic Elderly Lady: *(Looks at me suspiciously)* You have a library card?

Me: I do.

Angelic Elderly Lady: *(Angles her head to the side and squints her eyes)* You fibbin' me?

Me: Nope.

Angelic Elderly Lady: Let me see it.

Me: *(Show her the card and point)* Right there. Brand Library, Glendale, California.

Angelic Elderly Lady: *(Carefully looks it over)* Well, I say that's good for another five percent, Hon!

Despite the fact that it's a Thursday night, there's a raucous party going on four or five rooms away. I don't mind the mixture of noise and music, people having fun is fine by me. Besides, being a lifelong composer and writing a fair amount of music while sitting in front of a TV or in any number of diners, I've become an expert at ignoring audio distractions. Of course, the fact that I'm almost deaf in my left ear makes it easier, but hey, my right ear works just fine.

So there I am, alone in my room, answering some emails, wearing only a t-shirt and underwear, when I hear a knock. I open the door a crack, peak out and see a short and slender young woman dressed in a way that clearly displays her prodigious curves. (Have you ever wondered that the reason guys like curvy roads is that they remind them of curvy women? Me too.) Without looking at me, she pushes the door aside, walks under my arm and stands in the middle of the room slowly checking it out. After a full minute she turns around.

Young Woman With Prodigious Curves: Who are you?

Me: Name's Foster. What's yours?

Young Woman With Prodigious Curves: Tammy. Where's Carla and Cathy?

Me: I don't know.

Young Woman With Prodigious Curves: Oh. *(Continues looking around the room; even checks out the ceiling)*

Me: *(Silently watching her for a minute)* Uh, I'm sure it's none of my business, but uh, why are you here?

Young Woman With Prodigious Curves: There's supposed to be a party.

Me: Ah! I think there's a party down the hall one way or the other.

Young Woman With Prodigious Curves: Oh.

Me: What room were you looking for?

Young Woman With Prodigious Curves: They said 201.

Me: Aha! This is room 210.

Young Woman With Prodigious Curves: Oh.

And she leaves. Not an hour later, I hear another knock and it's the same gal. She walks past me, looks around, says, "Oh, sorry," and leaves. Forty-five minutes later, the exact same thing happens again. Tell ya what, the things that happen on the road are something else.

THE TANGIBLE AND THE TRANSCENDENT

The following night, Friday, I go to the Chicago concert and the place is packed with fans and so much energy that it feels like we're all levitating three hundred feet in the air. The band is amazing. Great musicians, flawless chops, and over the top excitement like it should be, like we all want it to be. And yeah, the food backstage is awesome.

I talk with Bobby Lamm afterward and he says that they do between 100 and 130 concerts a year. What?! That means they've played *Beginnings, 25 or 6 to 4, Saturday in the Park,* and all their other killer tunes thousands of times. And if this night in Richmond is any indication, they still play them with the freshness of a first performance, and with the fervor and mastery like it's the last time they'll ever be on stage. Cannot say enough good things about that band and the guys in it. Hat's off, my friends.

The following morning, Saturday, I head on over to Steel Horse Harley. Only the front tire needs replacing, but they're over-busy and can't fit me in until well into the afternoon. I get the bike around six o'clock, so I decide to spend another night at the Motel 8.

Then, wouldn't you know it, just before I get on the bike, it begins to rain. So here I am with a slick new tire riding ever so slowly over a slick bumpy road riddled with slick manhole covers while several big-city Richmond types speed past, but only after they angrily honk their horns.

As usual, I don't pay them any mind except for the one who cuts in front of me, missing my brand new tire by inches. The more worrisome issue is that there's something unsteady about how the Beast is handling, but I can't quite put my finger on it, finally deciding it's due to the bumpy road.

I'm eager to get going bright and early the next morning when, sigh, the Beast won't start. It's Sunday and Steel Horse is closed so I get the bike towed to Richmond Harley, which is in the northern suburb of Glen Allen. *[It's since moved a little northeast to Ashland.]*

It turns out that the stator needs replacing, but they don't have one in stock and because it's Sunday, I can't get a new one until Monday, which means I have to spend another night or two in Richmond.

Angel, the ultimately capable repair order writer, who actually looks like an angel—I mean, you know, wow—offers to give me a ride down the road to a motel. ("No worries, Hon, I'll take ya there.") The thing is I have to wait several hours until she gets off work.

So I go upstairs, buy a t-shirt, grab some popcorn and a soda and sit in one of the comfy leather chairs. Not a minute later, a gal named Bonnie Blu ("no 'e'") sits down and starts talking excitedly about all the supernatural goings-on in and around Richmond. ("You'd be amazed at what goes on in Richmond at nighttime, Hon.")

Bonnie Blu is familiar with every cemetery in the Richmond area and tells me that the Civil War bodies in all of them are slowly rising to the surface, and that she once saw a skeletal foot sticking out of the ground. (I'm wondering if that is what's really meant with the saying that the South will rise again.)

She also tells me about the Richmond Vampire, the Ghost-Bride at Tuckahoe, and the Civil War soldiers haunting Cold Harbor. But the story that most grabs my attention is one about a little girl and a black dog.

The story, as Bonnie Blu tells it, is that during the Civil War, there was a black, cast-iron dog next to the front door of a general store alongside the James River. A couple of times a week, a local mother and her four year old daughter would go to the store to get food and supplies. The girl would buy some candy with her allowance then, full of imagination and wonder, as little girls so wonderfully are, would go outside and "play" with the black dog while her mother shopped.

After a year or so, the girl dies of scarlet fever. The store owner, not wanting the dog to be melted down for rifle barrels or bullets, gives it to the little girl's family as a gravestone. To this day, the black dog guards the little girl's grave atop Black Dog Hill in Hollywood Cemetery. Visitors leave trinkets, toys, hair ribbons and other little girl things on and around the grave. They also leave coins so the little girl will always have money to buy candy. And then....

At sundown, after everyone has left the cemetery, the little girl and the black dog come alive and run and play together throughout the night.

After Richmond Harley closes for the night, Angel drives me down Highway 1 and I have her drop me off at a Knight's Inn. Knight's Inns are always a gamble. They're among the cheapest motels around, but you never know what you'll end up with. As with many other big chains, including Motel 6 and Super 8, they have two categories of motels: ones they actually own and ones that are owned locally and just have the Knight's Inn sign out front, presumably to get more business.

The ones that are locally owned will sometimes be, well, let me put it this way: You might have clean sheets and be able to take a hot shower. From my experience, Knight's Inn has more of the locally owned places than any other motel chain, but this one, thankfully, is clean and properly managed.

The best thing about the place, however, is that it's right next door to Aunt Sarah's Pancake House. Giant waffles, country fried steak, half-pound burgers, freshly squeezed orange juice, lots of bacon, pot roast to die for, solitary board games to play while you're waiting for your food, and prices so low you think you're making money instead of spending it.

Food-wise, it's definitely my kind of place, but also people-wise because the hostess, Tawana, another angel, calls me Hon and keeps giving me discounts. And free cookies with every meal. Chewy oatmeal cookies. Chewy oatmeal with raisins cookies. They're my favorite. I think I'm falling in love.

After dinner, I think about my conversation with Bonnie Blu, so I take the wooden chair out of my room and place it on the grass lawn in front of the motel. I have no method for calling up ghosts, but figure if I sit here in the gloaming for a while, placidly munching on cookies, and make myself open to the possibility, I just might meet a ghost or two. Maybe have a conversation with a Civil War blacksmith or schoolteacher.

The many healthy trees on the other side of Highway 1 gently sway in the light breezes and the sounds of the traffic fade away. I concentrate on the growing shadows for a while and soon come to the conclusion that there is, indeed, a parallel community here, the citizens of which are mostly friendly and in awe about all the electric lights and metal vehicles zooming past.

Monday comes around, but the stator arrives too late to get it installed, so Angel picks me up Tuesday morning on her way to work. I'm the first customer on the day's schedule and it's not long before the Beast is ready to go. I load up my stuff, say goodbye to the good Richmond Harley folks and ride off. However, as soon as I get out of the parking lot, that odd handling I'd noticed a few days ago becomes prominent. When I get up to around 25 MPH, there's a noticeable shimmy to the handlebars, and the faster I go the worse it gets.

I pull to the side of the road and check the bolts holding the front tire and they're all secure. I'm thinking maybe the weights balancing the tire were put in the wrong places, but I've no way to check that, so I turn around and head back to Richmond Harley.

On the way, I begin to wonder if this is happening because I made some ghost-friends and they want me to stick around for a while. Or maybe they just like bikers from Southern California. Then I wonder if I'll ever get to leave. But if I never do get to leave, it wouldn't be all bad because, hey, think of all those cookies I'd get from Tawana.

Angel introduces me to the mechanic, Mitch. I tell him about the shimmying and suggest he take the Beast for a ride. When he comes back he doesn't say a word, doesn't even look at me, and rides straight into the service bay with a hard and determined look on his face. I gotta say, it gives me confidence when a mechanic has that look.

Not ten minutes later, he invites me into his bay, which also gives me confidence because I always figured that if a mechanic knows his stuff, he doesn't mind you being there.

Mitch has put the front rim in a metal contraption and slowly rotates it against a small wheel that's connected to a dial, which shows that there are four places where it's off perpendicular. He pulls out a manufacturer's service manual and shows me where it says that you should never ride on a wheel that's more than .31 inches off. Two of mine are about a half-inch off and one is a whopping .89 inches off.

I guess all those tens of thousands of bumps and chuckholes finally took a toll. And the old tire wore out in conjunction with all those off-perpendicular places and that's why the ride had remained smooth—it's amazing all the things the Beast does to make my ride comfortable—and that explains why there was never a handlebar shimmy until the new tire was put on.

A new rim is pricey so I ask Mitch if he thinks I can make it back home to Southern California with a wheel this bent. He thinks a few moments and warily says, "You might make it." Well, it's the "might" part of the answer that makes me nervous so I tell Angel to go ahead and order a new one. The closest new rim is in Milwaukee and FedEx can't deliver it until after 3 P.M. the next day, Wednesday, so I'm to spend still yet another two days in the city of ghosts, angels and cookies.

Mitch puts the crooked tire back on so I can at least ride back to the Knight's Inn and ride around Richmond a little, which is what I do. I look at a map, take some tree-lined, manhole covered roads, get lost a few times, and finally, in the waning sunlight, find the entrance to the Hollywood Cemetery. It's closing time and the gate is locked, so I park in front of it, walk in through a sidewalk gate in front of a house and over to a groundskeeper sitting in a Jeep.

I introduce myself to John and tell him I heard an odd story and came to find out if it's true. Before I can tell him what it is, he says, "Black Dog Hill, right?" (I guess a lot of people come here to find out the truth of the story.) John tells me I'll have to walk there and that it takes ten minutes each way and gives me directions. He says he has about a half hour of driving around to make sure there's no one left in the cemetery (no one currently alive, that is) and he'll meet me at the front gate when he's done.

245

So I walk on up the road, go right then left, and there I am, standing atop Black Dog Hill. It looks just like Bonnie Blu described it, sprinkled with coins (I added some) and toys and little girl baubles. Alongside the grave is the black, cast iron dog looking attentively into the distance, and somewhere around, you just know it, a little girl is waiting for the sun to set.

On Thursday, my eighth day in Richmond, I shimmy on over to the dealership and Mitch puts on the perfectly perpendicular new wheel in no time at all. I thank him for his expertise, thank Angel for her hospitality ("Be safe, Hon") and make sure to tip them both. My next stop is Aunt Sarah's to say goodbye to Tawana ("You take care of yourself, Hon, and come back real soon!") and get a last batch of cookies. Finally, I'm taking a smooth westerly ride with the Beast hugging the road as is his wont.

45

A CIVILIZED PEACE

Freewheeling it out of Richmond is bliss. I met some wonderful people, both currently alive and not, and loved being there for eight days, but living on the road is the way I prefer to roll, and staying in one place for more than one night is contrary to that. I don't know the exact route I'm taking, but I do know I'm heading west. I pull over only once to take some photos and, by pure happenstance, happen upon the site of General Robert E. Lee's last encampment before arriving at Appomattox.

The Appomattox Court House is where General Lee surrendered the Northern Virginia Army to General Grant on April 9, 1865. I arrive mid-morning, the same time as a biker couple from New Jersey, and after a short and friendly chat, head into the site.

It is fitting that the whole area is peaceful and quiet because this is where the beginning of the end of the bloodiest war in U.S. history began to take place. To wit, in the four years of the Civil War, there were an average of over 400 casualties per day. Yes, *per day.*

While walking around the grounds, looking at the actual rooms and furnishings, reading the information plaques and watching the short documentary films, the thing that affects me the most is how civilized the whole affair was. Truly a surrender of honor and respect.

For one thing, when Lee, in his dress-up uniform, informed Grant, in his dirtied riding gear, that his soldiers hadn't eaten for days, Grant asked how many men he had. When Lee said 20,000, Grant replied, "Well then, you'd better order 30,000 dinners." And this was done *before* any truce was signed.

Because the North never acknowledged the South as a sovereign nation, there could be no formal treaty. Instead, Grant and Lee each signed a sort of letter, the generous terms of which were formulated by Grant himself according to the wishes of President Lincoln.

All Confederate soldiers were paroled and allowed to return home and none would be prosecuted, imprisoned or hung for treason as long as they abided by the conditions of their parole. Rifles and artillery had to be turned over, but the officers were allowed to keep their sidearms, and all Confederate soldiers were allowed to keep their horses and mules.

In doing all this, Grant had legally exceeded his authority—the letter should have come straight from the White House—and the generous terms angered some powerful political foes. For instance, Lincoln was assassinated only six days later and the new president and commander-in-chief, Andrew Johnson, with retribution on his mind, was quoted as saying "Let the hanging begin." Nevertheless, despite the political and career risks, Grant, along with help from many others, persevered and the Union followed through with its side of the agreement.

Two poignant anecdotes in particular demonstrate the civility of the truce. Grant suppressed any celebration on the part of the Union soldiers, later explaining, "The Confederates were now our countrymen, and we did not want to exult over their downfall."

The other involves Ely Parker, Grant's adjutant, the one who actually penned the letter of surrender. Parker was a member of the Seneca tribe of Native Americans and when Lee found out about this said to him, "It's good to have at least one real American here." Parker replied, "Sir, we are all Americans."

Walking back to the parking lot, I realize that in twelve days I'd visited five different war memorials and spent eight of those days in a city populated with Civil War ghosts and a good, hard ride seems to be the only way to untangle the labyrinth of thoughts and heavy emotions I'm carrying.

Besides, in those twelve days I'd done very little *real* riding and am in desperate need of something challenging other than compressed traffic on bad roads. Eager for some long hours of sitting in the saddle concerned with nothing but throttle and clutch, I take a quick look at a map and decide to head toward West Virginia.

Riding a motorcycle always carries with it the danger of death and it's that very fact that either spawns the freedom of riding or expands it. Or both. And that rush of freedom expands even more when we adopt a daring attitude, some would say foolhardy, and do things not within the margin of acceptable safety.

Like take to task curves we've never seen before even when we can't see the other side of a copse of trees or an outcropping of rock. What's there? A tightening radius? A stalled car? A patch of sand? Some plodding wildlife that's bigger than a motorcycle? Well, when you're in a daring mood you want to find out as soon as possible, concerns for safety only lightly considered.

Despite the recklessness, we all do it now and again because it's like a spark plug that ignites who you are. Your eyes water a little, the wind slaps your face and there's a tingle in your palms. You become hypersensitive to the changing smells, the small bumps and dips in the road, the subtle nuances of the engine's rumble, and that momentary slip of your back tire and the instant it catches hold. It's a real life blend of danger and freedom, and at the end of such a ride you are nothing more or less than yourself.

I take Highway 460 to Daleville then Highway 220 into the George Washington and Jefferson National Forest. There are a few white clouds, the temperature is slightly on the warm side, and the road is in very good to excellent condition.

Typical of the South, there's a rich kaleidoscope of greenery everywhere, including the loping hills left and right. It's content and quiet all around except for the Beast's rumble, which is especially thunderous when I roll on the throttle and cross the double yellow line to pass cars and trucks. In contrast to the calm surroundings, my heart is frenetically pumping adrenalin through my veins like Valentino Rossi heading toward the finish line.

Not long after crossing over the tree-crowded James River, I follow Interstate 64/Highway 60 west and it's here that the Beast cranks the speedometer needle over a hundred. When the two thoroughfares separate, I stay on Highway 60 and despite the colorful views, a multitude of trails and scenic lookouts, my entire attention is solely on the ride and I barely notice the landscape as it rushes past.

I manage to sidestep Charleston via state highways, roads that are a reflection of the anything-but-straight border of much of West Virginia. I whip by brick and mortar churches, mobile homes and wooden houses, some abandoned and some occupied, one-pump gas stations, neighborhood grocery stores, and a community named Foster.

I don't know if I'm hungry or thirsty and I'm not paying attention to the time of day or my rapidly changing locations, other than being pretty sure I'm headed north. When my jagged route takes me on a road too narrow for a middle line, I ride helmet-less and continue pumping the throttle like I'm drunk on speed, wind and engine rumble.

After a stretch of time that could have been moments or decades, I come to Interstate 64 again. When I get north of it, the late afternoon shadows of the Appalachian hardwood forest are covering most of the road and soon any vestige of sunlight will be gone. I settle down, look for a room, and come to rest in Point Pleasant well after sunset.

It's a special kind of relaxation you have after a day of hard riding and one I'm definitely feeling now. However, there is something different. I experienced the true freedoms of riding today, but despite the biker truism that a good, long ride will clear out your mind, as I sit at a small table in my small motel room writing this, I realize that that's not what happened.

Instead there is a combining of all the fine things I experienced with the heavy emotions from the five war memorials I visited, an entwining of the positive and the negative, the light and the dark. Still, there's something else, a mystery, something I'm missing and have missed on many occasions, and it has to do with soldiers and veterans.

As most of us do, as all of us should, I have a deep respect and gratitude for soldiers and veterans and feel special when I meet and talk with one. And that's when that "something missing" always pops into my head. I could never determine exactly what it was, but it seemed to be something personal, of the heart. Perhaps spiritual. And this feeling was especially strong when I visited the Vietnam War Memorial, the Wall.

I begin to think that maybe the reason for this "something missing" is because I was never a soldier. I've never pretended to be one nor have I ever claimed to know what it's like to fight in a war. During the Vietnam War years, I never once protested the war nor have I ever maligned the soldiers who fought it. I went to college for a few years but not to avoid the draft. No, I went to college to learn about music and how to compose it. That's all. Thinking about all this, I remember a book that had a huge effect on me.

I first read Stephen Crane's *The Red Badge of Courage* while in high school and again about twenty years ago. Published in 1895, it is unquestionably one of the best war novels ever written. I'm thinking that because, like me, Crane was only a writer and not a soldier, he might have some insight I can relate to, so I download his book onto my Kindle and begin reading random passages here and there.

It's surprising how much of it I remember, how much seems familiar, like I just finished reading it last week. After an hour or so, I finally find what I'm looking for, the thing I've been missing out on all these years.

> *There was a consciousness always of the presence of his comrades about him. He felt the subtle battle brotherhood more potent even than the cause for which they were fighting. It was a mysterious fraternity born of the smoke and danger of death.*

So that's it, that's what I've been missing out on. Brotherhood. I don't regret not having fought in a war, but I do regret that I will never be a member of that "Battle Brotherhood." I'm forever an outsider to something sacred.

While going to sleep, my thoughts go back to the Vietnam War Memorial, the Wall, to the 58,286 lives lost and to the hundreds of thousands of other veterans still alive, the Brotherhood, the only ones who truly know the story.

PART VI

A BACKWARD GLANCE OVER TRAVELED ROADS

As idly drifting down the ebb,
Such ripples, half-caught voices, echo from the shore.

The strongest and sweetest songs
Yet remain to be sung.

Walt Whitman

PART VI

A BACKWARD GLANCE OVER TRAVELED ROADS

46

INSIGHT

The Sturgis Motorcycle Rally is a blast. This is only the second time I've been here, but I am convinced that it is easily one of the most enjoyable events of any kind anywhere.

I've often said that everyone should attend the Sturgis Rally at least once if only to know how much fun bikers can be. And it doesn't matter who you are because there's something for everyone. For instance, say you have a studious, geeky, non-biker friend who likes to learn all about the intricate, inner workings of things. Well, just tell him this: The Jaegermeister Girls would make for an excellent study in anatomy.

True, if you do an internet search for Sturgis you'll see all sorts of photos of wild times. Even some violence, though it's safer than 85-90% of the rest of the country. No doubt those things occur, but overall, I find it to be a rather welcoming place pervaded by neighborly Midwestern hospitality. And let's face it, walking on a downtown sidewalk and seeing thousands of motorcycles and no cars at all is downright heartwarming.

I arrive on a Monday afternoon after an uneventful 1400 miles. Uneventful except for that stretch in the Mojave Desert after North Las Vegas where the heat got to me. All I can say is thank goodness the McDonald's in Mesquite (Eastern Nevada) has great air conditioning.

After checking in at the Buffalo Chip Campground, I find a spot and pitch my tent among families from five different states somewhere toward the middle of the northwestern quadrant. (The Buffalo Chip is so big you can legitimately use words like quadrant.) My neighbors are all good folks. In fact, right after I'm settled in, I'm invited to have a roast beef dinner with a big family from Montana.

Immediately, we're a week-long, get-along family except for the young couple from Orange County, California, who say they're going to leave the next day because there's "too much dirt." This gets me thinking, "Well gosh, it *is* called a campground, right?" But then, who knows, maybe campgrounds in Orange County, California are dirt-less.

While wandering around Sturgis, which is a mind-blowing thing to do, it's logical to conclude that the second most common item is food, the first being, of course, beer. As I look at all the menus, I come to admire the vast open-mindedness that bikers have for different kinds of food. Talk about a tolerant bunch. I mean, bikers are willing to accept any and all kinds of food dishes providing they're all derived from meat. To put it another way, you could accurately describe Sturgis, or any bike rally, as Vegan Hell.

However, there's one place in Sturgis that might be the exception to the rule. It's on one side of the concert area directly across from the stage and its entire menu is printed on twenty big plastic banners that are arrayed above the walk-up counter. It takes a while, but I read all of them and, to my amazement, you can get five different kinds of vegetables: French fries, sweet potato fries, deep-fried dill pickles, deep-fried onions and deep-fried green beans. Yeah, Vegan Hell. Gotta love it.

I'd say the third item on the list of common things is live music. Everywhere you go, there is live music and overall, the bands are damn good. The headlining acts are damn good, too. The Doobie Brothers may have aged a lot, but those guys still do it the way it's supposed to be done; vocals, solos, everything. Lynyrd Skynyrd, I've come to believe, cannot do anything wrong. (Batman and Elvis were at that concert on their Harleys.)

Kid Rock's show was rocking hard and pretty near flawless, as were the ones by Brantley Gilbert, Sublime, Alien Ant Farm and Fuel. Yin and Yang were at the Full Throttle Saloon again this year and those guys are pure energy. What a hoot it is to see all those overweight Midwestern bikers dancing their butts off to Hip-Hop.

Something interesting happens during Rob Zombie's concert. They're up there blowing everyone away with their chops, especially his lead guitarist John Hand. (Dang, that guy's amazing!) Well into the set, RZ says they're going to do a cover of *We're an American Band*. Sounds like a good idea.

So they're playing it and the place is seriously rockin'. Well, the second chorus is a double chorus, but a few of them go to the solo section after only half of it. But like the pros they are, the song gets righted in seconds and they all get this "aw, shit" grin on their faces. Afterward, RZ's laughing and says, "Yeah, I guess we should have practiced that."

My days are activity-filled. I watch an outdoor women's Roller Derby match, amateur and semi-pro MMA fights and a few bike pulls, which is two guys playing tug o' war with their bikes. I also take a test ride on a brand new Indian Chieftain. I overhear a couple of guys talking about the amazing torque of these bikes so when we're out, I get it into sixth gear, slow down to forty, roll on the throttle and it speeds right up without a protest. Love that.

Another event I witness is a guy trying to break a world record by riding through a 361 foot cardboard and chicken wire tunnel that was drenched with some sort of combustible liquid and set on fire. The rest of us are thinking the only good thing about this is having an ambulance and a fire truck waiting. Unfortunately, he doesn't make it. He blasts through the cardboard wall about two-thirds of the way and the firemen douse him with fire retardant.

One day I ride over to the shooting range east of the Buffalo Chip. If you ever go there, the first thing to do is get a set of earplugs because even with them snuggly lodged in place, it's explosively loud. I have a definite interest in the army-issued sniper rifles, which have a louder smack than any other gun I've ever heard, but I'm mostly drawn to the fifty-caliber machine gun so I go ahead and buy eight rounds.

Feeling the power come out of that thing is like nothing else. Right after the eighth round buries into the mountainside with a puff of dirt, the guy who oversees the shooting leans over and says, "Bet that was the fastest eighty bucks you ever spent!" He's right.

However, the most impressive thing I do is watch Patch McGillicuttey ride the Wall of Death.

The Wall of Death is a vertical structure that looks like a miniature grain silo made out of wood (some call them silodromes) maybe thirty to thirty-five feet in diameter and about thirty feet high. At the top is a flat, six-foot wide circular area where you can stand shoulder-to-shoulder with everyone else and watch Patch do his thing.

As an introduction, Patch tells us that he's 38 years old and has broken 36 bones and been on the verge of death in intensive care six times. (I feel like a lightweight; if you count my nose, I've broken only twelve bones.) Then he gets on a bike and rides around the wall until he's parallel with the ground. Yes, parallel with the ground! As in he's riding sideways! Then he does it again without holding onto the handlebars, then again while standing up, then again while leaning back with his feet up on the bars, like he's lying on a lawn chair sipping a brew.

I'd seen videos of this before, but in person it's impressively scary. I mean, he's going forty to fifty miles-per-hour and sometimes zooms about a foot under our chins. (Why isn't he getting dizzy?) By the bye, Patch holds the Wall of Death world speed record at over ninety miles-per-hour.

For the grand finale everyone holds out a one, five, ten or twenty dollar bill and Patch, still not holding onto the handlebars, rides by and grabs them one by one. But he doesn't just throw them to the ground, no sirree. Instead, he's a gentleman and zooms down to the bottom, and without slowing down, hands them to his wife so she doesn't have to pick them up off the floor.

I'm hoping good ol' Patch has a good ol' payday because he deserves it. I decide that if I ever start imagining myself as some sort of a badass on a bike, all I need to do is think of Patch and I'll be put back in my proper place.

Vest patches and tattoos are the Cliff Notes of philosophies of life and anyone going to a biker rally could easily come up with the conclusion that they're a requirement for attendance. This year I decide to pay more attention to them so I can, you know, learn more about life.

Most of the patches are the ones you often see: Live to Ride, Ride to Live; Loud Pipes Save Lives; If I Have to Explain, You Wouldn't Understand; The Voices May be Imaginary, but They Have Some Good Ideas; and so on. But I do see a few that reveal deep thought.

WHAT IF THERE WERE NO SUCH THING
AS A HYPOTHETICAL SITUATION?

MY WIFE COMPLAINS
THAT I NEVER LISTEN TO HER.
OR SOMETHING LIKE THAT.

MOTORCYCLES:
HELPING UGLY PEOPLE
HAVE SEX SINCE 1903.

Then there are the tattoos. Now, we've all seen tattoos where the art-work is so amazing you do a double take and that's certainly the case in Sturgis. But the best one I come across is simple and on the right arm of a guy from Alabama.

I love my ex-wives.
1. Cheryl
2. Katie
3. Sharon
4. Brenda
5. _____

Speaking of tattoos, there must be fifty places to get them (if that's an exaggeration, it's a small one), but from talking with Pierce, a righteous bartender at the Knuckle Saloon, I find out that the one place that's open in Sturgis year round is the Tattoo Cellar. Pierce just got one on his hand that looks great, so after eating lunch, I walk on over there to get mine. I call it the Freedom Firebird. It's on my right shoulder and I'm damn proud of it.

In the first *Freedom's Rush* book, I wrote about the fortune of meeting the superior mechanic and supreme raconteur, Vinni, whose shop is in

Douglas, Wyoming. ("Everyone knows where Vinni's is.") Well, Vinni, along with his lovely wife, Lindy, and their friend, Tanya, are staying over at the Bear Butte Creek Campground so on the fourth afternoon I ride on over for a visit.

Man, do these people know how to travel. I mean, they have everything, even a little trailer with a nice bed, food and cooking and eating utensils. Not only that, they had the good sense to choose a campground that has trees, which means shade, which means it's cooler than the Buffalo Chip, which means I'm a little envious.

Vinni shows off the paint job he did on his 1994 Fat Boy and I don't blame him. The work is so good you can drag your finger over where it goes from black to white and not feel a smidgen of a border, not the slightest bump whatsoever. And despite the fact that he rode it all the way from Douglas, it looks like it's just been detailed.

In the evening, Vinni takes me over to meet his friends from the Bear's Den, a great group of guys and gals from Wyoming. One of them brought along a bottle of bubblegum schnapps that he developed and brewed himself.

It actually does smell and taste like bubblegum and how that high of a liquor content can be so smooth and tasty is something I can't fathom. One sip gives me a serious buzz and while I'm sitting there trying to focus on the tip of my nose, I'm taken back to when I was a kid and collecting those baseball cards that came with a square slab of gum and get the money-making idea that if, instead of baseball cards, he hid famous biker cards inside the labels, he could sell a million bottles and start a whole new collectibles movement.

∞

As I said above, both times I've been to Sturgis have been enjoyable, violence free and friendly. But then, odd things do happen. Inexplicable things that have to do with golf carts.

I stay late at the Wolfman Jack concert area one night and get lost while walking back to my tent. And the more I walk, the more I'm lost. I'm seeing nothing that looks familiar but come across things, like a dirt race track, that I didn't even know were there. Finally, I see a golf cart with a guy in the driver's seat, and a girl and another guy sitting on the far back seat facing backwards.

I tell them I'm lost, describe where my tent is and ask if they know how to get there. They do know, but instead of giving me directions, they say they'll take me there, which is a real neighborly offer. I sit next to the driver and he gives me a roundabout tour of an area of the Chip that feels like it's from another world.

We finally get to my tent and I graciously thank the driver, but when I go to thank the other two, the guy is standing up facing forward and the girl is sitting in a very welcoming position still facing backward. Yep, during my long tour of the Chip, they were back there perfecting their skills for making babies. I thank them anyway, shake their hands and wish them a fulfilling night.

Then there's the time I'm walking home after the Kid Rock concert. Two very pretty twenty-something girls riding in a golf cart through the mud come up behind me. Well, two very pretty twenty-something girls riding in a golf cart through the mud is always a delightful sight, so I smile and nod.

They stop right next to me and the driver asks something I can honestly say I've never been asked before. And probably never will again. With big and round eyes, she leans over and in a hopeful, quivering voice asks, "Are you Lionel Ritchie?" I don't want to shatter her hopes so I say, "Uh, ya know, I don't think so, but hey!, you never know!"

Then, right after that, two other very pretty twenty-something girls riding in another golf cart through the mud pull up alongside of me. They're each wearing those X-ray glasses that have eyeballs connected to springs and it reminds me of the time I was a kid and had a pair. The passenger stands up, carefully looks me over with those X-ray eyeballs bouncing up and down and says, "I can see your penis." (I'm not cleaning up any vulgarity here, she actually uses the word penis.)

My first thought is that because I've had a few beers I maybe forgot to do something important after I went to the bathroom. So I take a look, but I'm packaged up all nice and proper. Evidently, the X-ray glasses they make these days work a heck of a lot better than the ones I had when I was a kid.

LEARNING STUFF

The main reason I ride is what many who ride will tell you, even if it's for only a mile or two: Riding a motorcycle is a freedom-thrill. But there are many other reasons, too, like visiting different states, going to places you've never been to before, even to places you've never heard of.

Sure, all of the states have terrific roads, jaw-dropping views, friendly people, oh you could go on and on. But you could spend your whole life in just one or two states and experience all those things. So why venture far away from home? There are many valid answers to that question including the one I like best: Why not?

So yes, there are many reasons for riding, too many to count probably, and it's during my rides through Ohio, Kentucky and Indiana that one of them comes to the fore: learning stuff.

Basically, there are three different ways to learn. You can read stuff, people can tell you stuff, and you can figure out stuff on your own. Many of the things I've learned on my own are things most any biker will tell you. Like the best time to pass a truck is when you're going uphill, duct tape and zip ties are a must, park so you don't have to back up while going uphill, and *do not ever* breathe within forty yards of roadkill.

Of the three ways to learn, learning stuff on my own is my favorite because it's efficient and I don't have to worry about anyone else pointing out the flaws in my conclusions.

As it turns out, my three-state ride of Ohio, Kentucky and Indiana is highly educational, being mostly a learn-by-figuring-out trip. For instance, while in Ohio, the first of those three states, I realize that some of its roads were designed by roller coaster engineers on pogo sticks. (Betcha didn't know that, didja?) Up and down, up and down. I mean, whew, this is fun! So here I am, pogo-sticking along, and where am I headed? Where else? The Serpent Mound State Memorial, which is about ten miles north of Peebles.

The Serpent Mound in Ohio is, as the brochure says, "The largest surviving example of an ancient animal effigy mound." In all the reading I've done, I cannot recall ever reading the term "ancient animal effigy mound," but it must be a big deal because, hey, it's in a brochure.

The item of interest is 1348 feet long, which is equivalent to four and a half football fields, which is over a quarter of a mile; and, as you probably guessed, it's a mound (three feet high) in the shape of a serpent fully equipped with a head and a tail.

The fascinating thing is that the bends in the serpent's body correspond to all sorts of celestial stuff, like the positions of the sun at the summer and winter equinoxes, and the northern- and southern-most wanderings of the moon. There are also a bunch of yet-to-be-explored caves underneath it, but the serpent mound experts have somehow determined that it's not an ancient burial ground.

From carbon dating done in 1996, we know it was built over 3000 years ago. Imagine! Over 3000 years ago, people right here in North America knew about serpents, equinoxes and wanderings of the moon. (There is, however, some evidence it's only a thousand years old, but still....)

The whole thing is built on the lip of a crater made by a meteorite 300 million years ago and there are magnetic anomalies all over, which means there are places where your compass will go haywire. Even migrating birds get lost in the area and will end up flying in circles for days and weeks. Also, if you project the outline of the serpent into the night sky, it aligns with the constellation Draconis as it was 5000 years ago, which is also true of the great pyramids.

The big riddle, however, is *who* built it and *why*? Because of the unusually high iridium content (whatever the heck iridium is), really smart astro-archeologists and astronaut theorists, along with really smart Native American Shawnee, have come up with some theories involving alien visitors. Theories abound in the mainstream scientific community as well and every now and again someone comes up with a new one.

Well, it may be a mystery to all those university-educated, super-smart effigy mound experts, but heck, I figured it out right away. Undoubtedly, it was built by a bunch of guys who had a lot of time on their hands and thought serpents were cool. This proves once again that if you want to find the real truth of something, all you need to do is ride a motorcycle for a while.

After all that learning, I get to do a little more Ohio road pogo-sticking (really, this is so much fun) and it makes sense that I end up in a town called Hillsboro enjoying a dinner at Frisch's Big Boy Restaurant. (No doubt how Hillsboro got its name.)

I hadn't planned to visit Kentucky, but the state has been calling me for a while. "Dude, c'mon, I'm right here, fewer than a hundred miles away!" So I backtrack a bit and ride on over there as a sort of reward for solving the Serpent Mound riddle.

I cross over the Ohio River on the Simon Kenton Memorial Bridge and ride into Maysville, home of Heather Renee French Henry, the 2000 Miss America Pageant winner. (Learned that from the city limit sign.) I take some photos then go southwest and pass through a place called Oddville, the name of which was chosen because someone said, "Oh, what the heck, why not?"

The countryside around here is rolling, lovely and untroubled. A few of the leaves have begun turning, but most are still a deep green, marking time on their growth as they watch bundles of autumn mist gather in the distance.

I pass by two Amish families in immaculate black carriages, each briskly pulled by two horses; the adults nod and smile, the children watch with innocent curiosity. For some moments, it's as if I have entered a land of timeless make-believe.

I continue south and spend the night in Paris. The following morning, I'm riding along with the morning commuters and the ambience is completely different from the countryside, which puts me back into the mood to learn by figuring out stuff and as I ride by some sprawling and upscale ranches, I figure out an amazing fact.

In Kentucky, there's a state constitutional amendment (there has to be) that gives horses preferred, upper class status. I'm not joking. Have you ever seen where those four-legged guys live? They're beautiful! And big! Trust me on this, if you ever have to live a lifetime as an animal and you get to choose which kind, choose to be a horse in Kentucky.

Two days later, I'm in Indiana close to the community of Cloverdale when I see a sign for the Cataract Falls. Waterfalls are cool so I get a room, unload, then head on over, arriving not long before sunset. The falls aren't that big, but they're situated such that you can climb over a fence with a sign on it that says, "Do Not Climb on Fence," walk down an embankment, across some rocks, and get within several feet of them.

There's a swatch of pale pink in the sky above a marvelous fog that serpentines its way through the trees while the puddles in the rocks are splashes of quivering silver. There's no one else around and as the sun sets, I feel like I'm isolated in a nearly colorless photograph.

I hang around for a while, taking photos and when there's only a trace of sunlight left, I head back to the Beast and fire him up. Getting out of the small park takes longer than I'd expected because I have to ride up this steep embankment that's as long as that serpent effigy mound. Going up a quarter mile long hill on a motorcycle is easy-peasy, right? Unless it's covered with leaves. Wet leaves. Wet, slippery leaves. Wet, slippery leaves in the dark with no one else around, like this one is.

It's taking forever. I mean, I try different speeds, even try duck-walking, but no matter what I do the tires keep slipping here and there. Even when I stop, the Beast is slipping backwards. I finally pull onto the dirt shoulder, park the bike, get off, and with my boots, scoot the leaves left and right making a safe, albeit wet, path.

The following morning, I jump on Interstate 70 and head home. Riding-wise, Ohio, Kentucky and Indiana have been trouble-free (except for those slippery leaves) and I get into a sort of silly frame of mind. Again. I've been on a roll for a while now, getting smarter by figuring out stuff, so I decide that this is the perfect time to ponder the imponderable, challenge the unchallengeable, search for the unsearchable. You know, stuff like that.

I end up tackling one of the more long-standing conundrums of life, the answer to which we've all yearned for as much as King Richard III yearned for a horse. This is it: How did it come to be that the number 7 is the only single digit number with two syllables?

Think about it. All single digit numbers have only one syllable, which makes sense, *except for the number 7!* Why, oh why? I mean, who does this number 7 guy think he is? Sitting there like he's all special, saying to all the other single-digit numbers, "I have two syllables so there, nanner-nanner."

I suspect sinister goings-on, think about it a while and, sure enough, the number 7 has been far from innocent for centuries. So much so that, dare I say it?, he has sold his soul for a syllable. Don't believe me? Consider these facts.

It starts with the letter 'S', which looks like a devil serpent. S is also the first letter of the word sinister. And Satan. (Coincidence? Hardly.) And that S is followed by e-v-e-n. But 7 is an *odd number!* By all logic his name should be the one syllable Sodd (S-odd), but instead, he's S-even. And when did this happen? The exact moment number 7 changed from being the bad guy (the 7 deadly sins) to being the "Lucky Number 7" good guy.

Convinced? Thought so.

48

A GOOD MAN

The purpose of life ...
is to be useful, to be honorable, to be compassionate,
to have it make some difference that you have lived and lived well.

Emerson

I met him during one of those long rides back home.

I take off from my motel in Tucumcari, New Mexico and immediately get onto Interstate 40 West. Along with a strong wind there's an off-an-on light rain so the road never gets dry. The car drivers, however, ignore the wetness and speed along like they're late for a romantic rendezvous, but at least they're not intrusive or abusive. I'm making good time, too, which is good because with a long and fulfilling summer ride behind me, I'm ready to be home. However, without planning it, I end up playing leapfrog with a double trailer truck.

Just west of Tucumcari, the I-40 has a series of hills. They're all low and quite long, so it's nothing your bike would notice, but it's a different story with double trailer trucks. I come up behind one on an uphill stretch where he's doing forty miles-per-hour at the most. Nothing unusual about that—he must have a full load—so I pass him on the left, then go into the right lane so the drivers racing to their sweethearts can pass me.

I'm on the downhill side for a minute or so when I look in my rearview mirror and see that the trucker is closing in and closing in fast. So I pull to the left again and he zooms past on my right going somewhere close to ninety.

This get repeated on the next hill and the next, and for me, it's fun because it gives me something to do while riding through the desert. However, I begin to wonder if this is annoying the guy. I mean, let's face it, you do *not* want to annoy anyone whose vehicle weighs a hundred times more than your bike, right?

So as I pass him on the next hill, I look up and he's got this big smile and gives me a thumbs-up. Guess he's having as much fun as me. Later, after the road flattens out, I pull off for lunch and give him a high five and he honks.

After that, nothing much happens. Until I get to Sanders, Arizona.

Sanders is an odd place. I'm sure there must be a town around here, a neighborhood or two, but if there are, you can't see them from the freeway. All you do see in the middle of all this desert is a gas station, a diner and a motel, all squished together like water bottles in an overstuffed saddlebag. And in the glow of the setting sun, it looks like something you'd see on Twilight Zone or in a David Lynch film.

I fill up my tank, get a room then walk behind the buildings a hundred or so yards to a double train track to take some photos. Just as I'd hoped, a pretty sunset graces the western sky as a train is coming toward me. Then, to make it even better, another train is coming the other way and they pass each other not more than twenty yards from where I'm standing.

Not only that, it happens again maybe a half hour later. I think about lying down on the narrow slip of ground between the two tracks so I can feel all that swiftly moving weight put a rumble into the earth. But I don't. I mean, it'd probably give me and the two engineers heart attacks.

After the sun sets for good, I go into the almost-deserted diner for dinner and sit in a booth next to the windows of the front wall looking toward the front door. At a table in front of me and a little to the right is a big, silver-bearded guy wearing overalls and wire-rimmed glasses. I take him for a trucker, smile and nod, and he does the same.

I finish my dinner and as I walk by him toward the cash register, he says, "Is that your Harley out there?" I say it is and after exchanging a few pleasantries, he tells me that the giant Goldwing with a trailer in the parking lot is his.

I sit across from my new friend, Bobby, and we share road stories for a good while. The thing he's most proud of, other than his family, is being the unofficial traveling ambassador for the Ride for Kids Program, which is where bikers raise money for the Pediatric Brain Tumor Foundation.

One thing the bikers do, and the one Bobby enjoys the most, is visit kids who have brain tumors and give them rides on their motorcycles. (During the holidays, Bobby dresses up as one of the most authentic looking Santa Clauses you've ever seen.) In fact, he loves doing this so much that he bought a motorcycle with a sidecar for that very reason. Bobby also tells me that he wants to, at least once, be a part of every Ride for Kids event in the United States and that's why he's on the road now.

The Ride for Kids is a simple idea and an effective one. The procedure is simple as well and requires nothing more than a willing biker and a kid snuggly strapped in. Now, they never ride fast or far with these kids, maybe twenty miles-per-hour at the most in a parking lot. Right before taking off, Bobby always looks at his passenger and says, "Do you feel the need for speed?" They always laugh and are giddy with excitement.

Except for this one eleven-year-old girl. When Bobby said his "need for speed" line, she didn't react in the least and kept staring straight ahead. But when the girl's ride was over, she had this huge smile on her face, "beaming like a light from Heaven." The nurses told Bobby that that was the first time they'd seen her smile in over five years.

We continue with our stories and end up talking for so long that he insists on buying me a piece of pie along with some ice cream for himself. I tell him that when we meet again, the pie and ice cream are on me.

The next morning, he's ready to take off into the wind and rain long before I am. He says he's eager to get going because in order to make it to the next Ride for Kids event on time, he has only two days to cover over a thousand miles.

Just before leaving, however, he hands me a small and simple brass bell that he made himself. He's made a bunch of them over the years and tells me that each one has its own unique sound and that every time one of them

271

rings, it's a blessing from God and lets the owners know that they are each also unique. He then tells me that to receive its full benefits, "It hasta go on your handlebars."

I genuinely thank him, we each agree we'll meet up again someday, and he takes off. I wonder how a brass bell will look on the nothing-but-black-and-chrome Beast but quickly realize it doesn't matter because a gift from another biker is sacrosanct. So I fumble around in one of my bags, find a zip tie and fasten it, just like he suggested, on the handlebars and decide that it will always be there.

For the next few years, Bobby and I stay in touch, sometimes via email but most of the time on FaceBook. He reads my book and enthusiastically promotes it a number of times. I always thank him for his travel writings and often urge others to get on his mailing list. Every time I see his ruddy face and white beard in a photo, I smile and say to myself, "There is a good man."

In February of 2016, I learn this.

Robert Louis Newman, 64, of LaPorte, IN
died Friday, Feb. 12, 2016, in Kendallville, IN,
as the result of an automobile accident.

I also learn that at the time, he was on his way to pick up flyers for another Ride for Kids event.

I go out to the Beast, take a long look at that brass bell and think about life and happiness, and how we are each blessedly unique. I think about helping others and about friendships; about the understanding that bikers have for each other and how Bobby extended that understanding to kids all over the country. And I think about the unselfishness of bringing joy to all of them. My eyes well up, but I smile anyway and say to myself, "There was a good man."

I still owe you a bowl of ice cream, my friend.

49

THE APPALACHIAN KID

He was older than the days he had seen
and the breaths he had drawn.

Jack London

Animosity is a rare thing in the biker world. Sure, you come across it now and again, but for the most part, bikers are a cheerful, sincere and helpful lot. There's a natural heartiness and kinship, too. Further, it's a world populated with an infinite variety of personalities and the infinite variety of characters you meet is one of the things that makes the motorcycling experience rich. And there comes a moment in every ride when you kick back and reminisce about all the people you met.

There were the two bikers I met in El Paso. For three hours, we drank beer, ate salted peanuts and laughed more than we talked.

The valet at the hotel in downtown Houston, a tall, lean young man with an easy smile. He told me that before he moved to the United States from Burkina Faso, Africa, he rode a Chinese motorcycle, but his dream was always to get a Harley. His is a soul unburdened by sin.

The couple in Alaska who had just ridden the 460 mile, gravel and flint Dempster Highway up to Inuvik in Canada's Northwest Territory. They still had a wide-eyed look of shock on their faces. And the couple who had only two days to ride the 1200 miles on the Alaska Highway from Toad River, British Columbia to Anchorage, Alaska. When I wished them luck, they each nodded and said, "We're gonna need it."

In Missouri, there was Tony, a man who has spent his whole life studying people. By observing me for just five minutes, he not only knew my exact age and ancestry, he knew I lived in the Los Angeles area. And his best friend, David, who talked about how much he loves to ride his golden Goldwing trike and how he wants to someday settle down in the Black Hills.

The lady in New Jersey who took twenty minutes out of her workout time to photograph me and the Beast against a pretty sunset. The mom at a roadside fruit stand who bought me my very first Georgia peach.

The check-in lady at a motel in Arizona who took the time to read every one of my patches and listen to the stories behind them. The check-in gal at a motel in New York who took ten percent off my bill because I'd brought her a piece of pie. The young check-in gal at a motel in Nebraska who, when I asked how she was doing, simply said, "Lovely" with one of the sweetest, most sincere smiles I've ever seen.

The dozen or so waitresses who each gave me a free piece of pie, and the Waffle House waitress in Alabama who brought me a free, tall glass of sweet tea as I sat outside on a curb next to my bike because, "It's hot out here, hon, you need something cold to drink."

The housekeeper in Vermont who ran through the puddles in a motel parking lot as I was riding away so she could give me the money clip I'd left in my room.

The children who stared at me wide-eyed and when I winked, they would hide behind their mother then take another peek at me with one eye and a grin.

I met too many people to count. I never learned many of their names and I've forgotten most of the ones I did learn, but I'll always remember them. The hundreds of bikers who greeted me with a smile and a firm hand-shake, and laughed at my lame jokes as I laughed at theirs; the thousands who wished me a safe journey; the older ones who told me about a long ride they did years ago, and the younger ones who promised they'd get a motorcycle "real soon."

But of all the memorable people I've come across on my trips throughout Canada and the United Sates, the one I think about as often as any other is someone I met at the Kirkside Motor Lodge in Bennington, Vermont.

The Kirkside Motor Lodge is a one-story building in the shape of a rectangle that's open at the side that faces Main Street. I arrive there late one afternoon, about an hour before sunset, and though there are many more vacant rooms than occupied ones, the owner decides to give me a room next door to an attractive middle-aged woman and a handsome, bohemian-like young man with thick curvy black hair to his shoulders.

They're quiet but friendly, greeting me with a smile every time we see each other. From what I can tell, there's nothing improper or strange going on, but there *is* something different with their relationship, but I cannot figure out what it is.

It's the first of a two-night stay and after a delicious dinner at Ramunto's Pizza, I go back to the motel and see the young man sitting on the porch in front of his room. I sit in front of mine and we talk for a while about football, books, and the differences between sunsets and sunrises.

All the while, he stares into the dark distance. It's odd. It's not as if he's ignoring me or wanting to end the conversation or trying to think of something to say. Rather, he's preoccupied. Too, his voice is distant, and it is as if his words are weighted down. We keep talking.

The following morning, the woman is up and about, but I don't see the young man and figure he's still asleep. I'm outside getting ready to ride around the area when the woman comes over, introduces herself as Mary, and we engage in some pleasant small talk. At the end of the conversation, she leans toward me, puts her hand on my arm and says she's Kyle's nurse.

That evening, I find myself again having a conversation with Kyle while he gazes into a distance far more vast than what is in front of us. He tells me that he's hiking the entire 2,181 miles of the Appalachian Trail and that he and Mary had come into Bennington to get supplies. I enthusiastically admire his undertaking and, still looking away, he offers a half smile.

He asks about my trip. I tell him I'd ridden from Southern California via Canada and, in turn, he admires my trek saying, "I'll bet it's amazing riding all around on a motorcycle." I say it is and he says, "Sounds like something I wish I'd done." I say what I often say at such a time. "Well, if you've ever imagined yourself on a motorcycle, do yourself a favor, get one and ride the hell out of it."

For the first time he looks directly at me, his kind eyes deep and clear and unwavering. "I'm dying." I pause for some moments. "You're going to die?" Again he looks into the distance, his future, and with a calm finality says, "Got an incurable disease. That's why I'm doing the Appalachian. It's the one thing I've always wanted to do. Probably the last thing I'll ever do."

50

THE BIG FIVE-ZERO

My non-planning ways usually pay off. Same with not making reservations or deciding on particular destinations to visit. What I like is the adventure of going somewhere, anywhere, and not knowing what I'll find until I get there. But like I said, this method *usually* pays off. Alas, my trip to Hawaii turns out to be one of those other times.

It's not until my flight lands in Kona (KOH-nuh) on Hawaii's Big Island that I realize I'm way on the other side of the island from my hotel room in Hilo (HEE-low). The Beast is in Hilo as well because that's the only place where the shipping company in San Diego would send him. (He insisted on an ocean cruise.) No one to blame but yours truly, so I shrug my shoulders and commence figuring out how to get there.

There's no shuttle or Uber service available so I check with a cab driver and he says it'll be about three hundred bucks. (Ouch!) So I check with the lady at the information desk and she tells me I can get there by bus and it costs only a dollar. Great! The only problem is that the nearest bus stop is about ten miles away and the only way to get there is by cab.

So my exotic Hawaiian adventure starts with a forty-dollar cab ride to a K-Mart, where I sit on a metal bench for an hour, then sit in a public bus for a two and a half hours, which is followed by a two-mile walk to my hotel. Tell ya what, if you're looking for a well-planned, reservations-made, know-everything-in-advance vacation, I am *not* your guy.

I get to my hotel room well into the evening and am immediately confronted with the first of two problems: I don't feel well. My sinuses are totally stopped up and my head feels like it weighs ten pounds more than normal. But hey, from the neck on down I feel fine!

The next day, I confront the second problem and it's a bigger one: the Beast needs a new starter. It should be simple: Find someone who can do a straightforward installation that should take an hour or two. But it's not.

Before getting here, I had called Big Island Harley in Kona, the only dealership on the island, but they are strictly appointment-only and the earliest one I could get was a week and a half down the line. Besides, they didn't have a starter for the Beast.

I called every other place I could find and there was only one guy (yeah, *only one guy*) who was still in business and willing to get his hands a little greasy. So I bought a brand new starter from Old Road Harley, the dealership closest to my home, and Fed-Exed it to him.

His name is Charles and he's been wrenching his whole life, including when he was a young man and some sort of motocross champion. He once helped his friend work on a Harley (just one) in the 80s, then was the service manager at a Yamaha dealership for some years. And to round out his résumé, for the past twenty years he's been working on nothing but mopeds.

Yeah, I know what you're thinking, but y'know what? He may not be a Harley mechanic, but he is a Tesla-like wizard with electricity and whenever he picks up a tool, his muscle memory is like Picasso's. Of course, he sometimes forgets where he put a tool, but hey, he's my guy and I'm behind him one hundred percent.

Charles meets me at the shipping place and his idea is that we push the Beast up an eight foot long, two by eight inch piece of lumber and into the back of his twenty year old Mazda pickup. Then back it down when we get to his place. I'm thinking, "Two guys pushing up a 700 pound bike on an eight inch wide piece of wood? Uh, no." So I figure, what the heck, I'll push the starter button and see what happens. And it starts!

This is a good thing, of course, but it brings up another problem and it has to do with the fact that when you ship a motorcycle, the gas tank has to be less that a quarter full. I know there's much less than that but figure (i.e. hope) there's enough to get to Charles's place, which is only fourteen miles away. And I don't want to stop for gas because the bike might not start again. So we take off. Yeah, you know what happens next.

With only two miles to go the gas tank is drier than Hawaii's Ka'u Desert. Charles goes to his place, fills up a gas can, comes back, and I pour in the two gallons. But now the bike won't start. I'm still not interested in rolling the bike up that board so I call a tow truck and it costs "only" a hundred bucks to go those two miles. Gee! What a deal!

But all of that is only the beginning. The woes of getting the Beast up and running are so many, so varied and so frustration-filled that I won't go into all the details because it'd make for an incredibly boring read and my thoughts would be spinning around so much I'd fall over and hit my head on a pile of hardened lava. But I will say that those frustrations keep mounting and mounting and end up bigger than the tallest mountain on the island, the 13,800 foot Mauna Kea (MAO-nuh KAY-uh).

It involves, among other things, a brand new starter that's slightly defective, someone selling me a wrong starter and refusing to take it back, waiting three days for a wrong part to arrive from the mainland, and waiting another four days for the right part to arrive.

Yep, I'm hemorrhaging money and time. But I do learn an important fact: overnight delivery to Hawaii means two to four days.

The chrome lining in all this is the staff at the Hilo Seaside Hotel. What wonderful people! They're always cheerful, quickly become like a second family, and never complain about having to make me new room keys because I keep forgetting to take mine with me.

Not only that, Karlene gives me a big bag of munchies, Lei expertly sews a patch onto my patch vest, and every now and again the waitresses in the Coconut Grill give me desert or an extra glass of lemonade for free. And there's Greg, a fellow biker, who schlepped me around in his open air Jeep so I could get what I thought was the right starter.

The most amazing display of friendship, however, is courtesy of another fellow biker named Wayne. Wayne rides the same kind of bike as the Beast and when he finds out my plight, tells me I can take whatever I need off his bike and put it on mine so I can ride. Man, that's something, isn't it? Only a few would make an offer like that to someone they just met. (And most of them are bikers.)

I should take Wayne's offer but don't because he'd have to drive all the way back home to Kona and end up missing work. Besides, I keep expecting the Beast to be ready the next day or two. Instead, the days keep going by and I'm still not riding. Major bummer.

I'm not into touristy activities but one day, I do manage to climb out of my funk and onto a bus for a tour of the volcanoes. It's enjoyable and enlightening because Frank, the driver/tour guide, is a walking/talking encyclopedia of Hawaii and Hawaiian history.

I'm the last one to join the tour and the first place we visit is a black sand beach on the east side of Hilo. Black sand beaches are a result of volcano activity so, yeah, there's a connection, but the next place we visit is a large macadamia nut farm and factory. What macadamia nuts have to do with volcanoes I don't know, but from hanging with Frank after we get there, I figure he just wanted to chow down a heaping helping of macadamia nut ice cream.

Mechanical mishaps keep happening and I end up having to extend my stay for four days. Yeah, more money hemorrhaging. But despite that, and the fact that my on and off sickness is mostly on, I'm having fun getting to intimately know the area around my hotel.

Early every morning I go for a short walk and try to catch a spectacular sunrise over Reed Bay and every afternoon try to catch spectacular sunset over Hilo Bay. Alas, it's raining and/or overcast almost every time so my photos are mostly gray, which is the appropriate color for the way I feel.

Also, I have become a regular at Ken's Pancake House and a walk-up counter called Verna's. (IF NO CAN—NO CAN; IF CAN—VERNA'S!) The most remarkable thing about Verna's is their burger patties. They actually taste less like meat than the ones you get from McDonald's, something I didn't think was possible. In fact, they're so filled with breadcrumbs, that a double cheeseburger is more like a spiceless, three-day-old meat loaf sandwich on white bread.

Once, while in an illness-riddled funk, I entertain the idea of shipping the Beast back home and getting it fixed there. It'd be cheaper, right? A faster fix, right? Smart idea, right? And I did ride twelve miles before running out of gas so *technically* I did ride in Hawaii, right?

But I decide against it because twelve miles doesn't constitute any kind of *real* ride, and a real ride on this island paradise is the reason I came here.

After two-plus weeks of frustration, the Beast is up and running and sounding like he's happier than me. I profusely thank Charles, the patient and tireless mechanic, for going far beyond what was asked of him. (He's so patient that throughout all of this, his only real annoyance was that his dog, Brix, fell in love with the Beast and was sad to see him go.)

Finally, I take off with a big and liberating smile on my face. I'm actually riding, *really* riding, in Hawaii! Yes! Then, not a half mile later, the clutch cable snaps. I start laughing. Uncontrollably. I mean, is this really happening?

I call Charles, he drives over, we winch strap the bike to the back of his pickup and tow it back to his place over a bumpy dirt and gravel road that's scattered about with mud puddles. It takes an hour of wrenching, but the good man figures out the problem, fixes it and fixes it for good.

The end result is that in the span of two and a half weeks, I get in only two full days of actual riding, about 450 miles. But despite the almost constant rain, I gotta say it's an amazing two days. Really. The Big Island is something else and I'm loving the paradise it is.

On my first riding day, I head down to a place called South Point. The road quality is lower than the usual not-that-good quality most everywhere else and at the end of the twelve-mile South Point Road it gets worse. You ride down a short and narrow, steeply sloped, broken asphalt driveway onto a dirt parking area embedded with rocks. And there you are at the southernmost point in the United States, about 350 miles farther south than Key West!

Several of the forty people are fishing, but the primary item of interest is a forty-foot cliff. The thing to do is jump off of it, gambol about for a while in the endless and deep blue Pacific Ocean, then climb back up a vertical ladder.

One of the young men does a half gainer and gets a big round of applause so I'm thinking this would be a good time to show off the Olympic-level form of my triple back flip. But then I realize that my boots would weigh me down and, regrettably, have to pass on the idea.

On the second day of riding, I cut across the middle of the island on Saddle Road, which is an excellent ride except for a half-mile of mud due to road construction. It starts out going through a sort of jungle then, after it gets into a lava covered desert, I hang a right and ride up to an information center where you can learn all about the world class telescopes on top of Mauna Kea.

While walking around, my heart is pumping faster that usual, I keep getting out of breath, and I start to worry that my illness is coming back. But as I'm leaving I look at the entrance sign and realize that the reason for all of this is that the altitude of the information center is 9200 feet. Then my heart rate jumps up another notch or two on the way back down. The combination of wind, rain, and patches of sand and gravel on a 17% grade will do that.

Afterward, I ride into Kona, which is a happening city, definitely more active than laid back Hilo. I buy a few t-shirts from the Harley dealership (gotta buy a t-shirt!) then head north on Highway 19 to Waimea (WHY-uh-MAY-uh), which is at the bottom end of a road I heard about from every Hawaiian biker I met.

Highway 250 takes you from Waimea up to the northern end of the island to the community of Hawi (HAH-vee). It is easily one of the better-maintained and most enjoyable roads on the island: wonderfully curvy with a nice surprise here and there.

And the views? A motorcycle on that road is like riding a cloud above the big valley floor, and toward the end you're hovering like a Hawaiian God 6500 feet above the shimmering ocean.

My flight doesn't leave until after 5pm the next day so I decide to spend the night in Waimea. It's after midnight, the rain has stopped and the clouds have found different locales, when I find a secluded spot free of lights and look heavenward. How different this sky is compared to what I'm used to!

Constellations whose names I don't know, stars sparkling wildly and pulsating in unfamiliar rhythms as if they're saying, "We've always been here and always will be. You should visit more often." And I should.

I walk back to the motel, sit on a bench in front of it and start thinking about where I am. Many have written that when we travel long distances or go out at night and look at the stars, we realize how small we are, how insignificant our lives are when compared to the expanse of the earth and the universe. I've no desire to be contrary, but I take the opposite view.

To me, when you get out, really get out and truly look at those vast distances, you become part of them and they become part of you, and you become as big or even bigger than it all is. Limits and boundaries, even the concept of a finite existence, become a sort of make-believe.

I go back to my room, but I'm too amped up to go to sleep. Heck, I'm not even sick any more. Instead, I think about riding a motorcycle and what it's all about and come to one of many conclusions, and that is that riding a motorcycle is about promises.

There are two types of promises: those you make to others and those you make to yourself. And if you think about it, when you make a promise to someone else, it's always preceded with a promise to yourself. True, if you don't or can't keep your word with someone else, they'll most likely forgive you, which is a testament to the fine character of your family and friends.

The brutal truth, however, is that breaking a promise to yourself is where the real damage is done because once you do that, breaking promises to others becomes easy. And as it is with making a promise, breaking a promise to another is always preceded by breaking a promise to oneself.

When you decide to ride a motorcycle, you *are* making a commitment, a type of promise, to yourself. And every time we climb on our bikes, we renew that commitment, the result being that we become much better at keeping our promises and commitments to others. Could this be the reason bikers, on the whole, are trustworthy? I believe so.

Is life a process of finding yourself, creating yourself or some combination of the two? The answer is something we each have to work out for ourselves, but whichever it is, it's of relatively small importance when compared to the multiple wisdoms you acquire when you ride; that feeling of being grounded and invincible, the certainty that you can depend on yourself, and simply knowing that you can keep a promise.

One other thing to tell you about is the "Big Five-Zero" chapter title, the meaning of which I'm sure you already figured out. This may sound like a brag, and I guess it is, but what it refers to is that the Beast and I have now ridden in all fifty states. And we did it with the same helmet and the same pair of boots, too. (And with the way I smell sometimes you'd think I did it all with the same pair of socks.) Add to that Washington D.C., seven Canadian provinces and one Canadian territory and you could say we've put in a few miles.

Riding in all fifty states wasn't something I thought about until three years ago, but once the idea came to me I couldn't let it go. I'm not the first to do it and won't be the last, but what makes it special for me is that the Beast and I did all those miles together. Plain and simple, I love that bike.

As with visiting all the Four Corners cities, riding in all fifty states offers no fame or money, but there *is* a feeling of accomplishment connected with it, a sublime satisfaction in doing something for no other reason than deciding to. A Grand Helluvit, if you will.

Honestly, it isn't that hard. All you do is carve out some time—two to twelve weeks a year—, ride every day and be willing to experience all sorts of weather on all sorts of road surfaces. And, of course, you'll need a motorcycle willing to experience all those things with you, which brings up yet another point.

Because of the courageous and cordial companion he is, I decided to give the Beast the best reward possible. I picked him up the day he landed in San Diego and we rode straight to Drew Surina of American Speed and Custom, who gave him a much deserved, thorough internal makeover.

After removing every nut, bolt and screw, Drew reconditioned, rebuilt, restored or replaced everything and the Beast is now bigger, better and more Herculean than ever, good for another 100,000+ miles. And believe me, we're going to ride all of 'em.

But no paint job. The Beast and I talked about it and came to the conclusion that because we've worked so hard for all those scuffs, scrapes and scratches, each one is a badge of pride and it just wouldn't be acceptable to cover them up.

THE LONG ROAD HOME

The best bike is the one you're on,
The best road is the one you're traveling,
The best destination is wherever you're headed,
The best time to get there is whenever you arrive.

db Mikkelsen

After all he's been through, the Beast deserves acclaim.

He's a Harley-Davidson Softail Deuce, born in the last year of the 20th century. When we first partnered up, his odometer read 14,600 miles and now, seven years later, he's over 108,000 miles old. He's had some electrical problems, any bike could, but what about engine and transmission issues? He's had none. Zero, zilch, nada. And after all those miles he still has enough torque to pull a fully loaded cement truck starting off in third gear.

As I wrote above, he's visited all of the Four Corners and the geographical center of the forty-eight contiguous states. And if that wasn't enough, he insisted on braving the mud and weather in Alaska then, as a vacation, took a laid-back tour of the Big Island in Hawaii.

Yes, he's now ridden in all fifty states. I don't know if he's the first motorcycle to do it or if he'll be the last, but he will forever be a part of the minuscule percentage that have. All of that, however, is just a surface look at what he's accomplished.

Twice he's been down hard, but he got up each time and ended up stronger than before. He's avoided collisions with triple-trailer trucks, maniacal sports cars and unobservant SUVs, as well as moose, deer, cows, bison, rabbits, dogs, cats, squirrels, porcupines and armadillos.

He's tracked through snow a foot deep, endured several hailstorms, stayed upright against 45 MPH crosswinds, been hit by windblown sand from countless miles of desert, sliced a straight path through deep mud hundreds of times, and successfully maneuvered around thousands of chuckholes.

How many times the rain has sizzled on his pipes, no one could count. And he once suffered a front tire blowout while going 60 MPH. Sure, he wiggled and wavered, but he refused to go down.

His rumble has been heard above 12,000 feet in the Rockies and below sea level in the Mojave Desert. He's seen surfers in the Pacific Ocean, waves crashing on Atlantic beaches, and felt the soft, warm waters of the Gulf of Mexico.

He's crisscrossed the Great Plains, the sprawling farmlands of Central Canada and the panhandles of Oklahoma, Texas, Idaho and Florida. He's brushed against giant redwoods in the Sierra Nevada, cornfields in Iowa, firs in New Brunswick, and pines in Georgia.

He loves riding over rivers and streams. The Mississippi, the Colorado, the Ohio, the Illinois, the Snake, the Columbia, the Platt, the Arkansas, the Tennessee, the Yellowstone, the San Joaquin, the Rio Grande, the Monongahela, the Potomac and countless others. But the Big Muddy, the Missouri, has always been his favorite.

He's done most of his miles alone but enjoys the companionship of other motorcycles, once riding with hundreds of thousands of them on September 11th, 2013 in Washington D.C.

He enjoys the challenge of winds, playing tag with dust devils and chasing the shadows of clouds. He derives a special peace while riding under a canopy of stars.

Most importantly, every single trip—*yes, every single trip*—he brought his weary, weather-beaten rider safely back home.

When you ride, you come to depend on many things. The first that comes to mind is the obvious one: your bike. In the morning it's there waiting for you, starts right up, goes wherever you point, cushions the bumps, slices a path through the wind, and gives you a thrill on every curve.

You depend on the roads to keep going, even if they're under severe maintenance; on the bridges to stay aloft; and on those yellow speed limit signs just before all those blind corners because, let's face it, they sometimes save your life.

You depend on the sunrise to fuel your passions, on the sunset to let you know you had a good day, and on the sun herself as she faithfully rises every morning and, without pause, traverses her path across the sky.

You depend on the breezes to cool your thoughts, on the trees to soften the edges, on the waters, both still and not, to remind you that there is great motion and great depth to life and all who participate in it.

You depend on your memories because you always learn something new from them; on your imagination to make the future bright and victorious; on your intuition because there are times it, too, saves your life.

You depend on that smile from the gal manning the cash register, on the directions from the guy who just stepped out of his 4X4, on the kindness of the motel clerk who looks over her glasses and says, "Looks like you could use a good night's rest, darlin'."

You depend on the nods and the waves you get from other bikers because they understand.

You depend on your friends to write an email now and again, on your family to answer the phone with a lighthearted voice, on your kids to always stay in touch, their last words being, "Love you!"

And your heart. You depend on your heart's continuous yearning for Freedom and its boundless ability to find it at every bend.

It's true that when I'm ready to get home after a long ride, I'm eager to be home and though I'm ultimately happy when I get there, I know I'm going to miss being on the road.

I'm going to miss the challenge of getting up every day to ride a motor-cycle, something for which I have no natural talent.

I'm going to miss packing my bags and strapping them to The Beast—the delight of precision, the discipline of sequence.

I'm going to miss the first roar of the engine in the morning; whatever dissonance I may harbor, whatever weariness I may carry, it brings me to the present, full of verve and hope.

I'm going to miss knowing how fast I'm going by the sound of the engine, knowing the temperature by the feel of the air on my neck, knowing the speed of the winds by the wiggling of the windshield, looking at a bridge in the hazy distance and knowing within a tenth of a mile how far away it is.

I'm going to miss a life where my only schedule is "checkout time is 11 A.M.," but if I politely ask the housecleaning lady, she'll let me stay a couple of more hours.

I'm going to miss the smells of alfalfa fields freshly harvested; of wild bushes of rosemary, lilacs and gardenias; of the coming rain.

I'm going to miss the might of mountains and the masculinity of winds, the bend of rivers and the feminine draw of a moonrise.

I'm going to miss how the sun warms my back after a cold morning and how the evening breeze cools my face; and lying on a bed after a day of riding, eyes closed, and listening to the soul of Sarah Vaughn and the honesty of Willie Nelson, the fervor of Liszt and the silky perfection of Ravel.

And I'm going to miss those times when you look, really look, at everything around you, near and far, and you become charged with an enormous strength so that you sit in the saddle like Helios on a great steed, and instead of rolling on the road, you pull it under you; instead of cutting through the wind, it splits apart for you; instead of riding past mountains and under clouds, they march around you like a procession of ancient gods.

At every curve, my friends, may the future turn with you.

Love and Respect,
Foster

ABOUT THE AUTHOR

Photo courtesy of Suzie Katayama

Foster Kinn (a.k.a. Dwight Mikkelsen) was born and raised in Visalia, California. He is the son and brother of Danish immigrants, the father of three, the grandfather of four, and a widower.

He has been a professional musician and composer his entire adult life, and has arranged and orchestrated for many artists, including Quincy Jones, Barbra Streisand, Chicago, Whitney Houston, Elmer Bernstein, Patrick Doyle, and George Clinton; and has worked on hundreds of films and TV shows.

His primary love, however, is Classical music and in the past several years has been busy composing ballets, including *Thumbelina*, *The Legend of Jack Frost* and *In Embla's Garden*. His arrangements have been performed by The Los Angeles Philharmonic Orchestra, the Civic Orchestra of Chicago, the Pittsburgh Pops, and the Vienna Opera Orchestra.

He describes himself as "fundamentally a Freedom guy, a Classical music composer, and a not-too-bad-raconteur, who wishes he had more time to ride his motorcycle."

INVITATION FOR MORE FREEDOM

If you liked my book, please go to www.FreedomsRush.com and send me a note. Really, I'd love to hear from you. And if you want, I'll put you on my mailing list.

When I'm out on my long rides during the summer, and only during the summer, I send out what I call TravelBlogs. Each one contains 8-1500 words and four to twelve photos, and I promise you'll get no more than two a week for a total of ten to fifteen a year.

Also, I have several fictional short stories available for download from Amazon.

If you are interested in the photos I wrote about, they can be seen and purchased at FosterKinn.Zenfolio.com.

Ride Big, Ride Long and Ride Free, my friends.

Love,